The evidence is now available.

Thousands of expert witnesses have contributed to our new understanding of the Earth's "mysteries" and "miracles." *Flying Saucers Uncensored* provides the *Extraterrestrial Perspective* we need to understand how our life has been affected by visiting spacemen from the outer-reaches of our cosmos. This book will change the perspective of everyone on Earth with the courage to judge the evidence.

FLYING SAUCERS UNCENSORED

H. T. WILKINS

PYRAMID BOOKS • NEW YORK

TO THE REV. IRENE FARRIER
OF CHARLOTTE, MICHIGAN,
*and to the many correspondents and readers
of the author's books, in Great Britain,
Eire, Holland, Germany, France, Australia,
New Zealand and the United States of America,
who have rendered valuable services to him in
the research into flying saucer phenomena.*

FLYING SAUCERS UNCENSORED

A PYRAMID BOOK
Published by arrangement with The Citadel Press

The Citadel Press edition published 1955
Pyramid edition published August, 1967
Third printing, February 1975

ISBN 0-515-03434-7

Library of Congress Catalog Card Number: 55-11618
Printed in the United States of America

Pyramid Books are published by Pyramid Communications, Inc.
Its trademarks, consisting of the word "Pyramid" and the por-
trayal of a pyramid, are registered in the United States Patent
Office.

Pyramid Communications, Inc., 919 Third Avenue,
New York, N.Y. 10022

CONTENTS

FOREWORD

A Curtain Raiser to the Most Amazing Drama of All Time

"FOR THE FIRST TIME man has it in his power to destroy all life on his earth. Will he be able to avoid some such form of universal suicide?" asked Lord Cherwell, a member of the British Atomic Energy Commission, speaking at Liverpool, on July 14, 1954. He added that, at present, we know very little of nuclear chemistry. Uranium is a relatively rare element. Can we induce protons and deuterons to combine and form heavier particles? If so, the energies obtained would be immense, and the raw material is available in unlimited quantities, but all these things are merely in the offing. None of them has yet been proved possible on an economic scale. They lie in the future which many of us may not live to see. It remains to be seen whether man will or will not use the vast resources of science wisely, or whether he will act so as to restore the surface of his puny planet to the primeval slime from which it has emerged in the last thousand million years. Perhaps the very near future will show.

Latin writers like Pliny and Seneca, Tacitus and Julius Obsequens, and the Renaissance encyclopedists, like Conrad Wolfhart and Lycosthenes, recorded sightings of unidentified objects in the skies over old Rome as early as the 4th and 3rd centuries B.C. Were the complete cuneiform records or the clay tablets and seals of old Sumer and Babylonia available, we should doubtless find that similar objects had been seen in their skies, as they were in the days of pre-Inca Peru. They appeared over old English abbeys in the 14th century; were seen, earlier, on land and sea in Angevin and Norman days; were seen, in Ireland, prior to the 11th century. Bewildered astronomers noted them in their 16th and 17th century ephemerides. The Royal Society annals take puzzled note of them, exactly as did the *Mémoires* of the French Académie des Sciences, years before the French Revolution. Seamen, coun-

trymen and townsmen saw them, in both Europe and the
Americas, on land and sea. Repeatedly mariners in the
19th century, on all the world's seas, logged them.

But there appears *one notable difference* in the plethora
of sightings and the tempo of events in the skies since
1944. And it must make one speculate that this results
from our liberation of the terrible energies locked up in
thermonuclear and nuclear-fission bombs. Those in outer
space know what, probably, we do not: that even more
dreadful cosmoplastic energies lie locked up in the sub-
atomic sphere. Then, too, the passing of the sonic barrier
by suprasonic planes has most certainly drawn them here;
for, it is said, that within the sphere or plane of these
etheric energies many of these fourth dimensional and invisible beings have their habitat.

In the past twenty-three centuries, in their visits to our
skies, they appear to have come in units at periods far
apart. Perhaps we had metals or chemical deposits they
wanted, and of which, what science we then had, took no
account. But they had then no reason to *fear* what we
might do in our crass handling of the great forces of nature. In the last ten years, whether or not there is a greater
awareness on our part, or our psychology has been affected
by two world wars, fleets and cohorts have been frequently reported, and, on occasion, even their vast space ships
have been seen within our own atmosphere.

There is considerable evidence to prove that these visitants are possibly established in bases on the moon, and
even on other planets, to whom may go reports as to a
cosmic general staff, and, perhaps, sea water and samples
of air, exported from our earth for purposes of study and
experimentation. We cannot for one moment doubt that
the artificial earth satellite to be launched within the next
two years—by the United States and/or Soviet Russia—
will definitely establish the existence of space ships within
our atmosphere.

The projected space satellites will establish, once and
for all, that the official scoffers who have, for years, denied the existence of flying saucers, space ships and all
other unidentified flying objects have simply closed their
eyes to the obvious truth. Fortunately, we do not need
to wait for the launching of artificial satellites to disprove
the official attitude. Nor is it necessary to do so by bringing forth a series of hoaxes or deliberately perpetrated
"spoofs." The evidence is here *now,* and it is of a nature
to make any serious thinker question the official attitude.
Much of this evidence, to be sure, is suppressed. But

enough seeps through to demonstrate the existence of cosmic intelligence.

From the thousands of reports that are brought to my
attention by correspondents all over the world, from accounts which manage to appear in the press—often de-
layed and frequently emasculated—and from scores of
other sources, I have sought to present the uncensored
story of the most amazing drama of all time: *the phenomena of the flying saucers!*

August, 1955

H. T. WILKINS

IT IS NO LONGER a question that the phenomena called flying saucers are real and objective, and not mere hallucinations fit only to be considered by psychiatrists or medical psychologists.

The corpus of evidence is now far too great. Too many sane and sober-minded men and women, of all professions and occupations, have seen these unexplained objects in the world's skies. They include police officials, patrolmen, men on the footplates of locomotives, manual laborers, physicians, housewives, engineers, scientists and technicians.

While official spokesmen of government departments, both in the United States and England, smile politely or frown portentously when told of sightings of unidentified objects in the sky, yet, "off the record," some have told reporters that higher quarters have the phenomena under careful consideration. No doubt they have, especially when one finds that R.A.F. commandants of airfields and bases have issued strict orders to pilots or groundsmen not to say anything to press or public about sightings they have reported.

I received a letter from a young man in Cheshire who telephoned an R.A.F. base about a strange object he and two others had seen in the sky. He got this answer: "I cannot comment on the phenomenon you saw last night (at 7 P.M., November 10, 1953); but I have forwarded a report to higher quarters." The officer ignored this correspondent's inquiry: "Was this object picked up on your radarscope?"

We now reach this significant stage in the drama of the flying saucers. It is summed up in a question which is by no means fantastic when one relates it to the now vast corpus of strange reports of unidentified objects of all sizes, some satellites, other appearing as main space ships: "Will these space ships land at some time?"

In this book I set down a corpus of *new* evidence relating to saucer incidents and sightings over England, Western

Europe, the United States, and Australia. It may lead some readers to speculate whether a general staff of some world, or even worlds, in outer space, may be operating over the Earth; and whether these operations are part of an over-lord strategy and cosmic plan, directed from vast space ships, distant from our atmosphere; with these satellite discs roaming over our own earth's skies carrying out tactical missions.

From pole to pole, these entities must have surveyed our earth in the last twenty or thirty years. Not a con-tinent have they left unvisited; not one of the world's capital cities have their aeroforms left unsurveyed.

There are those in the United States who say that the entities who send out these discs and "ether-ships" to sur-vey the earth are beings of the human order, but fifteen feet tall. This, of course, is what has been traditionally and in folklore said of the Mu-ans and Atlans—of the lost continents of Mu and Atlantis. The invisible, but real world of these entities is said to be similar to, though not identical with, the physical world of our earth.

I have seen a dithyrambic account of the world in which they are said to exist. It is called the Heavy World, on account of its extreme density, by analogy with the visible stars called "heavy" because of their great gravity. This "heavy world" resembles one of the apocalyptic visions of John of Patmos. Its size is stupendous; it is vibrating and pulsating with high energy, iridescent in colors, with a glorious plant and bird life. It has splendid colossal build-ings (they would need to be, with tenants fifteen feet tall!). Its tall beings are perfect in mind and body, synthesizing Hellenic and Roman ideals. Motion, there, is a function of the mind; that is, they can cross what we call the voids of space, and of time, traversing light-years, in an instant, and emerging into what one may call our third-dimensional world planes.

It has also been said, however, that *some* of these visi-tants are by no means, in outer form, the summation of the Hellenic ideal, as it had existed among the Atlanteans, "the beautiful mind in the beautiful body." True, their mind is of a very high order indeed; but the outer form is, it is said, not attractive, but bizarre. Such beings, probably, do not share our notions of ethics, or good and evil. They may be beyond *our* ideas of good and evil; but their in-tentions towards the earth are benevolent, or neutral.

Apropos of the above, I am still unable to say whether or not it was a vulgar hoaxer who, on October 8, 1953, was heard on the radio at Salt Lake City, Utah, saying:

"I speak from a space ship. You cannot reach me, but I can, with ease, reach you. If you saw me, I should appear so horrible in your eyes, that you would be scared to death."

In numerous sightings of saucers observers have reported that round these objects was an intense glow of radiation. The aeroform may throw off heat-radiation, at a colossal speed or rate of vibration, striking the atoms of hydrogen and oxygen of our own atmosphere. These heat rays may cause some form of combustion. As the aeroform, or saucer, starts to ascend, the temperature falls, creating a magnetic field around it. Forces of attraction and repulsion would then come into play.

Possibly, the quantum theory may be involved here, or the jumping of atoms in and out of their orbits. There may be attraction and repulsion at quantum rates. The "driver" of a saucer aeroform may reside in its skin. One terminal may be heated and cooled rapidly. The "waves" in the "drivers" may stand still, and there may be a luminous effect in the radiant dischare at one end, where the shape slips off the wave-form.

If this be the case, it is obvious that their science far transcends ours. We have not, so far, been able to understand, except dimly, what is involved in molecular motion. And most certainly, we, on this earth, have no idea of any material that could stand this terrific heat; for the heat-waves and oscillatory speed involved *must* be insulated from and have no effect on either the interior of the saucers, or whatever entities may be within them. It would have to be a synthetic substance. At this moment, we, here, know of no means of closing up and aligning the atoms and molecules in the substance of the exterior of any form of terrestrial space ship we might send to the moon. True, it *might* be done with powerful electrical impulses. *If* we could do this, the ship, so shielded from lethal cosmic radiation in space, might become weightless; putting almost inconceivable velocities within our power.

Whether that may be so, or not, unless this extremely difficult problem be solved, the consequences to terrestrial space-voyagers will involve something like cancer and certain immediate or lingering death.

A word about the various types of discoidal and satellite, non-terrestrial aeroforms which have been sighted in America, Europe and the rest of the continents, between 1946 and since.

Where do they come from?

There are those in the United States who say that the controllers and creators of some of the vast space ships, or carriers, are centered in the planets, Mars and Venus, or their etheric doubles. Among them are beings from a remote past age, from Atlantis and Mu, prior to the vast cataclysm which destroyed those continents. (Who can know?)

One is fully aware that statements of this kind will be received with skepticism or derision by the class of archaeologists and scientific historians—so far as history can be deemed a science. For, as Napoleon Bonaparte once said, history is fable about which there is general agreement. It is, therefore, very largely subjective.

Curiously, several American technicians who claim to have come into personal contact with saucers, if not their entities, have written accounts deposing that signs, glyphs and symbols have been seen within these aeroforms, or have been in some way communicated, that are singularly like, and, in some cases, identical with glyphs found in ancient sites, or on objects in North and Central and South America. However this may be, there are others, among them so-called "Etherians," who are *not* the transmigrated souls of Atlans or Mu-ans!

The vast carriers are of several types. One is said to be one and a third miles long, 500 feet in diameter, and to have a crew of some 2,500. These include technicians and pilots who control the satellites they carry or assemble! They also have weapons, but *not* for use against the earth, or her people. The vast carriers are said, incredible and fantastic as it must sound, to have a mechanism which can *teleport* them to the earth's upper atmosphere. There, in the wink of an eye, they can convert to the "vibrational level" at which they become visible. As the mechanism is very delicate and its control difficult, it has happened that some of these carriers "de-materialized" close enough to the earth's surface to have been observed. Testimony, his last on earth, was given by an experienced air pilot, Captain Thomas Mantell. On January 7, 1949, he was ordered by Colonel Guy F. Hix, commandant of the airfield at Fort Godman, Kentucky, to try to close with a vast space ship which had hovered over the airfield for more than an hour. Hix said the thing was "umbrella-shaped and had a rotating streamer of red":

"I now see the thing—almost seventy yards across . . . I'm very close to it . . . Its size is *tremendous.*" [*Spoken over the radiophone, after which Mantell's plane disintegrated, as if a "death ray" had been put on it. Every bone in the luckless airman's body was smashed, when he crashed to earth.*]

There is reason to suppose that, usually, these mysterious, colossal space ships remain far out in space, acting as base-ships and coordinating the activities of their satellite saucers or discs. They often, but not always, refrain from venturing into our atmosphere, so as to prevent optical or other detection, such as radar.

How are the flying saucers—the discs in our own atmosphere—propelled?

In several ways:

(1) A form of jet propulsion in which a ray is projected or beamed upon air in a sealed chamber, the air being intaken as the disc moves in our skies, and automatically compressed. It is, so to speak, "atomized," by the ray. In the skies of a planet having little air, or destitute of an atmosphere, other fuels, or metals may be used and "rayed."

(2) By electromagnetic drive which intersects with the field of magnetic force set up by a planet in rotation. But this device can be used only relatively near the surface of a planet. When used, one has the mysterious blanking out of radio transmitters or receivers, or wild spinning of compasses in airplane cockpits, when saucers have been sighted far overhead.

One other form of propulsion is used, but only in the vast space ships. It taps what are called "the energy flows" in space. The mechanism is in synchronism, or unison with these flows, but slightly out of phase with them. If used for long-distance flights of a type of flying saucer over a planet, it can generate a maximum speed of 270,000 miles an hour, or 7½ miles a second! (I have mentioned several cases of saucers, subsequently calculated to have attained this appalling speed, in the skies of the United States.) The speed depends on the phase used and on whether the aeroform travels with or against the energy flow.

We will have sightings to deal with of saucers that appeared to have no inertia, and could pass almost instantaneously from a hover to a fantastic speed of miles per second.

How is this phase attained?

Either (1): By a device generating a cone-field of electric energy, which can cause the "flow," or pull of gravity, to veer on all sides of the aeroform, and so annihilating gravity-pull and weight close to the saucer; or (2): by a downward-directed beam of electrons. This "diversion field" has been visible in some of the saucer sightings, when something like a corona discharge has been seen, a luminous envelope or skin of fire. The corona effect is also seen in the case of saucers powered by electro-magnetic energy.

Now, let us glance at some forms of the saucers detailed in this book as sighted by American observers: doughnut-shaped; fusiform or cigar-shaped, seen by myself, on July 23, 1954, over north Kent; spherical; rubber-heel shaped.

The *doughnut shape*: Seen over Maury Island, on the northwest coast of the United States by coast guards, at 2 P.M., June 21, 1947. It had an outside diameter of about 125 feet, with a cavity of some twenty-five feet, and thirty feet thick. It carries test equipment, very advanced technicians, and a crew of about fifty. It is used for technical experiments and observations. Drive: electromagnetic.

The *fusiform, or cigar shape*: Functions like a terrestrial escort or fighter plane—to protect the other types, if needed. About a hundred feet long and twenty-five feet wide, with a crew of about twenty entities. Its drive is the ray-jet, above, or the primary of space travel.

The *crescentiform,* or *rubber-heel* shape of saucer has about four types, and uses either the ray-jet or the electromagnetic system of propulsion. One of these types can be mistaken for a *fireball*. They are used largely for reconnaissance of this planet and *others*. The crew ranges from two to five.

The *spherical saucer*: About a hundred feet wide; a transport aeroform, carrying passengers and/or freight. Has a crew of twenty-five to thirty. It is driven by both ray-jet and primary space propulsion.

There are also global or spherical aeroforms, which are *not* manned, but remotely controlled from carriers or mother space-ships. They have devices for very long-range television-scanning and reporting. Some of them automatically collect earth, rocks, water and other things from this planet, for study. An American rocket technician at a base near the Oregon mountains, even declares that, in 1953, he was taken for a ride in one of these manless aeroforms controlled, he says, by posterity of old Mu!

In 1949, there were persistent reports of flying saucers shot down in both Mexico and the United States. Of course these reports are impossible to confirm. Imaginations have been busy with the dark side of our moon—the side we never see, except for an edge revealed by librations, or wobblings. None can know. short of an actual landing on the Moon, whether it has subterranean life, as H. G. Wells' space-novel imported. Some Americans hold that there is a way-station on the moon—perhaps on the dark side—and from it has come a carrier ship, with four-feet tall, humanoid beings manning satellite discs. These latter, it is said, were twenty-seven feet wide, with an aerodynamic surface of which the cabin occupied a diameter of sixteen feet. Propulsion was by earth-induction (electromagnetic). Their (pacific) purpose was to explore and gain knowledge of the earth. Somehow, their carrier ship went out of action, and the discs had no base or supervision. They could not return to the moon on their own, not being equipped for interplanetary flight.

A flying saucer from another world saw one of them over New Mexico, signalled it, got no reply and, believing it was hostile, caused it to crash on the earth. Several others were crashed by radar—it is believed, but not used for this purpose—by the United States Air Force. When their carrier ship did not return, saucers from another world, it is said, transported to the moon twenty-six of these thirty-seven aeroforms whose science had not shielded or could not insulate their propulsion and control from the interference of radar. Eight of these "lunar" machines crashed on the earth, and the fate of three more is unknown.

There is a vast, spindle-shaped, or cigar-shaped, cylindrical space ship of unknown origin, which was photographed over a blast furnace in Hamilton, Ohio, in 1950. It was also "snapped" by a young woman taking pictures of ordinary terrestrial objects at Hawthorne, Calif., when it was seen in the act of releasing satellite discs. It was seen over Denham, in England, and twelve hours later over Sweden, in 1949, again releasing discs which, at high speed, flew off in opposite directions. It is probably a space ship of hostile character and is suspected, both in England and the United States, of causing serious fires. In Europe, this weird space ship appears *solus;* in the United States such ships have been seen and photographed in squadrons of three.

Again, what in earth or sky, in our atmosphere, or in outer space, is the weird, vast white column of light seen, in one case, dropping reddish-yellow objects over Lake Geneva, in March 1763, and over the Cotswold Hills, in

July 1953? Or the mysterious white and vanishing fila-
ments seen to be dropped from high-flying visitants—not
planes—over southern France, in 1950? On such mysteries
we have no light.

One reason for the patrolling of the earth by these
visitants, who in some quarters are said to police the
solar universe, may be their fear of our rediscovering the
secret blast forces, arising from triggering off chain-reac-
tions, which destroyed a planet, shown by Bode to have
rotated between Mars and Jupiter. We see its remains in
thousands of asteroids and planetoids. This cosmoplastic
annihilation drove several planets off their orbits, and
catastrophically affected all the solar system, including the
sun.

Against this theory is another: That increasing cosmic
radiation is passing through our ionosphere, causing mu-
tations in the earth, and crystallizing her surface. Huge
chasms are formed into which the outer crust falls, causing great earthquakes. *If* that be so—and who can *know*
whether it be so or not?—these visitants may know that
man, whatever he does, is helpless to avert the decrees of
destiny, the writing on the face of the cosmos:

> "The cloud-capp'd towers, the gorgeous palaces,
> The solemn temples, the great globe itself,
> Yea, all which it inherit, shall dissolve;
> And, like this insubstantial pageant faded,
> Leave not a rack behind."

In that case, their purpose might be exploratory, to collect evidence of our scientific development, samples of our
choicest and peculiarly earthian productions. Again the
old Eastern wisdom must make her voice heard: "Live ye
as men. Sufficient unto the day is the evil thereof."

It is exceedingly unlikely that these visitants would seek
to destroy our planet. Beings of such great science and
wisdom would gain *nothing* by it. But they might have
plans of overlordship. The first move of some of these
mysterious entities may have been directed towards dis-
couraging our plans for space travel. They may have imposed the so-called "death ceiling" on British jet air liners.
They might deal with ground transport by methods of
thermal interference, or demobilization of locomotives. A
third movement *might* be towards fissioning such common
and indispensable materials of our civilization as glass
and metal. In what they did, or did not do, what may be
called enlightened selfishness would be their motivation.

What might be the purpose of a demiurgic cosmic power, indifferent to us and seeking the overlordship of our earth?

Our bodes they would *not* touch. There would be no gain for them in *that*. They would *not* spread carnage and chaos and disease over the earth, as we ourselves did in two terrible world wars. It might be our *souls* they would seek to annihilate—the soul of man. They might make spiritual helots of us. There might gradually grow up a race of earthians destitute of genius, but not necessarily of talent. Creative art and pure science, the godlike in man, would die out. There would be no mystery, no *ad astra* aspirations of man in the world of scientific discovery and creation, no parapsychology, no avenues for adventure; for the desire for that would be eliminated. To that end, a mutation might be created, a type of human being destitute of divine curiosity and dissatisfaction. In the phrase of Kipling's hillman, he would have *not* two separates sides to his head, but only one. Or, to vary the metaphor, the onion would have only one skin, not a succession surrounding a kernel or nucleus. The latter would symbolize the higher powers of the mind, extra-sensory perception, the divine, the paranormal, the parapsychological, everything transcending the normal, everyday world of matter and peeping into glory and power.

However this may be, it is as well to ponder any unqualified theory that *all* these elusive and mysterious saucers have arrived in our skies merely to help save us from the consequences of our own follies. The latter would be of little benefit to a planet that must work out its own salvation and learn from the results of its own follies. It is likely, indeed, that *some* of these visitants, perhaps *many*, are benevolent and helpful. It is equally probable that others are *not*. In any case, their ethics or moral concepts can hardly be ours, in view of the extremely advanced degree of their science. But if they force on us, or rather, the pressure of cosmic events forces on us world unity and the abolition of causes that lead to conflicting ideologies and wars, the flying saucer drama will have been more than worthwhile.

Nothing is gained by avoiding an overall view of facts, pleasant and unpleasant. It is the purpose of this book to try, however imperfectly and inadequately, to give a dim notion of what the vast corpus of the flying saucer phenomena suggests.

Earlier in this chapter, I referred to the "magnetic" propulsion of some of the mysterious aeroforms. Of course, the term magnetism is not used in the older, classical sense of that energy, which physicists regarded as more or less static. I have been told that American technicians have, for some years, been at work on a very secret device based on some form of "magnetic propulsion." All concerned with it are as much sworn to secrecy and as vigilantly watched and screened as are research workers concerned with nuclear-fission, or thermo-nuclear weapons.

As far back as 1934, the Westinghouse Research Laboratories demonstrated the peculiar property of cobalt steel, when prepared in the form of two magnets. It will float! Two ring-shaped magnets of cobalt steel are set in a frame, one above the other. The lower magnet is enclosed in a frame; the upper magnet is free to float up and down on a celluloid guide, coming to rest about an inch above the base. Given a push, this upper magnet bobs up and down, like a cork on a choppy sea, until it resumes its resting position.

To some extent, this peculiar action recalls that of a gyroscope which, of course, is itself linked with rotation of the earth, generating a "magnetic current." In this device, like poles are placed so that they repel each other; but the upward movement of the magnet is, of course, limited by the pull of gravity, which it balances. *But,* if we assume, as seems to be the case, that flying saucers can divert and neutralize gravity pulls, it must follow that their use of magnetic, or, as it might be called, electromagnetic "flows," or energy, far transcends our knowledge, and that we can hardly have touched more than the very fringe of this "new" physics.

In November, 1950, I was told of a Mr. Duncan Mackay, a mechanic employed in a factory of the British Road Services. He is said to have invented an engine working on a principle of magnetic force, which generates current and compresses air at a force of about 300 pounds to the square inch. One man could assemble this motor in a week. As a power unit, says Mr. Mackay, it could drive a ship. It is silent in operation, can be started instantly by a twelve-volt battery, and "there is no limit to its power capacity. It needs only lubricant and requires neither fuel nor water." He says it would run for ten years. In the Second World War, he put before the British War Office a magnetic bomb, effective only in a range of several yards.

Eighty years ago, a remarkable and now forgotten genius, John Worrell Keely, of Philadelphia, foreshadowed some of the powers of the very advanced science which appear to be under the command of these mysterious entities of the flying saucers. Keely found that the "corpuscles of matter" (atoms and molecules), could be "subdivided" by radiations which he called "certain orders of vibration." It was in November, 1874 that Keely showed twelve Philadelphia businessmen a "new and complicated motor," called "the hydro-pneumatic-pulsating-vacuo-engine." It appears to have brought him in many dollars, and he lived well and spent a great deal of time and money on his inventions.

But over Keely was the shadow of the hoodoo that so frequently dogs the man in advance of his age.

Keely had read MacVicar's *Sketches of Philosophy*, and a book titled *Harmonies of Tones and Colours Developed by Evolution*, whose author, Mrs. J. E. Hughes, was the niece of Charles Darwin. He began to "investigate the flow of magnetic currents from pole to pole," and later invented a motor that would use this energy and that of "etheric vibration." He then showed a machine that ran by some mysterious force unknown to the science and mechanics of the 1880's.

The press and the orthodox scientists ridiculed his claims. When he was backed by a Mrs. Moore, her friends got a court order to restrain her from spending her money on Keely's discoveries and researches.

In his workshop, Keely used some cosmic force which could start up a motor when he struck a note of music. As might be expected, that note of harmony soon called down on his luckless head the very cacophonous notes of the press and the orthodox scientists. But overseas in England, some hard-headed businessmen by no means shared this skepticism. They—the famous millionaire Barnato Brothers of the diamond mines of South Africa—commissioned a London engineer, Major J. Ricardo Seaver, to cross the Atlantic and investigate Keely's devices. In the presence of the astounded Seaver, Keely passed a bow across the strings of a violin and, ten feet away, the harmonic note started up Keely's motor, whose speed increased until it fairly rocked the bench to which the motor was bolted!

Seaver tried his own hand; but, for some time, he was unable to strike the correct note. In order to stop the motor, one had to strike discordant notes on the violin. Unfortunately, Keely had not anticipated the invention of the gramophone which would have recorded on a disc the precise note necessary, and so have equipped his amazing motor with an automatic starter. He said that the difficulty was that the "magnetic and etheric currents changed continually." Keely had also invented, it is said, a method of overcoming the pull of gravity. His invention consisted of three glass chambers, forty inches high, mounted on a glass slab. Each cylinder contained three metal spheres, weighing six ounces each. When a wire of silver and platina (platinum) was connected up with the glass chambers and linked with them to a "sympathetic transmitter," the metal spheres rose or descended in the chambers, or remained stationary at any point, and the motion of the spheres was as light as gossamer, floating on a still day in autumn. He applied his discovery to the model of an airship weighing 8 pounds. This, be it remembered, was in 1889 and 1890, twenty years before Bleriot flew the first plane across the Straits of Dover. When he attached a "differential wire" to the model, it rose and floated; and he could keep the model stationary, in helicopter fashion, and at whatever height he wished.

But the hoodoo was on poor Keely's trail. He had lost his backer, Mrs. Moore. He had the artist's contempt for money. Gradually, the poor devil sank under a load of debts, worries and frustrations. One winter night, in 1898, he was found dead in his workshop. A heap of charred ash represented all that he left to a perverse generation.

The story is told that the son of his woman backer, Clarence Bloomfield Moore, rented poor Keely's house after Keely's tragic death. Moore went ferreting, prying and rummaging down in the cellar, and lo, he found there an old, compressed-air motor to which an iron pipe and tubes led!

"Hola!" said Moore, "this fellow was an unadulterated rascal and fraud. Look at these pipes!"

"But," said Keely's old stockholders. "Poor Keely never made any secret to *us* of that old motor down in the cellar. We knew all about it long ago." They had seen his motor tear thick ropes apart, break iron bars, and shoot bullets through a twelve-inch plank!

I mention this ironical tail-piece, because an anti-climax of this sort was the fate of Keely's emulator, a man born in the same state of Pennsylvania, a year after Keely's death. Keely's mantle fell on one, Lester J. Hendershot, born in 1899, in West Elizabeth, Pennsylvania. Hendershot was a natural mechanical genius. It is said that in 1921 he had a dream one night in which there came to him the idea that a motor could be operated by earth or magnetic currents. After many experiments, he invented a motor that would "cut the magnetic field, east-west, and thereby develop rotary motion." It rotated at a constant speed. Hendershot, then living in Pittsburgh, Pennsylvania, called it a "fuelless motor, deriving power from the earth's magnetic field."

The invention so impressed Major Thomas Lanphier, U.S. Army commandant of Selfridge Airfield, Detroit, that he backed Hendershot. On this airfield, mechanics built a model which is said to have generated enough power to light two 110-volt lamps. A second model ran a small sewing-machine. With his fuelless motor Hendershot also made a model airplane fly at the airfield. There was nothing to conceal the mechanism and workings of the motor from the mechanics. It was run, too, for twenty-six hours when local broadcasting stations were at work, and also when they were off the air. As Lanphier said: "We got the same results. There is and was nothing fraudulent in this invention, and the power it used did *not* come from, and was not stolen from any broadcasting station."

Hendershot said—and as a poor man he had to be wary of his ideas being stolen: "The revolutionary feature of my motor is a hitherto unknown method of winding the armature."

But the hoodoo was now on Hendershot's trail. A Dr. Fred Hochstetter of a research laboratory in Pittsburgh, went all the way to New York, sparing no time or expense, hired a suite at an expensive hotel, convoked and "lushed up" the reporters to whom he declared: "I tell you, gentlemen, that this invention of this guy Hendershot is a fraud. It will destroy faith in science for 1,000 years!" No one knows to this day who stood coyly behind Hochstetter with the fee for this piper's tune. But it was not enough to "kill" the career of a brilliant young man. Singularly enough, as the final extinguisher on Hendershot, Hochstetter did exactly what Clarence B. Moore had done in 1898 to Keely. Hochstetter got hold of one of Hendershot's motors and "found" a carbon pencil battery hidden in the works.

Hendershot replied: "I put it there merely to stop visitors from too closely prying into my motor in order to steal the idea and invention of the device."

But Hochstetter roared on: "Here is proof of fraud and rascality!"

So, *was* it?

Now a very singular thing happened.

I quote from a Washington newspaper, dated March 10, 1928:

"Lester J. Hendershot, the inventor of the famous fuelless motor, has been admitted as a patient in a ward of the Emergency Hospital, Washington, D.C. He was demonstrating his motor in the office of his attorney in the Washington Loan and Trust Building, on Ninth and F Streets, when there suddenly shot from the machine an electric discharge of 2,000 volts, which has paralyzed his arms, legs and palate. He will have to remain in hospital for weeks to come."

Odd that a machine that Hochstetter so blatantly dubbed a "fraud" should inexplicably and unpredictably have shot out this powerful voltage! But what is just as odd is that not only from that day did Hendershot completely drop out of the news, *but his invention also!*

I am not here concerned with whether or not powerful vested interests in the American fuel oil industry and the vast field of the internal combustion engine and motor manufacturing trades saw themselves menaced, and played, *vis-à-vis* Hendershot, the part played in Europe, in recent years, in the matter of the perpetual match and everlasting, chromium-plated razor-blade. What I am concerned with, and the reason why I have entered at some length into the history of these two pioneers is that both seem to have discovered, independently, one of the amazing secrets of the propulsion of these weird flying saucers, which forty-six years after Keely's death, and sixteen years after the severe accident to Hendershot, began to appear in the skies over our earth.

I may close this chapter with a short reference to a remarkable, now forgotten theory promulgated in Berlin, Germany, as long ago as 1906, by a scientist named Levetzof, or Lewetzov. He held that space is filled with an unknown ray, whose waves and particles come from all directions, and create a balancing effect that neutralize each other. He said that each ray exerts a pressure on all bodies in space. Since this radiation comes from all sides, bodies in free space are rendered nearly weightless and freed from the normal pull of the gravity-field. But, he said, when two bodies oppose each other, this balance of zero gravity is upset; for the rays that have penetrated a body become greatly weakened. If man found a way artificially to weaken the force of these rays, he would have discovered a tremendous and almost inexhaustible source of energy.

Since the project of space-vehicles is one of considerable interest to "astronauts," as well as to those interested in the flying saucer non-terrestrial phenomena, I think the reader of this book may care to have some further detail about the "Levetzov" ray.

According to the *Frankfürter (am Main) Illustrierte,* of November 14 and 21, 1953, Levetzov's theory appeared to contradict the accepted classical laws of gravity—and of conservation of energy. According to those laws, the mass-attraction of a larger body, in suspension, causes a smaller one to fall upon it. He said that if a device, using this artificially weakened, natural energy, were attached to one end of a motor car, the car should "run forever; since the driving rays work only from the opposite end. The same would be true for aircraft. A combination of instruments on different planes of the craft would serve to raise, propel and steer it."

The magazine alleges that, in July 1929, under an exchange program, German officers were sent to the U.S.S.R., one of whom, a certain Horst Pinkell, an expert in high-frequency radiation, knew the theory of Levetzov. Subsequently, it is said, a Soviet laboratory was erected at which the existence of the Levetzov ray was established. In 1940, or 1942, instruments were perfected and moved to a laboratory at Magnitogorsk, where research workers formulated a theory that the Levetzov rays alternated, in a very short time, from pure wave characteristics to a corpuscular structure, and back again. The meson-particle fluctuations within the atom had now found a stable physical explanation. The rays penetrate the earth, but lose a great deal of their strength in the penetration. Nevertheless, they can lift an object from the earth, provided that the direct rays from outer space are prevented from pressing down upon the object.

In November, 1942, experts directed by a Russian physicist, Andrei Goryev, were at work for the Red Army on a secret test-site, in the valley of Belaya, in the southern Urals. It was hoped (vainly) that a revolutionary type of aerofoil, using the Levetzov rays, could be put into the air against the Nazi forces. What actually was created by Pinkell and Goryev (says the *Frankfürter Illustrierte*) was an apparatus in the form of:

"Two pieces of crystal that, when laid one upon the other, stop the penetration of light rays when their 'grains' are at right angles to each other. But light rays may pass when the 'grains' are in a parallel position. By turning one crystal, infinite variations of penetration may be obtained. A crystal which completely bars the penetration of the ultra-short-wave Levetzov rays does not appear to exist. The Russians found a metal alloy that had the required properties when specially prepared by a secret formula. This alloy may be used as a polarizer, or neutralizer of the Levetzov rays, for about two years. After that period, the alloy's metals fatigue."

By the Law of Conservation of Energy, established in 1847 by Mayer and von Helmholtz, perpetual motion is an impossibility. "Nothing for nothing," says Nature. But what the Ural experimenters did, it is said, was not to try to abrogate this law, but to create a machine that would run steadily without energy from the earth. Since the driving force came from outer space, however, a terrestrial view might be that at last an approach had been made towards a perpetual motion machine, limited by fatigue in the component metals. It is said that by Spring, 1944, a motor car was being driven by this ray from outer space.

A veil of mystery now fell over the experiments. In 1948, came reports of the arrest by the Russian Secret Police of Herr Pinkell and certain Russian scientists. Incarcerated in the prison island of Tohnay, Pinkell was forced to carry on work in a secret laboratory. Their crime appeared to be that they had frankly told the notorious Lavrenti Beria, Secret Police chief, that more time was needed to perfect the work. Although in 1944, ray-propelled aircraft had been constructed in Soviet Russia, Beria demanded instant results. He put the research under the control of the Russian Air-Marshal, K. Vershinin who, in 1948, was alleged to have at his command five planes flying at a then "almost unimaginable speed and service radius, in theory equal to that of half the known space." The phrase is cryptic, but one may guess what is meant.

By February, 1952, it is said there was under construction, in Russia, a "space island" of the American Forrestal type, intended to serve as a stopover for space craft from the earth. (Or so said the Zyalkovsky Institute of Kaluga):

"We take great care, in our advance work, with all parts and assemblies for this space-platform. We surround them with the same conditions that will be encountered in space. Basically, the space island will be an enlargement of a type of aircraft already past the experimental stage, and which is propelled by a newly discovered energy of extra-terrestrial origin. A trip to the moon is a problem that will not have to wait too long for an answer." (*Report by the Zyalkovsky Institute, February 20, 1952*).

It is possible—who really *knows,* outside the innermost ruling circle of Russia?—that there was more than mere propaganda hot air in this statement. In the same month, the official bulletin of the Soviet State Academy for Technology, called "SUK," published an illustrated description of a "space island."

The *Frankfürter Illustrierte* alleges that:

"Since the forces exerted in propelling a Levetzov ray-machine are several thousand times greater than any previously known, there appears in the discs a radiant glow. This arises from an excess of power, or waste of energy that cannot easily be removed, and appears as heat. So great is the energy developed, that things within a fairly large radius begin to melt. A method of transforming this energy-surplus into waves eliminates the waste without damage."

Follows a description of a *terrestrial* flying saucer on this Russian model, or, as it should be, German-Russian model:

"A disc is the ideal form; but we may have a structure that revolves around its centre at immense speed, and therefore appears discoidal. The main part is a bonnet-like cupola of a framework of metal, the spaces between braces being covered with a transparent substance appearing as ports, or 'windows.' On this hub are mounted fan-wise, six wings with a small positive angle. Each blade or wing carries on the first third, top and bottom, a housing shaped like a hump, containing the transformer discarding the surplus-energy. Set into the outer skin of the blades are polarizing sheets that, dependent on their mutual adjustment, propel the craft, let it hover, and steer. But this entire formation is also being rotated by the Levetzov ray, while the cabin for the crew is suspended within the hub, and more or less stationary. The crew do not experience any feeling of acceleration, or deceleration; since they and the entire aerofoil are shielded from the rays."

Professor Hermann Oberth, well known rocket-missile expert of former Nazi Germany, now in the United States, said in an interview:

"We know of a material that will, in practice, insulate from the pull of gravity any object covered by it."

If that be so, this *may* suggest, perhaps—there is no proof—that the United States has followed Soviet Russia in creating some form of terrestrial flying saucer. But it must *not* be supposed that flying saucers, *in toto,* are merely new and very advanced terrestrial aerofoils. There is, as I have elsewhere stated, far too long a history of unknown flying objects in the skies, going back as far, at least, as Roman annals of the third century B.C., as well as other phenomena that rule out such an extenuation, or annihilation, or "rationalizing away" of the existence of flying objects from worlds outside our own planet.

It may be that German and Russian, and probably American scientists have rediscovered one form of the energies used in ages past, by entities whose science is far older than our own, and who have repeatedly entered our own atmosphere and scanned our earth. There exists a very large corpus of historical evidence proving that this revolutionary statement is not figment of imagination, or anyone's hallucination.

My friend, H. K. Hotham of Melbourne, Victoria, sent me this clipping from the *Melbourne Sun,* dated August 25, 1954:

TWO NEW SATELLITES (NATURAL):
Two meteors had become satellites of the earth and were revolving with it 400 to 600 miles out in space, the latest issue of the American magazine Aviation Week said yesterday. The magazine said that the discovery of the satellites threw the air force into confusion this summer.

Alarm over the sightings ended only after they had been identified definitely as natural rather than man-made.

In another place I have drawn attention to a series of mysterious lights and formations on the moon, and in or around lunar craters and plains, seen by astronomers and reputable observers, from the end of the eighteenth century, and many times in the nineteenth and twentieth centuries. Splendid rocket-like discharges have been seen from the moon in times of eclipse. In late September, 1954, a Duluth (Minnesota) newspaper reported that Frank Halstead, curator of the Darling Observatory, said that while he, Halstead, was lecturing in another room, his assistant, using a nine-inch telescope with a sixty power lens, saw what looked like a "lunar road," in the crater Piccolomini (July, 1954). As this can be seen with telescopes of lower power, this may indicate that the "road" is very wide and long. There is no reason to suppose that either the U.S.A. or Russia has built and projected onto the moon any form of terrestrial space vehicle; it would be all but impossible to keep such a tremendous achievement a secret. Therefore, *if* this be an artificial road, one may ask, is it, perhaps, a launching ramp for space vehicles of some other world?

All one can do is scrutinize this crater with a telescope of much greater power.

A correspondent of mine, Miss Josephine Myers, a hospital nurse in Omaha, Nebraska, who owns a lower-power telescope and makes a hobby of selenography, writes me as follows:

"On October 19, 1954, some space-minded friends of mine were very excited at what they called their discovery of something on the moon. I rushed home when my duty-spell was over, and looked at the moon with my telescope of thirty-five—forty power. It looked to me as if there were a big crater, about the right middle side of the moon where I had never seen a crater before. Clouds have since cut off my observation. So I guess I shall have to wait till it's full again, in order to make sure."

No student of the history of science despises the work of amateurs. He or she knows that more than one important discovery has been made or suggested by them. What better advanced base for flying saucers, spying on the earth, than our own moon?

THE FOLLOWING WAS MAILED TO ME, in good faith but not undue credulity, by a well-educated Californian:

"In March, 1953, a Los Angeles journalist had a strange caller at his office, a tall man, dressed in loose and shoddy clothing, whose skin had a curious bluish pigmentation. He told the clerk in the inquiry office:

" 'I am a man who has recently landed in your state from what you call a flying saucer. We set it down on the floor of the Mojave Desert. I wish to have some publicity in your newspaper, for it would help both me and your earth.'

" 'Oh yeah!' said the clerk, with a grin which changed to a look of surprise as he took in the queer appearance of the caller. 'Wait a minute, pal, while I ring up the City Editor!' "

Now, newspapers are accustomed to queer-looking and eccentric callers, and on most of them a reporter is assigned the not always enviable job of tactfully getting rid of them. I have had this job in my own time as a London newspaperman, and well know the difficulty one sometimes has with them. I well remember one man with a wild eye and an unearthly manner who, when I asked him his name and business, presented me with a card on which was the one word "God!" I imagine that it was this not always harmless sort of caller that the City Editor had in mind, when the clerk gave his impressions of the blue-skinned caller:

"The City Editor rang up one of his reporters.

'Sounds screwball to me,' he said, 'but perhaps you'd better see him. He may be loco, but you may get a few lines out of him. There's been so much recently about these flying saucers. See what the guy has to say.'

"The caller told Jim Phelan, the reporter, that he would call back next day with another man who, like himself, came from the planet Venus. Phelan thought that would be the last he would see of this crackpot. However, the queer man called back next morning with another queer being. The two were as much like each other as two peas in a pod. Both were 6 foot 6 in height. Their skin had the bluish tinge one often sees in cardiac cases. But it later appeared that heart disease was *not* their trouble. Both were emaciated. The clothes they wore looked as if they had come out of a sailors' slop shop. Very loose in fit and shoddy. When the reporter looked closely at their heads, he was struck by their ears which were pricked, like those of a breed of Asiatic dogs. Their hands, too, were queer—seemed to be jointless."

" 'Where d'ye say you come from?' asked Phelan.

" 'Venus!'

" 'Huh, I s'pose you mean the planet of that name? How did you get here?'

" 'We landed our little disc-ship in the Mojave Desert, and walked and what you call hitch-hiked here from San Bernardino.'

" 'What happened to your saucer? Is it still there in the desert?'

"The 'Venusians' smiled, looked at each other, but did not answer. After a minute, one of them said: 'We find the climate of South California dreadfully hot and sultry, even in winter.' "

This must import that these queer beings did not come from the planet Venus, since that planet's upper layer of cirrus clouds, and its comparative proximity to the sun, much nearer than the earth, ensures that it receives twice the amount, or even more, of solar heat than does the earth. Whether they came from Venus, as a way station from, or in relation to some other possibly "etheric," or fourth-dimensional double of some visible planetary world (and the up-to-date astronomer now talks of "planetary doubles"), is something on which light may be thrown as the flying saucer drama moves towards its inevitable climax.

The interrogation proceeded:

" 'Why do you come to earth?

" 'We come to study your minds and your thought

and your scientific knowledge. That is why we travel through space.'

" 'What do you want from this paper?'

" 'We want publicity, as that will help us to travel.'

"Phelan explained that a story would get them more than they bargained for; that the publicity might lead to their being both shut up in a lunatic asylum, or put under detention in some camp controlled by the military or security authorities.

"One of them spoke quickly: 'Please do not give us this publicity.'

"Said Phelan: 'How come you speak English so well?'

" 'We learnt it listening to your radio and television broadcasts.' "

Then, according to my Los Angeles friend's story, a remarkable incident occurred. The reporter challenged them to prove that they came from some world in space:

"One of the 'Venusians' walked over to a desk made of very hard wood. With his finger-nail he scored in the hard wood a furrow nearly a quarter of an inch deep!

" 'Does that satisfy you?' he asked the reporter. 'If not, I can throw the whole desk out of the window onto the street below.'

" 'No, that satisfies me. Say, call back here tomorrow and I'll see if I can find you a job.'

"It appears that Phelan persuaded a pal to give these queer guys a job in a law office of a department run by the municipality of Los Angeles. While there these strange beings were given a piece of steel. In this one of them made with his thumb-nail an indentation more than one-half inch deep! It was found that these strange beings had peculiar powers of another sort. They were put on to trace lost and missing persons, and they traced them in two-and-a-half hours compared with the two to three weeks required by even the best departmental sleuths! Naturally, men who were working in the office, and had not been told about this story of their having come from Venus, were curious about their remarkable powers.

"Someone was so impressed, or so suspicious, that he communicated with the F.B.I., which sent an investigator. But, as if in some strange way, the 'Venusians' had telepathic powers, or some faculty of prevision, they did not turn up at the office. The F.B.I. have never been able to find them for questioning but I am assured there is a report about this queer affair in the secret F.B.I. files."

The steel, indented more than one-half inch deep, is said to have been sent for analysis to the laboratory of a metallurgical chemist. To have such an effect on steel, the report said, pressure of at least 1,800 pounds to the square inch would have been necessary, and the steel would have been fractured rather than indented! Moreover, what was even more remarkable, in the furrow made in the steel by the "Venusian" man, were fourteen elements not present in the rest of the steel. (It would be interesting to know if any of these elements are unknown in the Mendeleyev system, elements not yet known, or not actually existing on our own earth!)

What comment is one to make upon this story?

This: That one of the men, circulating it in an American magazine, is a highly imaginative freelance writer. In 1953, this gentleman was told, by another Californian gentleman, another story of an alleged landing of saucer entities, which the former wrote up very nicely, not to say transcendentally. From this, it appears that the second gentleman is, or was a plastic worker in a factory, manufacturing plastic installations for American Air Force radarscopes. Homeward-bound, on May 24, 1952, after his night-shift, he became the reluctant hero of a strange adventure. He was driving his car when he saw ahead of him, in the sky, a glowing red object which appeared to be trailing him, and radiating something which gave him a "queer prickling electrical sensation." Suddenly, the strange orb shot up into the sky, hovered, and released two small green, fluorescent discs which came to rest a few feet above his car. Out of the discs came a voice speaking perfect English:

"Have no fear, Orfeo, for we are friends. You are communing with friends from another planet."

The discs then projected a sort of screen on which appeared the radiant heads of a most noble man and woman, with whom Orfeo had "telepathic talk" lasting for the rather unprecedented space of two hours by the clock. One of the telepathic "communicators" made the astounding statement that every man, woman and child "is recorded in our vital statistics on crystal discs!" (*N.B.* Back in 1938, the estimated population of the earth was about 2,000,000,000).

The communicator added, as has been the case in other alleged encounters of saucer entities by California gentlemen, that Orfeo was specially favored, he "being one of three human beings selected for communication." The others live in India and Italy. It is to be noted that this communicator gave Orfeo a singularly inaccurate account of the death of Captain Thomas Mantell, killed in January 1948, when his plane distintegrated over Godman Airfield, near Fort Knox, Kentucky. Mantell had been ordered to close with an unidentified flying object of *vast size,* but the communicator told Orfeo it was merely a *small disc.* It may be presumed that the prodigious "crystal recording discs" are not *quite* invariably reliable as "vital statisticians."

At the end of this two hours' talk *by telepathy* the discs vanished into the blue, after promising to contact Orfeo later. But it was not until 10 P.M., on July 23, 1952, that, on a "vacant lot," Orfeo saw a thirty-foot-wide object aground. He entered it, and by telepathic command, sat on a translucent chair. Orfeo was then taken for a ride into the empyrean from which he looked down on a huge globe enhaloed by rainbows. "It is your earth," he was told telepathically. Then he saw, out in space, a thing like a vast dirigible, at least a thousand feet long and ninety feet high. From it came the music of the spheres. There were three decks, but no visible occupants. It had "rotors" of flame at each end. He was then returned to earth in the United States, and commanded telepathically to tell the scoffing earthlings about his adventure. He was then started on a nationwide lecture tour under the spiritual sponsorship of a Buffalo (N. Y.) elder who habitually broadcasts to the sound of trumpets and shawms and quartettes of "quiring" ladies and gentlemen who nightly make the welkin ring with loud hosannas.

Orfeo had another encounter with the saucer entity about 2 P.M., on August 2, 1953. This time, a gentleman came out from under the shadows of a road bridge, clad in a seamless blue suit. Orfeo was given a glance at prehistory, and some account of an Elysian world from which man fell when he blasted the planet Lucifer, rotating between Mars and Jupiter. The entity discoursed on a neo-Oriental, Maya illusion of a world of sin and sorrow, and on communism and left-wingerism with which venomous snakes were compared greatly to the detriment of the reds. Oddly enough, the saucer entity ended this edifying conversation by asking for a drink. Orfeo departed to fetch from the nearest drug store a bottle of pop, hesitating apparently to demoralize "Neptune," as he called his etheric visitor, by treating him to a flagon of the stronger brew that comes from Milwaukee.

The Santa Monica, California, gentleman who imparts the atmosphere to this sprightly story, himself tells another about a strange man who rang *him* up from Los Angeles:

" 'Call me Bill,' " said the stranger. " 'I am coming over to Santa Monica just to see you.' "

At 6 P.M., on a day in June, 1953, "Bill" appeared "out of the blue," dematerializing, so to speak, close to a bus stop on the Santa Monica boulevard. According to the imaginative Santa Monica freelance, "Bill" also proved to be a six-foot-sixer, with a strange whitish-blue skin and complexion, high cheekbones, a sort of Oriental countenance, and psychic qualities, "full of vibrations." One gathers it was "Bill" who put the Santa Monica freelance onto Orfeo, of whose existence the Santa Monican was previously unaware. According to "Bill," Orfeo was the first terrestrial gentleman ever to make a trip to outer space in a flying saucer.

(*N.B.* This claim will be violently and vehemently denied by other Californians who allege that they anticipated Orfeo's adventure by two to three years. Theirs, they imply, is the only true story, all others being shams, as the old Newgate Gaol chaplain said of his ballad books and last dying speeches of old English pirates about to be swung off scaffolds.)

"Bill" said they, from outer space, had commissioned him to request the Santa Monican freelance to act as a literary "ghost" to Orfeo, whose own education was not quite equal to the task. "Bill" also put the Santa Monican in touch with a Los Angeles newspaper reporter who rather reluctantly spilled the mystic beans.

However the truth may lie, in regard to the mysterious entity who could, with his bare fingers, cut his name and address, had he so wished, in cold steel, I must leave my reader to form his or her own opinion about the cold objectivity, or the warm and vibrant romance of Orfeo's and the Santa Monica gentleman's narrations. All I wish to say is that another Santa Monican resident writes me that after reading "Bill's" story, he got on the telephone to the other Santa Monican, and made an appointment to meet him. Alas! the freelance failed to turn up as he promised, and has never since communicated with his telephone friend and candid inquirer.

From documents reaching me by the courtesy of American correspondents, it appears that many of these concocters of romantic stories appear to be backing each other up, apparently on the assumption that if they do not hang together they will hang separately. How much pure or impure psychopathy is intermingled with these romantic stories it would be unprofitable to say. I particularly hesitate to do so in the case of a Palomar "Venusian" who has as his energetic coadjutor a young Irish son of a well known Irish knight and writer. The son had graciously and without my permission, or prior knowledge put under contribution, in the service of an obvious and lucrative flying saucer spoof, two South American books of mine. But this I *may* say: these far from veracious stories do cover a very serious theme with ridicule, and the derision of scoffers who are thus given an appearance of justification.

At this point, attention might be drawn to the singular story told, in 1953, by Mr. Truman Bethurun, a California mechanic. In that year, he claims he had contacts with the woman commander of a "scow," or space ship from some world in space, which she seems to have designedly misled him into supposing was behind our Moon. I have not seen his interesting book, "Aboard a Flying Saucer," but a friend has sent me extracts. These give me the impression that the woman was from some fourth-dimensional world. Bethurun records eleven visits with her.

I summarize the extracts:

"She called herself Captain Aura Rhanes. She and her crew had come to the earth for education and also to 'replenish our atmosphere tanks; for when we travel in space we, in our scow, are sealed-in tight.' (Why she called her disc ship a *scow,* which Webster defines as a large flat-bottomed boat with broad, square ends is not clear, unless the word is used metaphorically.) She adds that they come here for 'relaxation.' They do not wish to interfere with our planet; although they have no high opinion of us. They have seen and admired American fleets on maneuvers in the Atlantic. 'The only water in your deserts must be those from human tears.' Captain

Rhanes is a fine figure of a woman in looks, and has a masculine mind. She wears a black and red beret.

"When her saucer takes off, the door shuts noiselessly. Then the craft vanishes in sunshine as if it had been a pearl, or opal turning into vapor. Bethurun saw no propellers, no vents, no wings, and it left no wake of gases. He was aboard the space ship for half an hour. No sooner had his foot touched ground, than, hey presto, the 'scow' had gone! At other times he had seen Captain Rhanes and her crew of men go into and later vanish into nothingness in a Nevada roadside café, where apparently they drank nothing stronger than lemonade.

"Should terrestrials attack her scow, she said, they would disappear, and she demonstrated by causing a flashlight of Mr. Bethurun's to vanish, as if it had teleported. 'Yes,' said she to the naturally astonished Mr. B., 'you will see it no more. It has gone forever! That is how your people would go, if they attacked us and our scow.'

"Bethurun says the 'scow' was about 300 feet long and thirty feet thick. The impression one gets is that it and the crew converted to a vibration rate beyond our perception, and that in a short space of time."

(In other words: " 'Reality is no anchor for your soul. It is of the stuff of shadows.' Has not Bertrand Russell (and I do not infer that Russell would champion the flying-saucer riddle) said: 'An electron is a wave of probability, with nothing to wave in. All scientific theory is just statistics of probability.' *Au.*)

"Captain Aura Rhanes laughed at a question of Mr. Bethurun. 'We kill nobody. Why should we? Our enemies just fall and disappear. If they have done no real damage, they may rise up and go about their own business. We go away.' She added that teleportations 'is a fact . . . but one foreign to your comprehension.' He says she wrote a note in Chinese, in answer to one in French. Bethurun took the note to a Chinese cook, who looked at it and shook with agitation. 'No can read. No come from here.' The Chinese pointed to the ceiling, 'Come from up there.' It seems that the note read: 'Chinese women hold their husbands with love. If not, they put them in chains.' "

I do not know what a Sinologist would say to this epigram. One thing seems clear: the world from which

Aura Rhanes hails must be a matriarchate, in which women do not merely play at being soldiers.

If this book of Mr. Bethurun appears in an English edition, I advise my English readers to study it and form their own opinion on it. I must, however, be absolved from any supposition that I, in any way, endorse this unproved or unprovable story.

Here follows a mystery of an alleged abduction by flying saucers, only *one* aspect of which may ever be cleared up by some desert roamer stumbling over a man's corpse. Even so, the strange glyphs left on the walls of a garage of one of the two missing men may never be deciphered. The mystery, and the moving spirit, in this case, is the personality of a certain Karl Hunrath, an American citizen of Magyar antecedents. Nothing has been heard of him since March 23, 1954:

March 23, 1954: The authorities of Gardena airport, Southern California, inform the author of this book that nothing has been found of the plane hired for one hour by Wilbur J. Wilkinson, radio technician of the Hoffmann Radio Corp., and Karl Hunrath, electrician, both men residing at Los Angeles, California. It took off on November 16, 1953. The men did not file a flight plan. It may have subsequently crashed in wooded mountains, burnt over by forest fires, or in lonely *cañons,* or in a California desert.

Note by the author: The wife of Wilkinson, who has three young children, told a local newspaper that she believes her husband "has been abducted by flying saucers in a California desert." The glyphs were left on the walls of a garage by Wilkinson, who hired this plane. Hunrath was apparently the moving spirit in this mystery. The glyphs appear to purport that these two men had "contacted a saucer of the fleet of the planet *Maser,*" which Hunrath alleged had landed in a desert. It seems that Wilkinson had what are said to be tape-recordings of talks with entities from *Maser,* and that he was compiling an alphabet of *Maser,* received on his electronic equipment.

The "Dead Letter" office of California returned my letter to Hunrath's relatives with the notation that the parties could not be found. In it I asked for information on whether Hunrath had been a student of prehistoric American petroglyphs. Among the above curious glyphs alleged to emanate from one "Prince Reggs, of the planet *Maser,*" are glyphs and symbols singularly like a petroglyph found in the jungles of Brazil; a second resembles one found on La Plata Island, off the western coast of South America; a third resembles a prehistoric glyph for cataclysm and water; a fourth resembles the double sign of coition found in ancient Mu, a drowned continent in the ancient Pacific; a fifth resembles a prehistoric glyph found in California.

A Californian correspondent writes: "These two men took off for an hour's flight just round the airport, but evidently sneaked away for a supposed contact in the desert, which could have been done in about two hours' flying time, if they went straight over the mountains." Another California correspondent tells me that a well known "medium of deep trance has heard from a control that the hired plane crashed and both men were killed. The control promised to find out the locality."

My friend, Frederick G. Hehr, adds:

"These two guys, Hunrath and Wilkinson, rented a small plane like the *Moth*, ostensibly for a flight of an hour round the airport which is as flat as London. But they must have taken off for somewhere else, and either fell into the Pacific, or were caught in a downdraught on the mountains and smashed in some inaccessible *cañon*. Even big planes disappear and are not found for a year or two, unless they happen to crash near a travelled road or railroad. Around are plenty of mountains from 6,000 to 14,000 feet, most with deep snow all the year round, covering three sides of the Los Angeles basin. On the other side is the ocean, with a few mountainous islands occupied by wild pigs, goats or sea-birds. Only last week a Navy jet fighter plane vanished after the pilot radioed he was bailing out. His body was found, but only because a farmer reported a heavy crash up one *cañon*. At least half-a-dozen such planes vanish every week, and are not found for years. The highlands of Scotland, compared to this wild region, are overpopulated. Telepathy is something the saucer entities possess. I have had proof that they can read the thoughts of people with accuracy fifty miles away. Identification of certain no-good people, like brutal militarists and politicians masquerading as statesmen, is easy for them."

Since I have no hoax to get across with the aid of daily gossip columnists, "strip tease" sensational weeklies, hosts of charlatans and impostors, operating on suspicious photographs with strange "biometric" devices unknown to any laboratory, or "revelations" made on the radio and to clubs of saucer fans and nuisances, I fear I must end this Hunrath-Wilkinson story with what sounds like an anti-climax.

There has appeared a book in which two gentlemen speak of using the Ouija-board and short-wave radio contacts with saucer men from *Maser,* said to be the planet *Mars.* Thence they proceed to automatic writing, in the course of which pops up this same Prince Regga of Mars, called Prince *Reggs* above. There also appears the portentous figure of one Zo, a gentleman with seven children, said to hail from the planet Neptune, but with a stop-off bungalow on Mars. It is also curious—and here is one of the pitfalls of saucer fantaisistes who drag into the saucer theme "leit-motivs" from American pre-history, that these two gentlemen profess to be philosophers and scientists. One, who has appended his signature to an affidavit attesting the veracity and authenticity of still another gentleman's alleged stop-watch talk by telepathy and gesture with an entity in a landed saucer from "Venus"—a hoax. impure and unsimple—is said to be an anthropologist, or prehistorian, and an authority on Indian dances (as he may well be, for aught I know). His collaborator merely professes to be a "student of philosophy and science," employed, very oddly in relation to these studies, on the Santa Fé and New Mexico Railroad. It seems that some time before their book appeared, the publisher in California was sorely stricken with threats from someone to blow up his printery, and with dire menaces from another, suspected to be *Wilbur J. Wilkinson,* who alleged that all the material in this book was "snitched," or as the Artful Dodger said in *Oliver Twist,* "prigged" from him.

I am reminded in this mystery of a comic song which was howled, roared and barrel-organed when I was a boy, in the years of the Boer or South African War of 1899-1901. It had a refrain, a very pathetic refrain, as follows:

"Bill Bailey, won't you *please* COME HOME?"

My friend, Mr. Gray Barker, who at Clarksburg, West Virginia, runs a spritely little magazine called the "Saucerian," says that in 1920 there was a song in America, of which the refrain ran:

> "Mr. Gentle-man
>   Tell my Mammy to come back home.
>   I'm so alone."

I advise these gentlemen, as also another Californian who claims to have had a very remarkable ride in a saucer from White Sands proving grounds to New York and Washington, D.C., and back again, *not* to adventure onto the shifting sands of ancient American history and Atlantean archaeology, when indicting these veracious books. Such adventures tend to draw the malign eyes of skeptics their way.

In April, 1954, I received an air-mail letter from a friend in California reporting a startling event in the flying-saucer drama.

> "An unconfirmable report that President Eisenhower, in a recent visit to the Edwards Air Force base, California, was informed that a recent investigation of five types of flying saucers by experts and technicians there, has thrown them all into confusion and consternation. It is alleged that the experts have reported on the materialization and subsequent dematerialization, into a fourth-dimension of invisibility, of some of the mysterious types of non-terrestrial aeroforms, or unidentified flying objects."

There may be doubt whether President Eisenhower visited the Edwards Air Force base in person. It may be that he delegated a general to go there on his behalf. But from a reliable source in Southern California, I am assured that these five saucers actually did land *voluntarily* at this Edwards Air Force base. They were discs of different types and their entities invited the technicians and scientists to inspect their aeroforms and witness a demonstration of their powers.

Says my informant, who has a doctorate from an American university:

> "I can positively assure you that a friend of mine visited Edwards Air Force base, soon after this demonstration. He was accompanied by (1): a man prominent in the Hearst news syndicate; (2): a bishop of either the Methodist or the Episcopal Church; (3): a

former confidential adviser of ex-President Truman. I cannot release to you their names at this moment.

"I have also confirmatory reports by two other persons, but these would not carry weight by themselves. The story has gotten out all over the U.S., but NOT in public prints or newspapers. It was, of course, given the horse-laugh by the Pentagon and the Air Command at Washington, D.C. But the basic facts are that some of our technicians and scientists have actually 'gone off the deep end' mentally, when the saucer entities confronted them with new, and to them, inexplicable physical data. The entities demonstrated before their eyes that they could dematerialize and materialize themselves—become alternately visible and invisible. All this for our bright boys—now you see it, and now you don't!

"I congratulate you on the fine work you are doing in the flying-saucer field, and for the open-minded scholarship and distinguished public service in these Days of Confusion. I have nothing but admiration for it, and the almost endless labor of collecting and organizing such difficult material. It is certainly an exceptionally fine piece of work."

This learned gentleman adds that he firmly believes that *all* these non-terrestrial aeroforms we call flying saucers, are *Mutants*, who can and do change size, shape, color, mode of action, etc.:

"They also become transparent or nearly so—all while under observation. This points to the fact that the matter of which they are composed is not matter as we know it, but is, in fact, the etheric prototype— etheric steel, etc. Years ago, the Mark Probert communicators told us that it was correct to speak of etheric and/or astral copper, etc., from which our own terrestrial metals are derivatives. Thus, all the aeroforms (from space) may be said to be, as you say on page 296 of your 'Flying Saucers on the Attack,' of an order of matter akin to our own, but actually, only in a limited way. The matter is of extreme etheric density and high frequency of subatomic motion—hence, susceptible of mental control. So, *etheric and etherians* are legitimate terms for the whole body of these phenomena.

"In the long run, the matter of mental control will be found NOT to conflict with their use of—on occasion—elaborate apparatus. And, as you know, the theory of doubles is ancient and sound metaphysics and makes good science. The attempt to divorce physics from metaphysics, in dealing with these phenomena, is a pure dichotomy and can only delay and mislead. Incidentally, I may add, as you realize, that there is nothing 'mystical' about the use of paranormal means of information, so long as one is not subservient to the communications. . . ."

As there has been, in some quarters in the United States, a tendency to align these saucer entities with ghosts or excarnate entities from our earth, what this writer says is of interest:

"We find that what are called ghosts, or average excarnate humans in the world beyond our plane— the world of the so-called dead—or astral entities, have no knowledge of, and know nothing about these Etherian races and cultures of the flying saucers. The latter phenomena are entirely out of *their* vibratory range. But a few highly developed excarnate humans can and do study these Etherians. They gave us the fourth dimensional (4 D), or etheric account in 1946; and while the basic ideas have been expanded, they have not been contradicted by any subsequent data— a good test of any hypothesis. These saucer phenomena will never be understood until this thesis is grasped and understood. As a matter of public service, we MUST make the interpretation at least reasonably clear, and at least offer it to the public without propaganda. It has run us and our society into the red often, and we make no profit. I am very much interested in making the fourth-dimensional explanation clearly intelligible to persons like yourself, with a most superior mental equipment and a wide audience. The trouble is that the 'new' physics is new, and does not go along with the old text-book physics, the latter having come to an impasse. What is wanted is a new start, rather than an attempt at re-working the old concepts."

The writer accompanies his interesting letter with a diagram based on data communicated, he says, by the Etherian guides and instructors whose aeroforms are of the fourth-dimensional pattern, convertible into the third dimension of our own world, and back again. It shows that the plane of the Earth, or Terra, is penetrated, or crossed at right angles, by an etheric double or invisible, but real world, "the greatest heights of whose etheric mountains are the deepest parts of the earth's own seas; while the mountains of our own globe rise into the etheric and descend into other planes," making a fixed or right angle with them, as the higher mathematics might say.

N.B. I pass *no* opinion on this diagram!

A word about the Mojave Desert of Southern California may interest readers who have never been there. It is the location of this Edwards Air Force Base, or another highly secret base called the Muroc.

Says a Californian who has often traversed this desert:

"Saucer sightings have been frequent there. The area is as big as all England and Wales, from the latitude of Liverpool down. Visibility there is usually 150 miles *plus*. The few people there are outdoorsmen and outdoorswomen, and very observant. Here are located the Edwards and Muroc air and naval bases, where all the latest devices are tested. The atom bomb testing ground lies just over the northern rim of the desert. No wonder, then, that plenty of flying saucers have come over the area to give the flyboy competition the raspberry, and thumb them with the freemason sign! Also, to keep an eye on what is going on around there."

Has the following curious and bizarre incident anything to do with the landing of a saucer? It is not easy to say: It comes to me from a woman friend in Santa Fé, New Mexico.

May 7, 1954: The U.S. Army and White Sands proving-grounds are puzzled by a report of two women that, on a sand dune near an extinct volcano named "Kilburne Hole," strange tracks have been found. These numbered about thirty, and are shaped in the form of four concentric circles, with a dot in the innermost circle, and two straight lines, running from the outer diameter of the outermost circle. These form a sort of bracket, at whose terminals appear four impressions like pads, at whose ends are three fingers, or claws. The impressions vary in diameter, the largest being two feet. They seem to have been formed by a metallic object.

On the three incidents below, my reader must use his or her own judgment. I unhesitatingly dismiss them as hoaxes, but I give them here, since some reader is sure to ask me whether I have heard of them:

May 21, 1954: More "prairie fire" stories start in the Middle West about alleged encounters with saucer entities "from Venus." A Chicagoan is said to have quit his regular business in order to meet up with flying saucer entities. One who was called, or called himself "Garcia Sai" was a three-dimensional being of human, or humanoid type, with a scar on the left side of his face.

A second story is about one J. Seneca Sinelk, who had parked a nice new automobile on a vacant lot. A "Venusian saucer" landed close by, and out of it stepped a long-haired man, with dove-like eyes and more ineffable sweetness than is customarily seen in a pinup of a film star. The Venusian is accused of speaking ancient tongues, including the long-lost tongue of Atlantis. He says to Seneca:

"The all-powerful, supremely omniscient (PLUT) of Venus may commission me to buy many automobiles like your own. For we, on Venus, have none of your terrestrial means of locomotion. Hear me, O Seneca Sinelk. I shall shortly return from Venus with an extra *viamana* (*sic*) such as the one you now see, which together with 1,000 *spoles*, I will give thee in exchange for thy so-adorable automobile machine."

Author's Comment: A *vimana* (not "viamana"), in the Secret Doctrine of India, is a very ancient air-vehicle used in time of cataclysm or by ancient "Great Kings." It seems to be, in ancient Sanskrit lore, a memory of the flying machines used by both the ancient Mu-ans and the Atlanteans, to which dim legends and old Keltic myths refer.

On what an American friend writes me (July, 1954), quoted below, no comment of mine is called for:

"The editor of the magazine 'Yankee,' which published the story of Seneca Sinelk's adventure with a gentleman from Venus now admits it was a hoax; but it would (perhaps?) surprise you how many innocent saucer enthusiasts took and swallowed this story hook, line and sinker. The editor now wants no more to do with 'saucering'; he's had so many letters from wild-eyed addicts."

My friend adds that, on being informed by a woman "mystic" that she had been hearing "revelations" from crickets chirruping in the walls of a farmhouse he went her one better. He informed her that he had encountered a strange gentleman with an unearthly look, who was fingering an unlit cigar. He offered a match to the gentleman, who took it, "lit up" and promptly vanished. By next post, the mystic lady informed my friend that her "spirit controls" had confirmed my friend's suspicions that the strange gentleman was from the planet Venus, and would be back again one of these days:

> "Of course, this was all imaginary about the meeting with the strange man and the match; but it has shattered my faith in this particular medium; and my hopes of actually breaking bread with a man from Venus are also sadly fading."

I have advised my friend *not* to embark on any debunking of "Messiahs," nor "to get into the act by cooking up a few saucer-hoaxes" of his own. Did not Emerson, many years ago, counsel that all such spurious folk should be left to "debunk" themselves? They do, in time —after what the Marx Brothers call the "moolah" has been collected and safely banked.

On the stories below, I venture no comment:

May, 1954: Mr. Dan Frey, a scientist, tells the "Washington Post" that he had a ride in a saucer to New York, that he heard a voice from inside it that seemed to speak in his own head, and that the saucer was under remote control. (*Note*: There seems to be a blend of the 3rd and 4th dimensional planes in this story.)

There is also a story about an American stockraiser, who says a saucer hovered over his head in a field at night, was of the third dimension, and yet had such a psychical effect on him that it changed his personality.

Many of the flying saucers, seen anywhere in the world, impress the observer, as I have said above, as either being manned by entities utterly indifferent to the sensations of people on the ground, or to have no visible control mechanism. Here are two from Australia:

June 1, 1954: Weird thing, variously described as "like a white balloon," or "an umbrella, or mushroom-shaped object," with a long tail fining to a terminal, flew at amazing speeds towards the ground at Melbourne, 5:45 P.M. Seemed to have some entity inside it. A second object, seen the same evening, carried a revolving red light. It was silent, floated in the air, and then shuttled back and forth. Next, it spun three times like a plate on end and vanished.

At East Malvern, Australia, seven people saw an oval-shaped flying saucer *with entities inside it.* It flew at fantastic speed above the tree-tops at 12:25 A.M. Then it ascended rapidly. It was seen on May 30 and 31, at the same place, at 8 P.M., when it swooped, banked, flattened out, and looked like a "white football." One man said it left a train of sparks; another that it was as big as a railroad coach, and had entities inside it. Speed varied from a "floating grace" to vertiginous velocity, when it shot upwards. As it dived, it jetted out a yellow gaseous matter. Three of these objects were seen the same night. One suddenly faded away as if a light had been switched off; the second glowed dully; the third hovered, then dashed sideways for two miles. Visible twenty-five minutes. (Said the Australian Air Force: "We do *not* pooh-pooh these reports.")

The incident below is curious:

June 7, 1954: Three German tourists who entered the vast Lamprecht Cave, near Lofer, in the Salzburg mountain region of Austria have never been found. Their automobile was left locked outside the cave.

Author's Comment: The above may very well be merely a case of amateur speleologists getting lost in labyrinthine caves, although it is unusual for *three* men to vanish in this fashion. But I must risk the charge of being accused of fantasy or moonshine, when I say that both in England and the United States, there are regions of limestone caverns and mountains from which, in the last three years, queer phenomena associated with white lights descending to ground level from great altitudes have been reported!

I myself, after a curious experience in the early morning of July 23, 1954, wonder if the phenomenal object I saw had any contact with some quiet place in southeast England, and had landed entities. (I have, however, no reports of such landings!)

At 5:15 A.M., I was awakened by the drone, far overhead, of R.A.F. planes engaged in summer maneuvers. My house stands on a low hill some twelve miles from Charing Cross, London. It commands a fine view of about six miles of open country, bounded to the south by the low wooded hills of Kent. About twenty minutes later, after the sounds had died away and the planes were out of earshot and out of sight, I suddenly caught sight of a strange object flying at about 3,000 feet, silently, some six miles to the southwest. It was of elongated shape, like an airship, or cylinder rounded at both ends, was flying on a level course, and from end to end, flamed with a most eerie, red glow. It was most certainly no airplane—this region is a regular route for R.A.F. jets of the latest type and airliners and commercial planes bound to and from the continent. And it was most certainly no weather or cosmic balloon, with which I am thoroughly familiar.

I watched it for a second, and then jumped from my bed to get my binoculars. As I trained the eye-piece on the mysterious thing, it vanished into a low cloudbank, in the southwest, where my view was cut off. The sun was shining in the east, having risen at 4:10 A.M.; but the southern skyline, from about ten degrees upward, was rather cloud-barred. When I first saw the object it had come from the southeast, from the direction of Chatham and the Thames estuary. The course it was taking would pass over Bromley, and would take it towards Wimbledon and Staines. It would not, thus, pass over south London. It was travelling rather faster than a jet plane. When I saw it, it was above and on my side of the low hills towards Chislehurst, silhouetted against the cloud and hills.

What was it?

I think it was a *space ship*. At this time of the morning, only postmen or patrolmen or railroad workers would see it. Time: 5:25 A.M., and duration of observation about thirty seconds. It made no attempt to evade observation, or use cloud cover. Anyone abroad after 5:25 A.M., on the course it was taking to the southwest, must have seen it, since the eerie red glow would certainly attract the attention of any person with normal vision.

It was the last thing I expected to see. I think its dimensions were too large for those of any satellite disc of the saucer type. It seemed utterly indifferent in relation to any terrestrial observer.

I stress here, as I have done elsewhere in this book, my view that these visitants deliberately appear in such a way as to make clever use of the fact that any ground observer, knowing that Air Force maneuvers are on in his region, will assume them to be maneuver formations and dismiss them from his mind. But should he assess them for what they are, he is strictly forbidden by the R.A.F. to inform the public of what he has seen, and its real nature.

I ask: How much longer is this higher official nonsense to continue? Is the Royal Air Force and the British Air Ministry proposing to start an *ostrich farm?*

It may be noted that the course of this weird space ship would have taken it right over the spot (in the field of Bunker's Hill farm, Bexley, Kent) where the Army Engineers found the mysterious solid iron object which had splashed a crater in the ground, but was *not* a German or any other bomb. Might this weird, glowing fireship have been looking for a "planetary Marker," like this one? Who knows? (*See* Chapter 5, page 112, for the account of this Bunker's Hill Farm, Bexley mystery.)

A month later, the same or a similar unidentified object of cigar or fusiform shape, was seen over Evreux, on the Seine, France. Late in August it was sighted by the Italian Air Force for an hour, over the coast near Rome.

What was it that Robert Frenhoff, a science teacher at a school in Yonkers, N. Y., said he saw while hosing his lawn, at 9:40 P.M., on July 30, 1954?

"I happened to glance up into the evening sky, when I was surprised to see a queer thing like a child's gyroscope or spinning top, whirling along at a great altitude. It was mainly yellow, but had a crimson glow at the edges, which might have been an exhaust. I shouted to my wife and she and neighbors rushed out to look at it. It moved around in a fantastic manner. One moment it would hover near the Great Bear constellation, apparently, and then in a sudden rush, dart away at an angle of ninety degrees; then stop short as if it had hit a brick wall. There was no way of estimating its immense height in the sky. It repeated these hovering and rushing maneuvers until close on midnight."

Opinions range all the way from a new type of saucer to a terrestrial space-station of some home or foreign government; but it seems more likely that this gyroscopic object may be a cosmic aerofoil linked with the elusive flying saucers. No one knows—outside a very narrow military and aeronautical circle—what any Government may, or may not have achieved towards establishing space vehicles.

The editor of "Nexus," a very interesting, mimeo saucer-sheet published at Fort Lee, New Jersey, kindly draws my attention to two news items: (1) The "sacking" in August, 1954, from his job, of the free-spirited newscaster, Frank Edwards. He is said to have incurred the displeasure of his sponsors, the American Federation of Labor, by dwelling on the theme of saucer sightings and what is being hidden from the public by the American defense authorities. It appears that the A.F.L. have been displeased by the avalanche of letters sent to Mr. Edwards by people who have seen saucers. (2) The alleged concealment, in official cold-storage, of a saucer and its parts, forced down near Columbus, Ohio, and hidden at the Wright-Patterson airfield of the American Air Force.

Concerning (2), Mr. James W. Moseley got on the trail of a woman he calls "Miss Y.," who, as a civilian employee at a large military and air base in Ohio, acted as night girl on the teletype, decoding messages and handling classified material. About August, 1952, she saw in the photographic laboratory twelve prints of a non-terrestrial flying saucer, which the cameraman said he had taken on a recent secret assignment to a location in Ohio, where an interplanetary saucer had come to grief. Some days later "Miss Y." handled official messages which said that the saucer was passing through her base under guard, *en route* to the Wright-Patterson airfield in Ohio, which is the location of the secret Flying-Saucer Investigation Bureau of the U.S. Air Force. She also found that, both before and after the transit, a Red and White Alert was on, indicating official fear that the landed saucer might have communicated with its space ship.

Two weeks later, after official experts had examined the captured saucer, the Alert terminated. According to the reluctant witness, "Miss Y.," who would appear to have been talking too much, either for her own comfort or that of the authorities, the saucer was thirty feet in diameter, but had no "bubs" or blurbs, although there was a rim, or flange where the sections of the disc joined. She said its metals were riveted together and she had heard that the saucer had ports of a one-way vision, translucent material; that is, the entities could see through it without being seen. "Miss Y." further alleged that the U.S. experts had penetrated the saucer with considerable difficulty, and found that its metals were of alloys "unknown on the earth." No living creatures were found inside it. It appeared to have been remotely controlled. She also alleged that she had heard—of course, this is *not* evidence in any law-court or judicial sense—that dead bodies of humanoid creatures, five feet tall, had been found in other saucers previously captured and photographed. She said the saucer had floated down, not crashed, as if its magnetic propulsion had failed, or been cut off.

As one would expect, Mr. Moseley received a denial from the officers at the Ohio base that *any* saucers had been seen, much less photographed. He was also told by a high officer that the Department could not understand how "Miss Y.," an efficient member of their personnel, had come to make such statements. However, Mr. Moseley, who personally interviewed the lady, was impressed with her sincerity, and did not believe she was fantasying, or hoaxing.

All one can say is that while there is no smoke without fire, and the U.S. air and military authorities would, no doubt, take a very "dim" view about alleged hoaxes by one of their personnel—these authorities, like those in Great Britain, are exercising a rigid censorship. For publicly reporting flying saucers seen from 1952 on, any officer would risk court-martial and possible degradation in rank.

Follows a story of a singular encounter in Norway:

August 24, 1954: The chief of police at Mosjöen, in the province of Helgeland, Norway, lat. 66 degrees N., has been told by two Norwegian women, sisters, aged twenty-four and thirty-two, that they were in the hills near Lake Rösvatn, picking blueberries, when a dark man, clad in a sort of khaki overall with no buttons, came up to them and motioned them to follow him into a little valley. There, on the grass was a flying saucer-disc about sixteen feet in diameter. They said: "It looked like one saucer on top of another." The entity made gestures and showed them drawings, but neither he nor the women could understand each other, although they tried in Norwegian, English, French and German. Seeing he could not make them understand, the entity climbed into the saucer, which hummed then rose into the sky at great speed and vanished. Police will visit the spot in order to see if the saucer has left any traces.

Next day, the Norwegian Air Force told the press that the two women, Miss Edit Jacobsen and Mrs. Aasta Solvang had encountered only a big helicopter manned by an American, flying it for the Norwegian Air Force. An Air Force official alleged that the two women had been reading "a book on the invasion of the earth by space ships from another world."

But the two women strongly deny this allegation. One of them said: "It was not an American airman. It was a Martian, and we had an amazing experience. We offered him blackberries. He would not take them and spoke in some unintelligible jargon. We tried to shake hands with him but he laughed and climbed into the ship."

Author's Comment: If the being *were* an American airman, it seems singular that, as the women spoke to him in *English* and three other West European languages, he did not understand, but answered in what the women say was "unintelligible babble." Again, *if* he were an American airman, and had lost his bearings and wished to find from the women where he was, why did he fly off without making another attempt to find someone else to tell him what he wished to know? Why, too, is the American's name not mentioned and *his own account* of the encounter given?

An Oslo (Norway) newspaper adds:

"The stranger tried to communicate with the two women by drawing circles and pictures of what looked like 'heavenly bodies' on a piece of paper. He opened a hatch and entered by crawling into the disc. It began rotating, first slowly, then with great acceleration and vanished into the sky at incredible speed."

No one in Great Britain has reported an encounter*
with space-men from a flying saucer. But, on or about
September 5, 1954, two men in France reported such encounters. One was M. Marius Dewilde, a steel-worker,
aged thirty-four. He says he saw two space-men three
feet tall, in his garden! Dewilde, says the Paris "Soir," is a
serious man who neither drinks nor smokes. Nor does he
gossip and is not noted, in his community, for the dramatic or humorous:

"He has told the police of this village that at 11:30
P.M., on September 10, 1954, his wife had gone to
bed, and he was reading in the kitchen, when his dog
'Kiki,' tied up in the yard, started yowling horribly.
Then, suddenly, he heard footsteps approaching, and
the dog grew frantic and strained at his leash.

" 'I shone my flashlight,' said M. Dewilde, 'to see
who was coming. About three yards away, I saw two
figures walking, one behind the other. A metallic
gleam came as my light shone on the leading being.
He appeared to be wearing a diver's helmet. Both were
little beings with enormous heads. As I started to
walk towards them, there came a violent glare of
light from a shape behind them. It was a green ray
and it paralyzed me. I was rooted to the ground. I
could not move my legs.

" 'The two beings turned and walked back to the
green ray. It was now switched off, and the shape
rose up vertically like a helicopter. I heard a swish-

---

* I am told that an American pilot, Bill Faurot, said to be
at a depot in Stuttgart, Germany, alleges *he* was the man
these women met, and that he was flying a helicopter. Apart
from the ingenious theory that Uncle Sam's airforce controllers in Germany have developed a *terrestrial* flying saucer,
in emulation of the Russians, one does not know why Faurot
did not understand the English spoken to him by these
two women; unless, of course, he speaks a brand of American
that no foreigner could understand. I gravely doubt if even
the most trusting among American aeronautical higher-ups
would sanction the flying over foreign territory of a *secret
device* like this. The description given by the two women,
who do *not* appear to be foolish, was of an aerofoil like a
saucer, and not just a helicopter. Moreover, will brash and
backsliding flying saucer enthusiasts take note of the fact that,
what are called non-terrestrial flying saucers, have a very long
history going back at least to the time of Pharaoh Thutmosis
of old Egypt, say *circa* 1500 B.C.?

ing noise, and wakes of black smoke came from the thing, which rapidly gained height and went west. The thing was semi-circular. It was some eighteen feet wide and about nine feet thick. As it vanished, it glowed with a red light.'

"The police were told but could find no one else who had seen the thing. However, the ballast of the nearby railroad track was dented and stone pitted, as if by some radiant heat. The police say this might have been caused by pressure from a bolt or screw on the sleepers or ties. The folk of the village may scoff, but Dewilde says he saw saucer-men that night. Two others have come forward to say that they also saw them."

A few days later there came a report from Clermont Ferrand, in the lonely mountain region of the Auvergne, 342 miles due south of Lille, that a M. Antoine Mazaud, walking in the dusk along a lonely footpath towards a hamlet called Ussel, met a being in a helmet, about four feet six inches tall, who shook hands with him, and in Gallic fashion, kissed him on both cheeks. The being spoke a strange tongue, then turned and jumped into a cigar-shaped object, twelve feet long, which took off vertically into the sky, and vanished west at great speed.

M. Mazaud notified the police, who merely shook their heads and told the keeper of the local bistro, whose customers made very merry at M. Mazaud's expense. M. Mazaud, not unnaturally, was angry. While the tipplers were tittering, there was telegraphed from a village fifty miles from Lille, a report that Emile Renard, a builder, and his foreman, Yves de Guillerboz, had been cycling home along a country lane, when glancing at a stubble field, they saw a strange object parked among the oats.

Said Renard:

"I do not frequent bistros or estaminets, but I tell you we saw, on the field, a metal disc, blue-grey, thirty feet long, and nine feet high. It took off at the speed of a helicopter and smoke came from its rear. It made no noise and vanished into the clouds."

Neither M. Mazaud nor the police explain how a being in a helmet performed the feat of kissing a gentleman on both cheeks. It is not said that he had his visor down. Probably, the newspaper reporters "improved" the story.

The information that the machine came from Mars was certainly their addition. Neither Dewilde nor Mazaud advanced any theory as to the provenance of the saucers.

The Portuguese newspaper, "Diario de Lisboa," published on September 28, 1954, a story of "two aluminium-suited beings" who descended in a flying saucer onto a verdant Lusitanian mead, in order to cut flowers, snip off branches from trees and bushes, and put them into a gleaming box! The story is told by Senhor Cesar Cardoso. In the absence of any witness or corroboration, my reader must believe it or not. It looks to me like a hoax.

He says in a letter to the newspaper:

"I was near the village of Almaseda, when I saw a flying saucer, out of which stepped three beings in suits of shining aluminium. They were six feet seven inches tall. They picked and cut flowers, snipped off twigs from bushes and put them in a shining box. I and three friends were invited to enter the saucer, but when we refused the beings did not insist. They climbed back into their saucer and ascended vertically at an immense speed, emitting a shower of sparks."

Senhor Cardoso is meticulous about the stature of these beings, and no doubt, if pushed to it, his three friends, like the witnesses to similar claims in California, might be persuaded to come forward as signatories to an affidavit sworn before a notary public.

Next day, all over France, there were said to have been some lively saucer doings. I summarize them. It is likely that *some* of these stories are veracious:

A Chambéry doctor and fifteen witnesses say they saw a "flying saucer circus" (presumably this means a fleet) in the skies over Lyons, France. He said what he saw was a dark grey mass hovering over a 6,000 feet high mountain. When the grey mass lost height it looked like an inverted plate, light in color with darker patches.

Not far from Feyzin, near Vienne, south of Lyons, a young fellow saw a dome-like saucer hovering close to the ground, and emitting a magnesium-like flare.

At Valence, lower down the Rhône, in Drôme, a woman said she saw a whistling saucer in a field. She rushed to find eye-witnesses, but it had gone when they came, leaving a circle of crops, nine feet across, crushed down by something that had landed.

A farmer, Yves David, of Châtellerault, (Vienne, and 180 miles, as the crow flies, southwest of Paris) said that a creature, dressed in scaphandrical attire (like a deep-sea diver) came up to him on a lonely road, burbled unintelligibly, paralyzed him with a green ray, and raced back to a saucer which took off silently into the sky. He was unable to describe the aerofoil.

The first week of October, 1954, saw a veritable snowstorm of flying saucers all over France:

A farmer near Grenoble saw a glowing, lighted "engine" moving at great speed. Yvette, his daughter, said that it made a slight snoring sound.

In another part of France, 2,000 people saw twelve saucers "dancing a ballet in the sky."

Two people near Mulhouse (Haut-Rhin, Franco-German border), saw a cigar-shaped luminous object surrounded by twelve smaller satellite fusiform objects.

Over the beach of Carry-le-Rouet, three women saw a "half-cigar in the sky," throwing out smoke.

A "flying mushroom" object, with three tripod attachments, was alleged by a motor truck driver and friend to have landed in a field at Faremoutiers (Seine-et-Marne, east of Paris). It "put a ray on him that caused his body to prickle and come out in a cold sweat. His head swum dizzily." One version said it was a "green ray." He could not move an inch, until the thing rose slowly into the sky and flew off.

In the Bay of Biscay, seamen on a freighter saw a moving disc with a green glow.

Over the Invalides airport, in Paris, the actress Michèle Morgan saw a glowing disc.

A girl at Drôme, west of Grenoble, scene of other reports, says: "I saw a thing the size of a child with parent sack. The thing went back to the saucer, a human face, who was shrouded in a sort of trans- which rose vertically into the sky."

At Marcilly-sur-Vienne, west central France, the foreman of a quarry alleged that "a small helmeted and booted entity, carrying a sort of ray-pistol, fired at him and six of his mates, with a "luminous and paralyzing ray."

At Blanzy (Saône-et-Loire), two men saw a cigar-shaped thing in a freshly plowed field. It was about six feet long with a pointed yellow terminal. The rest of it was dark brown. As they approached, the fusiform object rose into the sky vertically.

Eight people, including a policeman and a grocer, saw an incandescent cigar-shaped object at Agen.

At Belesta, in the French Pyrenees, a marketman says he saw a brilliant ball shoot through the sky, leaving grey smoke behind.

A ferryman near Rouen saw spherical objects in the sky. In the valley of the Garonne, a butcher saw a saucer high in the sky that seemed to be using the river as a *point de repère* (bearings).

No wonder a French deputy, Jean Nocher, asked the French Air Minister to set up a body to sift the truth from hoaxes and objectively investigate these phenomena! At the same time, far away at Patna, India, near the Ganges, the keepers of the burning ghats where bodies are in-cinerated in honor of Vishnu, looked up, as did 800 other people, to watch a flying saucer "descend to within 300 feet of the ground. It was about fifteen feet wide, dark grey, and smoke jetted from its two sides."

On October 2, 1954, the French Air Ministry ordered an official investigation, since 267 people in widely sep-arated areas of France, reported seeing saucers. *All* of them could not be liars. They included railroad engineers, weathermen, seamen, doctors, and farmers:

The French government meteorological station of Morvan saw an oval-shaped craft going at amazing speed, 3,000 feet up. Cigar-shaped objects were seen at Coulommiers, sixty miles south of Paris, and police photographed marks left by a strange mushroom-shaped object. Madame Simone Geoffroy of Diges, a hundred miles south of Paris, said: "I saw a curious engine like a cigar pointed at both ends on the ground in a field. Standing near it was a being like a tall, dark-skinned man in a khaki hat. He looked at me but said nothing. I was terribly scared and ran away. People who went there two hours later saw nothing."

However, everybody who regarded these disturbing visi-tors as merely the sport of hoaxers, "spoofing dupes," took heart of grace and confidence again, when the police of Lille trailed a rascal of a miner at Beuvry-les-Bethune, who said he had made saucers out of strong grey paper soaked in gasoline, and having lit a fire under them, sent them—1,000 of them (sic)—into the wind, with yellow and red lights. The police found one on a haystack. While this may be *partly* true, it would be distinctly unwise to jump to the conclusion that what these people saw all over France, a pretty big country, were just a miner's prank.

The furore died down again, until October 17, 1954, when the owner of a café at Toulon, named Rappellini, told the Toulon police the following odd story:

"I was motor-cycling between Hyères and Toulon, on the Mediterranean coast, when I saw a being step out from a disc-shaped saucer. He was dressed in some sort of overalls. I said to him: 'Are you from Mars?' He said: 'No, French.' With me was my engineer-friend, Monsieur Ottoviani, who will corroborate what I say. The being asked where he was, and when told, made a rapid vertical ascent in his disc."

My reader must form his or her own opinion of Rappellini's story, as to whether this may or may not have been some secret terrestrial machine.

Far away at Salisbury, in Rhodesia, Africa, a certain gentleman got on the radio and rashly vouched for the authenticity of some decidedly dubious photographs, published in a German newspaper of Cologne. One of these photographs depicted what looks like a wax mannikin held up by the arms by two gentlemen in trilby hats, such as might be worn by detectives on a spree. Behind them stand two handsome ladies. The caption informs us that the mannikin is not quite 28 inches high, and comes from Mars. An unnamed "War Department" is alleged to have said that: "It is not proven that he comes from Mars, but we are positive that he came from one of the planets in our solar system, or from a neighboring star."

People in Salisbury and Bulawayo write me asking: "Is this fellow a dupe or a plain liar?"

Curious incidents have been reported, both in the United States and in the North Pacific, between 1950 and 1953. These may import that some flying saucers which have no human or humanoid, or any kind of entity aboard, may have been engaged in some kind of exploration or reconnaissance. For example:

Was a satellite disc—a flying saucer with no entities on board, and possibly controlled from some unseen space-ship—rammed and sunk by a specially equipped American plane in late April or May, 1953?

It looks like it, and the affair occurred in the waters of the North Pacific, off Tinian, one of the Marianas Islands, formerly mandated to Japan. On this island, it may be noted, are mysterious ruins of colossal, columned tombs which may be the monuments of one of the colonies of the lost and very ancient Pacific continent of Mu.

"In the last weeks (late April, 1953), our ships and aircraft have sighted numerous flying objects of un-known origin. Their flight courses were plotted and permit conclusions about their take-off and landing bases. Near the island of Tinian, one of these pro-jectiles was rammed by a specially equipped airplane and sunk in the sea." (*Report of the Chief of the U.S. Defense HQ., D., Tokyo, May 9, 1953.*)

Tinian has an up-to-date military airfield from which flew the atomic bomb-carrier planes sent against Japan in 1945. Although a passage in the above report might seem to imply that these objects were terrestrial in origin, it seems pretty clear that the American authorities were forced to conclude that they were, in fact, a type of flying saucer.

Among the reports of alleged, forced-down saucers, is a blatant hoax published in the September, 1954 issue of the sensational New York magazine, "Sir." In this hoax, which cited names of fictitious "scientists" for "vraiesem-blance," it is mendaciously stated that recently, on the is-land of Heligoland, off the western coast of Germany, a flying saucer crashed. It was found to carry "firing instru-ments" capable "of shattering glass with magnetic rays." Slumped round the crashed saucer were the incinerated bodies of seven humanoid beings, five feet eight inches tall. The saucer "was made of metal that even a tempera-ture of 15,000 degrees Fahrenheit could not melt."

The only comment I would make on this impudent and clumsy lie is that, if the late Mr. Pulitzer had left a prize for journalistic mendacity, the concocter of this hoax would certainly have won it, as the sporting gentlemen say, "hands down."

On the other hand, I do not think the incident below is a hoax, although I do not know the exact location of the affair. I have the information from my friend, Mr. Gray Barker, who runs an intelligent amateur publication, the "Saucerian," at Clarksburg, West Virginia. He tells me that the account came from a teen-ager, Rose Murphy, whose letters are all read by her parents before she posts them.

She says, and for a teen-ager, she certainly is unusually fluent:

"On the night of May 21, 1952, I and seven friends were trailing, riding a narrow path between a dry creek-bed and a dense wood. The moon was up. Suddenly, Hank's horse, which was leading, reared up and as he had never acted that way before, he caused the other horses to act skittish. One of our party got his mount under control, then looked up and started to laugh. He pointed to what he said must be a circus light, or an airport beam in the sky. At that point I guess we ought all to have turned back on the trail. Now, afterwards, we all realize that.

"But we went on riding, although the horses began to snort and quiver. It was about ten minutes before anything happened. This time my mare reared straight up and pawed the air. *Now I saw it!* A huge, light-blue, saucer-shaped object was less than 200 feet from the ground, and was descending rapidly. The horses seemed frozen in their tracks. So were we. The thing landed and hit a tree with a resounding crash, and an eerie blue light illuminated the whole countryside. Just before it crashed, it took on a dull glow on its underside, as if it might have been trying to avoid hitting the tree. The noise seemed to break the spell that was over us, and I heard Ellen, who was behind us all, turn her horse. I didn't wait. I don't think my mare ever ran so fast. We were supposed to open Lingenfelter's gate when we raced back home, but we went right over it. Since Hank's house was closest, we stopped there to talk over the experience. Hank has a very respectable position in the city government, so for fear of ridicule, we did not tell the police.

"Next day we went back on foot to the location. We found many trees down, some broken in half neatly. In the sand we saw an enormous indentation, that is, in the creek-bed. It was a dark brown, you might say, a cocoa-brown, but the flood waters from

the creek have since washed it away. I firmly believe
that the 'searchlight' we saw had something to do with
the saucer. There was no carnival or circus in the
area, and we are more than ten miles from Peoria airport.

"Besides, the light appeared to originate in mid-
air, all by itself, and not from the ground."

There was a singular sequel to this incident, although
I suppose horse-lovers might say that there could be other
reasons for what befell the mare:

Miss Murphy wrote to Mr. Barker about August 10,
1954:

"I am real scared! I can't help thinking that what
since happened came from the saucer. My mare's
last year's filly, three months old, has died. We thought
at first that she had lockjaw. She seemed to respond
to treatment, then on July 1, she just literally dropped
dead. I didn't think anything of it at the time, but
today I had a letter from Frank. Both Lou's and
Coaly's foals were born dead. The foals were not de-
formed. They looked perfectly healthy, average size,
weight, etc.

"Here's what scared me: Lady had been bred eight
times this year. When she came in heat again yesterday, I took her over to the veterinary. They gave her
smear and other tests, which proved that my mare,
Lady, is now sterile. The veterinary men can find no
reason for it. A seven-year old mare, perfectly healthy,
just goes sterile! You will probably think I'm 'off' for
supposing that the saucer had anything to do with
this. Well, if you do, I won't get mad.

Sincerely, Rose Murphy."

It will be remembered that one of the dire consequences
of exposure to *atomic radiation is sterility*. Was this
"crashed" saucer, which caused the Murphy party to gal-
lop away in terror using "atomic power"?

Your guess is as good as Miss Murphy's, or as mine.

I most devoutly hope that none of the humans in this
party may experience any ill effect as a result of their
adventure. Radioactivity is no respecter of persons.

SILENT SPHINX OR ROARING CHIMERA?

WHY ARE SOME of the flying saucers eerily silent, while others are noisy? Is it that the former hail from some "etheric" or fourth-dimensional world, a "planetary double" as perhaps a few astronomers might call it? Do the later come from some three-dimensional world, whether or not within our own solar system, or from outside it? No one can answer these questions with certainty.

My researches include such old Roman annalists as Titus Livius (died A.D. 17), Julius Obsequens (fourth century of our era), Pliny the Elder (died A.D. 79, during an eruption of Vesuvius), Seneca (died A.D. 65), the Irish *Mirabilia* and the *Book of Leinster,* Conrad (Lycosthenes) Wolffhart (1518-1561), and others. These show that both types of interplanetary visitants have been recorded as surveying the skies of the British Isles, and Western Europe, and even Arabia, *in the last 2,000 years.* Yet we are today no more in sight of a solution than were the old Roman annalists, the monks in the Middle Ages, or astronomers of the modern age of Kepler, Halley, or Herschel.

Let me summarize some recent incidents connected with the "silent saucers," between November 13, 1953, and July 12, 1954:

1953: Two British R.A.F. pilots say, on a television newsreel, that they saw, while in the air, a saucer whose speed was fantastic. As it moved it jetted flames, or a light that appeared brighter at the periphery than at the center. At 7 P.M., a circular object, blue in the center, was seen over Southend, Essex, trailing sparks. Altitude not very high, course horizontal, N-S. At 7:10 P.M., the same or a similar object was seen, glowing, to pass over Guildford, sixty-five miles away. Probable speed: 360 miles an hour.

"Timberline," organ of lumber interests, reports

object seen from motor truck, by Decker and Bunch (two ex air-force men). It rotated, radiated lights, was round and also seemed discoidal, flying low over Flagstaff, Arizona. Speed was about 350 miles an hour. It was silent, and visible for thirty seconds an hour after sunset, after which it dropped below hills.

At 4 A.M., bright blue light crossed Yuba airport, California, at varying heights (150 to 250 feet). From speed of a conventional airplane, it accelerated rapidly, flew in a flight pattern impossible for a terrestrial plane, then decelerated rapidly. Visible one and a half minutes in clear sky.

1954: (January-July) Golden-hued discs, very high and in a V-formation but *not* birds, seen 30,000 feet over Brighton golf links, Victoria, Australia. At 7:30 P.M., moved slowly east, vanishing in four minutes, but seen later some miles away at Armadale, 20,000 feet altitude. One observer, Mr. A. C. White, says he saw "boomerang-shaped black smoke ribbon at 7:40 P.M., about 20,000 feet high, speed of saucers being 300 miles an hour.

T. C. Drury, of the Australian Civil Aviation Ministry, was filming cloud formations with a movie camera equipped with telephoto lens, when a strange object suddenly emerged from a cloud and ascended rapidly, leaving a vapor trail. His film, when processed, showed a very small, light-colored object moving across sky.

Very strange unidentified object, very high, moved with undulatory motion over Seattle, Washington, shaped "like a bird," glowed golden-red, was translucent, sped with great velocity but no sound.

Twelve saucers pass over Auckland, New Zealand, and create sensation.

A woman at Kyneton, Victoria, Australia, saw at 6:15 P.M., a very bright object in the sky, visible three seconds.

Mr. Hair, permanent-way inspector for an English railroad, sees thing with blue flame, travelling at fantastic speed, between Glasgow and Edinburgh. (Scottish newspapers say it was seen by day and by night.)

From Bognor to London, people see on two following days, before and after midnight, very bright unknown objects high in the southern sky.

Beautiful object, like an orange ball, apparent size of setting sun, seen 12:20 A.M., over Lower Ferntree Gully, Victoria, Australia.

Brilliant gleaming, silvery thing "like flying dust-

bin lid," seen speeding at terrific rate over Chelten-
ham, England. A woman of North Glostershire village sees things like "inverted pudding-basin," in
sky.

The following incident is taken from the diary of Mr.
P. F. Sharp of "Abbots Leigh," Knutsford, England:

April 12, 1954: "Mr. C. Evans, a former member of
the R.A.F., was having tea in his house at Macclesfield, at 6:15 P.M., when chancing to look out of the
window, he saw to the north a flying saucer, which
did a slow turn and then passed a cloud at a speed
faster than a jet plane—say, 700 miles an hour. It
then vanished in the east. The object was silent. He
said the thing was like a balloon with a flat top—but
it was *not* a balloon of any sort, nor an astronomical
phenomenon. Its course was about 45 degrees from
the horizon, wind about ten miles an hour, west to
east. *Apparent* size about six inches. He assures me
that there was no window-distortion that would have
created an optical illusion.

"I wrote to the R.A.F. air base at Ringway, but the
commandant there said: "I can make no comment
on this phenomenon. I have forwarded a report to
higher authority."

Author's Comment: Three months before this incident, the British Air Ministry and the British War
Office ordered soldiers and airmen to tell the public
nothing of saucer sightings.

May 25, 1954: Reports come from Brisbane, Australia,
that at midnight people sighted a mysterious object,
about 150 feet in altitude, flying over a 100-mile
stretch of road, 318 miles west of Brisbane. A grazier
said it turned when over his house. It was yellow, as
large as a sedan automobile, and noiseless. A stenog-
rapher said it seemed to be V-shaped, with two red
rear lights. Fishermen say it shot into sight at a height
of 200 feet, then ascended rapidly. No planes were
in the area at the time. Earlier on the same day, a
butcher reported seeing a mysterious object "like a
long white sausage," which hung in the sky for three
minutes and vanished.

There are saucers which emit crackling, hissing and
buzzing noises and of whose provenance no man knows.
They have been seen over England, Australia, New Zea-

land and the United States. In some cases, there seems to be a periodicity about their appearances.

On May 9, 1954, I received a batch of saucer reports from correspondents in the United States, Canada and Europe, covering the period between October, 1952 and December, 1953. In some of these sightings there appeared a real or apparent synchronism with a nearer approach to the earth of the planet Mars, whose orbit has considerable ellipticity. It is, however, *not* at present possible to say whether or not an apparent proximity of Mars with the earth is related to the periodicity of saucer sightings. I set down these reports in chronological sequence:

October 12, 1952: Two boys, Jim McKay and Jim Robinson, both eighteen, were walking along Sunshine Road, Melbourne, Australia, when a strange object, making a "terrible whistling noise," suddenly swooped down from the sky and "hurtled towards them." The frightened boys looked around for shelter, and ran for a house. They said they saw the object distinctly, and it was colored red and blue. The Melbourne Weather Bureau said it was "not lightning!"

June 13, 1953: For about fifty minutes, at 5 A.M., an American, Mr. J. Weger, his wife and daughter, watched from a highway in the middle west, a strange, round object as big as a street light, emitting a noise, so loud it made the air vibrate. It had neither wings nor fuselage, and moved up into the sky at an angle of fifty degrees with the horizon.

December 6, 1953: In New Zealand, saucers with crackling noises were seen and heard.

December 30, 1953: A blue saucer making a crackling noise flashed and then hissed over an American air base at Bentwater, England.

January 12, 1954: At 5 A.M., over Hart's Range, 100 miles from Alice Springs, in the Australian Northern Territory, aborigines heard a strange whine coming from the east, from across the vast Australian Central Deserts. Then, from under a cloud, came a screech and something streaked across the sky. The natives know the sounds of planes very well, and were sure it was not a plane but a saucer. It startled them so that they rushed to the camp of an Australian prospector, Mark Mitchell, and woke him and his wife. It is the first time a saucer has been reported in this region.

June 10, 1954: Fourteen people at Melbourne, Australia, report sighting an oval-shaped object "as big as a railroad car," making a loud buzzing noise when passing in the sky over the town's suburbs.

I am informed by a lady, the widow of a former editor of the *Autocar* of London, that one summer night in 1952, she saw, high in the sky, three flying saucers passing silently over Wandsworth Common in London. There was no sign of any occupants. She wondered if they were remotely controlled from some invisible space ship.

It is such a silent flying saucer that appears to be responsible, as I pointed out, for the removal of millions of gallons of water from reservoirs in West Virginia, August, 1953, and from Lake Sawbill, Ontario, in July, 1950; and on trout streams and quiet brooks all over south and eastern midland England. They deposited a curious spray that became black in a warm room (April and October, 1953).

Follows another incident of a mysterious aeroform seen close to a reservoir in Massachusetts.

June 15, 1953: Two men, R. Lambert and F. Toupance were driving a truck to a reservoir near Pittsfield, Massachusetts, when at 8:45 A.M., they were startled to see a gleaming object like a cylinder with round nose and "open tail," from which were jetted puffs of blackish gas. It drifted over trees which were ahead of the truck, travelling at about fifteen miles an hour, and was about seventy feet long. The day was sunny. The object had no wings, made no sound, and had neither louvers, ports, or windows, except that near the nose was an aperture like a shutter. As it was only some four feet wide, the men concluded that no human beings were inside.

June 19, 1954: The twin-engined "Convair," of the Swiss air lines, took off from Geneva on a flight to London, and came down about a mile and a half from the beach off Folkstone, Kent. Two women and a boy passenger perished. The pilot said his instruments were in perfect order, but that the fuel gauges showed an extraordinarily low amount of fuel in his tanks. Both engines stopped. He told a London newspaperman: "I just can't understand what happened to the petrol. Out of 700 gallons we siphoned aboard at Geneva airport, 400 gallons are missing. Did we spring a leak after take-off?"

On June 28, 1954, the executive committee of the

Swiss air lines stated in Geneva: "We have discharged the pilot and co-pilot who did not effect re-fuelling at Geneva. They were guilty of a grave infringement of the flight rules."

One cannot help thinking that, *if* this be the case, it is no more understandable than for the driver and fireman of an express passenger train to start off on a long run on a main line without noticing that the bunkers in their locomotive tender lacked the proper amount of coal. Both incidents would strike one as incredible.

The eerie red apparition like a bar of glowing steel is not the least enigmatic of the types of silent flying saucers. I shall mention, later on, one I saw myself in the skies of north Kent in July, 1954. Some of these cosmic riddles may vanish as one looks at them but others travel on, horizontally and heedlessly, for many miles.

August 20, 1945: At Ulithi, or Urushi, ten degrees North latitude, 140 degrees East longitude, in mid-north-Pacific, in the Caroline archipelago, a red light like a bar of heated steel, apparently a foot long, was seen by an American Navy vessel. It appeared from the east, then travelled almost due north towards Japan. Time: after sunset.

February 13, 1954: American airline pilots report seeing five to ten flying saucers every night of their flights. American intelligence service asks the pilots not to discuss these sightings publicly. On March 24, 1954, an American Air Force spokesman admits that reports of saucer sightings reach the U.S.A.F., but the public is to be told of nothing.

April 1, 1954: At 6:45 P.M., people called the police of Anardarko, a township in Oklahoma, to watch a reddish, oval-shaped object, pink on the inside, with a blue glow on the outside, which appeared very high in the sky. After thirty-five minutes, it slowly faded out. It seemed to be moving slowly northwest, and left no wake or vapor trail.

Says a correspondent from Cincinnati, Ohio, on April 27, 1954:

"You would be surprised to be told that municipal officials of one of the biggest cities east of the Mis-

sissippi, have become so worried by the frequent
apparitions of silent, unidentified objects seen in the
skies over their rooftops, between February and April,
1954, that they have called on a scientist from Washington, D.C., to investigate. Meantime, not a word
has been uttered by these officials who say they fear
to create panic and hysteria, if the press report what
is happening."

I, surprised?
God bless you, NO! my friend. The surprises—and painful they may be—will come when these same officials discover that they have created and intensified the very panic
they fear. This policy of official silence will defeat its own
declared, or unavowed purpose, *when* the shock may
come.

MESSAGES FROM OUTER SPACE?

Nation shall speak peace unto nation? Yea, and
world speak unto world across the voids of unutter-
able space!
A New York newspaper states, in September, 1954,
that a leading American aviation company is experimenting in interplanetary radio communication.

I NOW POSE THE SENSATIONAL QUERY—which many may,
not unreasonably, deem fantastic—inspired by mysterious
incidents in the sightings of flying saucers, beginning with
the strange affair over Maury Island, in the Admiralty
Inlet, on the Pacific coast. In June, 1947, American coast
guards saw six doughnut-shaped flying saucers, one of
which, in distress, discharged tons of hot metal. This was
followed by a very mysterious encounter of Mr. Kenneth
Arnold and a U.S. coast guard with an unknown person
who appeared to have had personal contact with the entities.

My query is: HAVE THE SAUCERS TERRESTRIAL SPIES AND CONTACTS?

I conclude that they may have! There is historical evidence going back to at least the third century B.C., that flying saucers appeared in the skies over old Latium of the Rome before the Caesars, and in the skies of medieval England and Western Europe. It might, therefore, be supposed—proof there is none—that at one time or another, in the far past, contacts *were* made with or by saucer entities and the earth. Fantastic as it sounds, one might speculate whether there may have been, and still is something in the nature of a secret society which, in the last five or six centuries, may have established such contacts, and maintained them to this day. In 1953, I was informed that the U.S. Air Force intelligence considered it possible, from certain reports, that mysterious people in remote regions of the U.S.A. had met saucer entities, and harbored them. It had been positively told me, by a friend in a Middle Western town, that these stories were under investigation.

On January 1, 1954, there was found in the muniments room of the hôtel de ville, or city hall of the ancient town of Arras, in the Pas-de-Calais, France, a late medieval document reporting a weird thing in the sky, hanging for fifteen minutes over that old town, on the night of November 1, 1461. It may be taken as certain that this extra-terrestrial aeroform must have surveyed other places as well.

"In this year of our Lord, 1461, on the day of All Saints, November 1st, there appeared in the sky a brilliant object like an iron bar, long and wide as half the moon. For fifteen minutes it hovered motionless. Then, on a sudden, the strange object began to rise in spirals, and twisted and writhed like an uncoiled mainspring of a watch (*horloge*), and after, it vanished in the sky."

Since the next day was All Souls Day, dedicated to prayer for the souls of the dead, it is probable that the chronicler of this apparition assumed that it came from the land of shades.

It might be surmised—no man being hanged or beheaded for the supposition—that the learned and secretly unorthodox among the Roman Catholic monks and laity, in the fifteenth century and even earlier, may have had contacts with saucer entities such as described in the document above. I say: *Quien sabe?*

A very likely man to have had such an experience was the remarkable monk, Roger Bacon, said to have been born at Ilchester, Somerset, in 1214, and to have died in 1294. He had studied at the universities of Oxford and Paris, and his experimental science, his peculiar knowledge of astrology (forerunner of astronomy), discoveries in pure chemistry, knowledge of the optical basis of astronomy, the lens as applied to the telescope, and his prevision, in the field of mechanical science and aeronautics, of ships that would move without sails, and boats without oars, cars without horses, and machines that would fly in the air, led to his expulsion from a Franciscan abbey in England, and exile to France.

Here, in Paris, a liberal-minded papal legate, Guy de Foulques, afterwards Pope Clement IV, enabled Bacon to finish his *Opus Majus*, part of which deals with experimental science and perspective.

But obscurantist rulers and theologians were on his trail. They had his books burned and his body cast into a gaol, wherein he languished for fourteen years. There, however, as he would *not* have been able in a *modern* English prison, he continued to write! He was freed in 1292 and died about two years later. It is no undue straining of the facts to assert that the problem of life on other planets, or worlds in space, would have surely interested a man of his amazing intellectual powers. Suppose one day there were to turn up, like the medieval document at Arras, some lost manuscript of Roger Bacon, containing such speculations? Less likely things have happened. Be it noted here, that while Roger Bacon was alive and in the plenitude of his amazing intellectual powers, there appeared the following "signs and portents," recorded in monastic annals:

1239 A.D.: At a very great height, a strange object flying at great speed over England (*Matthew of Paris: Historia Anglorum*); *1254,* at midnight, a thing like a large ship high in a serene sky, visible for a long time until it slowly vanished (*Matthew of Paris*); *1258:* a flaming globe that came down from the sky and reduced to ashes two villas, a mile apart, in Scotland (*Chronicon de Lanercost*); *1290:* in bright noonday, a round, silvery disc that flew over the great Cistercian abbey of Begeland, in the North Yorkshire

Riding, and terrified the abbot and monks in the refectorium.

This document was discovered very recently in a muniments room at Ampleforth, near York. It is dated 1290 A.D., and can be added to other late thirteenth century sightings of flying saucers. In this case, the chronicler clearly considered the visitation a celestial intervention in rebuke of clerics who had dined on, no doubt, very sweet but stolen mutton. One may quote anachronistically, Johnson's warning that a man who minds not his belly minds nothing else:

"They say that sheep were stolen (*susceptos*) by Wilfred on the feast of the most holy Simon and St. Jude. But when Dom. Henricus, the abbot (of Begeland monastery) was about to return thanks (say grace at the high table in the refectorium), a certain brother monk, Joannes, entered and reported an amazing portent to be seen outside. Then they all rushed into the open, and behold, there was an awful thing. A nearly circular object of silvery appearance, not unlike a *discus* (*disco quodam haud dissimilis*) *flying slowly* above them all (*lente e super eos volans*). It excited among all the greatest terror (*atque maximum terrorem*). Wherefore, Henricus, the abbot, cried out that Wilfred had fornicated with women. . . ."

Apart from the small detail that it is not clear why a monk who stole sheep should have risked hotter hellfire by seducing women, it is crystal clear that the slow-motion disc which scared these monastic monks out of their lives, was exactly what was seen 660 years later in modern England and the United States.

Who can disprove that Roger Bacon heard from other monks about these incidents above?

We ought not to pass from this curious topic without mentioning that as early as 1066, when Norman William, bastard son of the Duke of Normandy and the daughter of a tanner of Falaise, had landed his low-browed, steel-helmeted banditti on the Sussex shores of old England, there was talk of experiments in aeronautics. Ranulf Higden, who died in 1364, wrote in his *Polychronicon,* which so pleased Bishop William of Wykeham that he ordered it to be read by a monk while the brethren were digesting their dinner in the refectorium, of a "conying man, Olyver, monk of Malmesbury":

"He was grette in the sterres (well up in astronomy), and a man of letters and grete age. In his youthe . . . hee fondede for to flee (tried to fly) and stood on a hyghe towre, where he tooke the wynde to fligh the space of a furlong and more. But he was aferd (scared) by the grete strengthe of the wynd whirling, and also of his awne folie dede (own foolish action) and fel downe so that he was lame in his thyghes for the term of his lyf."

Unfortunately, we are not given any indication of the aeronautical machine the monk experimented with. It may be presumed to have been some form of glider, or some wing-substitute such as was devised by Daedalus, for himself and his son Icarus who crashed into the sea named after him. It is not necessary, by the way, to suppose that even successful flight is a phenomenon of only our own twentieth century. We seem to have been anticipated by the scientists of old Atlantis.

Higden also tells us of this monk of Malmesbury that:

"seven days before Maye, this Olyver, when a sterre with a bright blasynge crest was i-seie into al the world wyde, continually for seven days blasynge, told that it was destroying of this contraye (country)."

No doubt, this monk of Malmesbury, who tried his wings and studied the skies had seen things like flying saucers swing into his ken off the top of that tower.

I hope the reader will pardon me for this digression before we pass on to a problem which attracted the late learned and liberal Bishop Barnes of Birmingham, England. At the Congress of the British Association for the Advancement of Science at Westminster, in September, 1931, he answered the question: "Do beings from other worlds in space communicate with the earth?"

"There are many other inhabited worlds . . . and on some of them beings . . . immeasurably beyond our mental level. We would be rash to deny that they can use radiation so penetrating as to convey messages to the earth. Probably such messages come now. When they are made intelligible, a new era dawns in the history of human knowledge . . . I should like to be alive then . . . we might get a truer understanding of the beginning of the universe."

Hardly four months after the death of this far-seeing man, I had information which may import that this very thing is now happening!

I summarize here what I have heard:

June 22, 1954: A very strange television signal mystery has puzzled engineers in Houston, Texas, and Lancaster, England. It seems to have first been noted by Mr. Charles Bratley of London, who operates a private television set. In July, 1950, there was operating at Houston, Texas, a TV station with the call sign "Klee-Tv"; but, in August, 1950, the Houston station changed the sign to "Krpc-Tv." No other station anywhere in the world has ever used or adopted this call sign, "Klee-Tv." Now, more than three years later, at 3:30 P.M., Daylight Saving Time, on September 14, 1953, Bratley in London picked up the call sign "Klee-Tv" on his set. A few days later, and on several occasions since, engineers of the Atlantic Electronics, Ltd., Lancaster, England, have also seen this obsolete Houston call sign on their receivers. What is the explanation of this mystery?

Paul Huhndorff, chief engineer of the Houston TV station cannot explain it. He says, what is really irrelevant, that signals from one station can be and have been received thousands of miles away. But that is the normal occurrence caused by a rebound from the layer of the atmosphere known as the ionosphere, and in such cases, even a time-lag of thirty seconds would be reason for great surprise. Here we have a time-lag of more than three *years!* Mr. Huhndorff dismisses the possibility of a hoax by amateurs; but he thinks it would be a mathematical miracle if, more than once, the obsolete "Klee-Tv" call sign may have rebounded from some celestial object more than 1½ light years distant from the earth. In fact, he says, "it is too fantastic for belief." (Yes, but so are many of the saucer phenomena; and yet they happen!) He hazards a theory that some intelligence on a world in outer space has received the obsolete signal and has re-transmitted it in the hope of communicating with our extremely far-away world! In that last theory, he may be near the fantastic truth. Who can say? *Quien sabe?* But here, above, are the "fantastic" *facts!*

In the vast territories of the United States, a series of strange incidents and mysterious phenomena have had

psychological effects. But it would be manifest nonsense
to dismiss, therefore, all flying saucer phenomena as
manifestations of aberrant mentality. On November 20,
1953, a woman mailed to the U.S. Air Force Intelligence,
Wright-Patterson Air Force Base, Dayton, Ohio (the seat
of the flying saucer phenomena investigation) a registered
letter containing this communication which, she said, she
had on Friday, November 6, 1953, received from one
Ashtar, commander of the Vela space fleet, to be sent to
"Your Offices of Government":

"MESSAGE TO THE PEOPLE OF EARTH:
    "Greetings in the light of love and peace, I am
Ashtar, Commandant, Vela Quadra Sector, Station
Schare. I bring you Zolton, Commandant from the
center of the Sector System of Vela.
    "I am Zolton. I extend to you, people of Earth
planet, the greetings from the combined federation of
our people in the Vela Sector System. The information I am about to give you, you shall record to be
advanced to your office of Government at the time we
instruct you to send it.
    "Our craft have prepared and charted facilities for
landing on your planet in numerous remote areas.
We have given sufficient demonstrations of our abili-
ties in speed and performance. We do not expect to
convert non-believers at the moment. There is no
need to fear of panic among your people at our approach and landings. For we shall previously condition the minds to accept us. The present destructive
plans formulated for offensive and defensive war are
known to us in their entirety. The surface of your
planet is in our photographic records in detail.
Through the control of light forces we can instantly
terminate production, transportation, and communication at any time, at any place upon your planet. Our
methods do not require that we destroy any single
thing. Our laws do not permit us to take human life.
They do not however, forbid us to control minds. The
present trend toward destructive war will not be in-
terfered with by us, unless the condition warrants our
interference in order to secure this solar system. This
is a friendly warning."

In this age of confusion, those who anchor their souls
upon "normality" which forbids the adduction of a paranormal theory of causation when one, more rational or

"normal," might appear to answer will have their opinion of this "warning." Others will or may think that, whether or no a purely subjective element be involved in this communication, it links up with some very queer occurrences of an objective nature of which the *official* explanations cannot be called solutions. Since I have no idea how this communication from "Ashtar" was obtained, I pass no opinion on it, one way or the other.

The warning from *Ashtar* recalls a Middle Western story in a newspaper dated about January, 1954, which was as follows:

> "In a car parked in a Middle Western town, a 'dead' radio receiver suddenly came to life and a voice said: 'I wish no one to be afraid, although I speak from outer space. But if you do not stop preparations for war, you will be destroyed.' On a radio hook-up last night, a newscaster says this message has been heard both in Los Angeles and Los Alamos."

It may be recalled that something very similar happened over a radio transmission line at the London airport in January, 1954. The mystery of that transmitting voice remains unsolved.

Author's Note: I have mentioned above the amazing English friar, Roger Bacon. In 1912, a dealer in literary antiquities, Wilford W. Voynich of New York, found a manuscript written in cipher on vellum, and illustrated with drawings of astronomical symbols, plants, herbs, and nude women! (One well knows the fascination the last would have for immured men.) It appeared that 26 pages of this originally 272-page manuscript were missing. On the last page was a puzzling sentence in Latin: "Thou wert opening to me many gates (*portae*)."

Some sought to explain away the nude drawings as erotic red herrings to put ecclesiastical sleuths off the scent of "dangerous thoughts." In 1921, Professor W. R. Newbold, of the University of Pennsylvania, announced that he had succeeded in breaking the cipher. It was an ancient Greek system of shorthand, and the medieval writer had probably used a lens to help build up a composite system of almost microscopic symbols. Since one passage in the manuscript tells of a riot arising between friars and collegians of Oxford University where Bacon had lectured, and gives an account of the explosion of *gunpowder*—of which he was the first European discoverer—it pointed straight towards the author as being Friar Roger Bacon. The manuscript says that the rioters thought that all hell had opened up when the gunpowder blasted off.

This manuscript indicates that Bacon had used a lens in a microscope in order to study cell development—this before 1294 A.D.! And also in a telescope, for the manuscript contained an accurate drawing of the Great Nebula in Andromeda showing details invisible to the naked eye. The writer stated that he had used an instrument (from the description, a reflecting telescope) with which he had corrected an error in the calendar! Bacon's lens was as powerful as the one used four centuries later by Leuwenhoek and Hamm in the rediscovery of biological data known long before to Roger Bacon! Bacon's diagrams showed microscopic cells, nuclei, and even spermatozoa; he had studied embryological phenomena; he knew that the human foetus was created when the ovum united with the sperm; and he taught that the world was round. All this centuries before the Renaissance!

I do not know how this remarkable thirteenth century manuscript survived the vandalism unloosed by Henry VIII, and renewed by Cromwell. Valuable libraries and archives were burned or torn up or sold to butchers, grocers and soap-boilers to wrap up commodities.

It is very probable that in this destruction there perished scores of records of strange phenomena in the skies. And not all of them could have been explained away as mere meteors, *cometa,* or thunderbolts. In Gibson's edition of "Britannia" of the Elizabethan antiquary, William Camden, there is a lively description of a "wyld fire" from the skies that killed many people and cattle, "spontaneously" consumed barns and hayricks, *even poisoned grass,* in a manner suggesting that some hostile entity from space was demonstrating upon the fields, farms and woods of old England, a heat ray projector. John Evelyn, the diarist (1620-1706), records a similar "fiery exhalation" on April 22, 1694.

Identical mysterious phenomena occurred in England in A.D. 1032, 1048, and in 1067. (*Vide* the Anglo-Saxon Chronicle, Simeon of Durham's "Historia Ecclesiae Dunelmensis," and Gaimar's "Lestorie des Engles.")

There seems little doubt that a vast corpus of sightings of strange phenomena in the skies—*not* always meteors, mock suns and moons, or *cometa*—has perished in the abyss of old Time. Records made by the ancient Babylonians, Sumerians and Chaldees, and peoples perhaps more ancient still, must have perished or may still be lying under the sands of Iraq or Egypt. In this connection, the vast archives of the Great Vatican Library must hold startling secrets. I cite from a badly decayed papyrus found among the papers of the late Professor Alberto Tulli, former director of the Egyptian Museum of the Vatican. The Tulli papyri were found still untranslated. Tulli's brother, Monsignor Gustavo of the Vatican Archives, allowed Prince Boris de Rachewiltz to see one dating from the Middle Kingdom. Prince Boris published his translation in the pages of "Doubt," the magazine of the Fortean Society of New York.* He identified the papyrus as part of the annals of the Pharaoh, Thutmose III (*circa* 1600 B.C.). This papyrus was damaged and has many gaps. The writing is, of course, hieratic or priestly. Prince Boris has chosen the most interesting part, which tantalizingly begins with a broken off section relating to some other prodigy:

. . . "In the year 22, of the 3rd month of winter, sixth hour of the day (*lacuna* after "day" to "might") (Might be between 11 A.M. and noon, in either February or March, *H.T.W.*), the scribes' archivists, or annalists, of the House of Life found that there was a circle of fire coming in the sky . . . (but) it had no head. From its mouth came a breath that stank (smelt abominably). One rod long was its body and a rod wide, and it was noiseless. And the hearts of the scribes became terrified and confused, and they laid themselves flat on their bellies (*lacuna*) . . . They reported to the Pharaoh. His Majesty ordered (*lacuna*) . . . has been examined (*lacuna*) . . . and he was meditating on what had happened and which is recorded in papyri of the House of Life. Now, after some days had gone by, behold, these things became more numerous in the skies than ever. They shone more than the brightness of the sun, and extended to the limits of the four supports (quarters) of the heavens (*lacuna*) . . . Dominating in the sky was the station of these fire circles. The army of the Pharaoh looked on with him in their midst. It was after supper. Thereupon, these fire circles ascended higher in the sky towards the south. Fishes and winged animals or

* An organization honoring the memory of Charles Fort and continuing his work. Fort collected material on phenomena left unexplained by scientists.

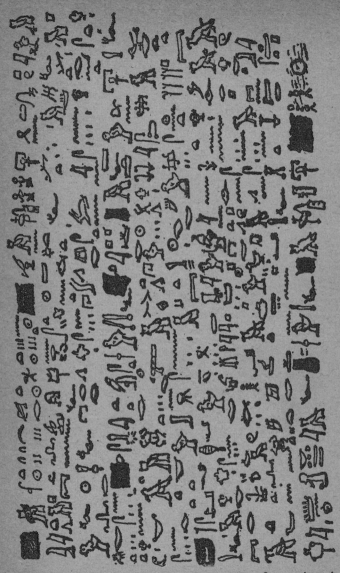

The world's earliest record of a flying saucer fleet, written in ancient Egypt, 5,500 years ago on a papyrus.

birds (? *volatiles,* French equivalent of the Egyptian word; might also mean volatile substances, animals or birds being the older and obsolete connotation. *Au.*) fell down from the sky. A marvel never before known since the foundation of this land! And the Pharaoh caused incense to be brought to make peace on the hearth (or earth) . . . (*lacuna*). And what happened was ordered by the Pharaoh to be written in the annals of the House of Life . . . (*lacuna*) so that it be remembered forever."

Recall an American report of September 12, 1952. A woman, her five boys and a young National Guardsman notified the police that at Flatwood Hill, West Virginia, they had been scared into panic flight from the hill-top at dusk by a thing dressed in a sort of "scaphandrical," or space dress, that landed from a discoidal flying saucer. It had exhaled a horrible stench, which caused them to vomit, probably an irritant gas. A local editor and five other men armed with guns, who went to the hill-top an hour later, reported a depression in the soil, indicating that something had landed there; and the odor was still strong enough to send them reeling back.

The "rod" mentioned in the papyrus is an Egyptian measurement anciently equivalent to 100 cubits, and the cubit is customarily equivalated to eighteen inches. Thus the real, or apparent size of the strange objects in the skies would be 150 feet. But it is difficult to understand what is meant by "one rod long, and one rod wide" in the case of a *circular* object.

The "House of Life" seems to have been a temple, or *naos,* where *scribae* or archivists were trained. The "hearth" may mean the altar of the god Ammon-Ra, Sungod of Egypt. It is not unlikely that some day other papyri may turn up, or some cuneiform tablets or cylinders recording similar "prodigies."

"Reality is no substance on which to anchor your soul; for her substance is of the stuff of shadows. She has no existence outside your own dreams. The concepts one is willing to accept into his category of thinking and to regard as natural, change with the epoch." (*Dr. W. F. G. Swann,* in "Engineering and Pure Science," U.S. Govt. Printing Office, Wash., D.C.) *Author's comment:* One of the "changing concepts" is that relating to fourth-dimensional types of flying saucers, alternately visible and invisible.

A REVOLUTIONARY CONCEPT is being forced upon us by the behavior of certain types of flying saucers. It is that there may exist worlds of another matter than our own, whose beings, although real are imperceptible to our terrestrial, "normal" senses. This belief is probably no more acceptable to the conventional or official scientist than to the hierarchs and priests of any organized or State church, or even dissident and non-conforming Christian sects. In fact, in England and in the United States, the silence of the latter in relation to these saucer phenomena is marked. It may be that they realize that the concept of an invisible but living world—(*not* one of dead souls)—must make hay and havoc of cherished dogmas. So, here, we may find the orthodox votary of religion joining hands with his old enemy, the orthodox scientist in a conspiracy of silence about revolutionary facts unpalatable to both. Indeed, what can they say in regard to a world which may be mathematically postulated to exist in the fourth dimension, but which in the skies of this earth, does not appear to "care a damn for us." And moreover, one whose entities appear to regard us with Olympian indifference.

Moreover, these fourth-dimensional world saucers, or

intra-dimensional aeroforms* demonstrate their powers to become invisible, or dematerialize. Under pressure of facts so inacceptable to the official or orthodox—it is becoming impossible to retreat down a psychological alley. One cannot dismiss as mentally deranged those very "fit" air pilots, or engineers who have been forced by the evidence of their own eyes to concede that these aeroforms can become visible one minute and vanish, inexplicably, the next. It is strange that men who will admit that there are pathogenic organisms so infinitely small that they cannot be photographed even by our ultra microscopes; that some astronomers who acknowledge the existence of "planetary doubles" balk at concepts like the following:

"Some of these saucer entities and their aeroforms are constructed of 'etheric matter,' extremely dense and therefore intangible and invisible. It becomes tangible and visible when its vibratory rates are converted, or 'lowered.' It is subject to the play of subtle energies, including the energy of thought. The aeroforms are thought-constructs, or mind-constructs. As such, they are, in effect, the vehicle of the actual body of the Entity who creates them. Just as our own terrestrial minds rule and become identified with our bodies, so does the entity of the Etheric world make for himself a vehicle or body out of etheric substance. This body may be of any shape or size, any one of a hundred *mutants*—such as the indefinite and changing shapes reported by observers of flying saucers throughout the world. The shapes may be a wheel, a globe, a fusiform or cigar shape, a fireball, or vapor, or gases. It may have any density, any rate of vibration desired. The impenetrable steel of landed discs, or flying saucers is, as it were, a sort of etheric isotope of our terrestrial steel, or we may call it 'etheric steel.' The shapes and vehicles and the entity operating them form one being, just as a human being is a psycho-physical mind-body

---

* Mr. John F. Bessor, of Pittsburgh, has asked me to note that he is the originator of the term *aeroform*. I have pleasure in doing so, since Mr. Bessor is a pioneer worker who originated the materialization and de-materialization theory in connection with certain types of saucers. Of course, as this book has stated, there are other types of saucers of matter akin to our own.

unity. The body of this Etherian entity is a thought-form which can go anywhere, and penetrates our earth and sea as easily as our air."

The distinguished American, Dr. Meade Layne, who formulates the above, is as well aware as anyone that it foreshadows a new synthesis: physics, not the text-book sort, which must some day be fused and interpreted by a new metaphysics. He is also well aware of the derision and opposition it must expect from the orthodox of both academy and church.

In the Spring of 1954, some 4,000 citizens of the town of Birmingham, Alabama, watched a very large, cigar-shaped "saucer" hover over the city for a full hour. Forty planes went up and circled it during that sixty minutes. At times the object faded out, then it reappeared, as a *mutant* would do. The bemused local newspapers saved themselves, exactly as do the official scientists, by alleging that: "It was only the reflection of light from gas-furnaces, or if you wish, lights from a small private plane!"

There is the fantastic question suggested by the numbers of British airliners vanishing over the Atlantic, between Bermuda and the West Indies, and over the Chilean Andes, in 1947 and 1948. Prolonged searches by land, sea and air yielded no trace. Were they abducted by cosmic entities aboard colossal space ships of the type that killed the U.S. pilot, Thomas Mantell, and disintegrated his airworthy plane over Kentucky, when ordered to close with a vast, unknown flying object? This tragedy happened *in 1949!*

Abductions of human beings, animals and objects may have taken place in the past, and even recently. I have been told that the ancient races of the Berbers of North Africa, who may have been one of the helot races of the old Atlanteans, have secret traditions about large-scale abductions of peoples of the earth by extra-terrestrial entities. There may have been decadence in the remote past and use of destructive forces, analogous to the H. and "L." bombs, which caused these entities to take action to avert grave cosmic disturbances.

Here arises a very grave question: How far have our own physicists gone towards a realization of the existence of what may be called *sub-atomic* forces? Do they know (probably some of them do) that, pent up within the atom are forces as yet untouched, which if unleashed would turn our whole solar system into a nova, and all matter into something loose or nearly dead, floating in space. Our atom bomb releases only about one-tenth of one per cent of the potential blast force.

Some think gravity has no pull in or on the nucleus of an atom; that within are only electronic forces. But is this really so? Infinitely minute as is the atomic nucleus, that nucleus probably *does* feel the effects of gravity, which may create a surface disrupted when the atomic nucleus is torn apart in chain reactions.

Invisibility is *not* intangibility in the sense of "nothingness." An infinitely minute body has within it bundles of force of incalculable pressures, like a sun whose parts are held in place by gravitational pull. If the gravity field is torn away from the atom, such tremendous pressures are released as would shatter the earth.

One might regard this world of atomic and sub-atomic forces as analogically like the skins of an onion. In the deeper layers, as yet untouched, lie fields of intense waves of energy. Here (according to some speculations) the beings who man some of these types of invisible, or fourth-dimensional, or intra-dimensional world aeroforms have their being.

If this be so, one can discern why these Etherian aeroforms are here in our skies. They may aim to prevent man from the consequences of that last infirmity of mind by which he deems himself a god and empowered in nihilist fashion to destroy himself, his world, and all that therein is. And these highly evolved beings may plan to prevent us. They are coldly and entirely disinterested in our -isms and -ologies. To prevent the disruption of the solar system, which they may share with us, or whose shattering may affect *them*, are they ready to root out mankind?

However our scientists or philosophers may regard these cosmic "theories," there are reasons why the man of good will and decency should ponder what is implied in them. The "theory" may be "all to blazes," but the *practice* is far too near to what may be appalling truth. One may sum it up in one pregnant though platitudinous sentence: "MAN, CONQUER THYSELF, OR THOU SHALT SURELY PERISH FROM THY EARTH!"

I am unable to offer any comment on the "objectivity," or otherwise, of reports in Middle Western newspapers that "a dead radio on a car, parked in a lot, suddenly came to life, and a voice announced that it was speaking from a flying saucer in space. Later, the same voice was heard on several radio networks." It is curious that, in the autumn of 1953, a mysterious voice called over a radio network at London Airport, announcing something about " 'your planet, Luna' (the Moon)." No one on the airport's signalling staff was found to have been guilty of a hoax—for which the penalty would undoubtedly be instant dismissal—nor was it ever established whence the voice came, or how it contacted what is really a private radio or loud-speaker station.

In a Flying Saucer Convention, held at Giant Rock, California, on April 4, 1954, speakers to an audience of some 3,500, alleged that:

"The entities of the space ships and saucers can and do read the mind of a radio operator, exchanging communications. They know when he is several yards from his set, and will give him time to reach it before they signal. They do not signal if they know—as they do—that he is already standing by his set. In one case, involving something in the nature of mind-reading at a distance, these entities gave the answer to a discussion going on in a room and not taken up or referred to on the radio."

What *proof* there may be that such long-range thought-reading takes place between saucer entities and terrestrial radio operators, is better known to the speakers above than to me. I must certainly not be taken as endorsing these allegations!

galaxies and constellations from our comparatively in-
Vast, incalculable light-year distances separate the significant earth. But the problems of space travel—time-space, gravity, cosmic (lethal) radiation—do not exist for the fourth-dimensional world, or worlds, of some of these aeroforms. They merely convert from one space-time frame of reference to another. And the "emergence into the new state of being" may not be a space-time phenomenon.

An invisible disc may be composed of "etheric" substance, or of another order of matter. It might be theorized that the change in vibration from invisibility of great density to visibility, or much lesser density, is brought about by pure thought!—the play of mind-energy on these ethers. They may then "emerge" into our perception, our spectrum of color and tangibility. On reconversion the saucer fades out, as witnessed in the case of a space ship with seven satellite discs, near Goose Bay, Labrador, on June 30, 1954, at sunset, by pilot Captain James Howard, flying a British Stratocruiser airliner from London. Howard was amazed to note fluctuations of shape and final fading out into invisibility. Apparently the entities knew that about forty miles away, U.S. Sabrejets were flying to intercept them.

A passing reference to the production of invisibility, on which the late H. G. Wells wrote a fascinating science-thriller, may be made here. We, on this earth, have accomplished this scientific marvel on a stage in London in the 1920's; and more recently (March, 1954), at Toronto, Ontario, perhaps by warping light.

I cite from the "Toronto Telegram":

"Eberhardt Matuschka, an Austrian engineer, has accomplished the scientific marvel of making human beings disappear, and not by the use of lenses. At a demonstration in the Toronto Hungarian House, the inventor picked out a girl from the audience, seated her in an ordinary kitchen chair placed on his machine, and began to twirl dials. The girl's body grew hazy, and the back of the chair could be seen through it. Finally, she disappeared entirely from view, and only the chair could be seen through where the body had been visible. After several partial materializations and mock alarm on the part of the inventor, he brought her back fully into visibility. During the whole time, the girl talked to the spectators and told them she could still see them. Witnesses say there was no possibility of any mirrors or similar stage gimmicks, and no pre-arrangement with the subject. The inventor declined to reveal how his machine worked. A clue is seen in the fact that he is a lighting expert of considerable note in Austria. There is no practical use for the invention at present, and he plans only to use it for stage illusions, and will soon take it on tour."

While disc aeroforms, capable of flight in our own atmosphere, can be constructed by us, true space flight by any aeroform we can now construct is beyond our power. And yet, among these flying saucers one may see revealed a new and revolutionary science, not merely reaching out towards, but attaining concepts of space, time, and matter as yet almost unimaginable to us. True, if our human mind continued to evolve, we might eventu-

ally achieve these marvels. *Not,* however, if deeming ourselves gods, and seeking to prove our "divinity" by un-
leashing vast blast forces, we wreck ourselves and our
solar system—*if* we are allowed to do so.

The following incidents appear to involve objects that
may be of the fourth dimension, or of an order of matter
not ours:

September 16, 1953: At 10:30 A.M., two brothers in
London, Ontario, saw from their car what they called
"a chunk of stuff hanging in the air, twenty feet
ahead of us and ten feet off the ground. It was dull
white, about ten inches wide, and irregular in shape.
We drove past it, looked round, and lo, it had
vanished!"

September 24, 1953: An unknown aeroform continually changing its shape was seen by civil defense
watchers near Carlsbad, N. M. Mr. Evrage, an observer, thought it was about 25,000 feet high. Another observer, Mr. Gilliand, watching it through
field-glasses, said: "It seemed to throw out a tail,
even two tails, and then grow round again. I've never
seen a weather balloon as high as this was."

Queer glowing object, red then white, seen moving
slowly over Detroit. In one description by a policeman it was said to look like a white-hot bar of steel.
When a plane flew under it, it vanished, *to re-appear
when plane had gone.* Vanished towards Canadian
border.

June 2, 1954: A mysterious white-green ball, with
yellow tail, descends from great height to roof-tops
in a settlement sixty miles from Melbourne, Australia.
It then "blacked out." Some say it looked like a
large car; others like a pointed balloon with point
towards the ground. Speed tremendous. It also
showed a tail like "an airport wind-sock." At 8:24
P.M., it split into two sections and vanished.

The "Journal Maritime" (Marseilles, France), reports flying saucers, recorded on radar screens in
French North Africa, that were invisible to the naked
eye. Squadrons of fighter planes flew with impunity
through them. French military observers believe these
entities hail from Mars.

There is reason to suppose that one type of saucer may
use alloys that, in certain conditions, generate energy.
This is suggested in the following:

April 26, 1954: Sunlight, striking on silicon found in sand and clay, generates electricity. (*Bell Telephone Laboratory, U.S.A.*)

Author's Note: Silicon is one of the thirteen or more constituents of a mysterious alloy dropped from a flying saucer in distress—shaped like a doughnut—over Maury Island, Washington State, on June 21, 1947. A silicon battery, held up, even to a clouded sky, generates current enough to operate a small radio transmitter.

Again, while these mysterious objects enter our own atmosphere, there have been occasions when astronomers have witnessed out in space what look like cruising fleets of interplanetary craft. The following incident has been reported to me by Mr. Leonard H. Stringfield, editor of C.R.I.F.O., (Newsletter of the Civilian Research Interplanetary Flying Objects) of Cincinnati, Ohio. It may be observed that something like this (except that the mysterious objects numbered more than 200) was seen by Señor Bonilla of the Astronomical Observatory at Zacetecas, Mexico, in daytime on August 12 and 13, 1883:

August 10, 1954: Amateur astronomer Edward Heinhold was observing Saturn with his four-inch reflector telescope, when he saw in that area six lights moving in a straight line. They were evenly spaced, except for two which were near together. Going east, they covered horizon to horizon in fifteen minutes—up to 11 P.M. His station is at Cedarhurst, Long Island. The front lights suddenly disappeared, then two more lights followed suit, and thirty seconds later, the remaining lights vanished while still above the horizon. Their altitude "must have been terrific."

What were these mysterious objects? To what world do they belong? One might as well ask who or what controlled the brilliant white light that in June and July, 1954, repeatedly "quizzed" two U.S. Naval planes flying north of Dayton, Ohio:

8:15 P.M. (*9 July 1954*): A brilliant white light flashed under an FG.ID Corsair plane. Speed very great. It then pulled up and climbed rapidly out of sight north, flaming like burning magnesium. *9 P.M. same night:* Same light reappears 12 o'clock, stays motionless relative to the plane, then dives and pulls up ahead of the plane, and climbs out of sight. Similar object seen in same area by another naval plane, June, 1954. Neither of the pilots got close enough to see a concrete shape.

Some of these weird objects appear to take impish advantages of a solar eclipse to mask themselves:

July 1, 1954: Flying in an airliner, 13,500 feet above the Hardangervidde plateau, Norway, during the total eclipse of the sun, a photographer named Bjornulf, took a color film from the window of the cabin, as did two other cameramen. When the pictures were processed, all the photographers were surprised to see in the center, below the solar corona, an oval glowing white disc standing out against the blackness of the sky. This disc moved rapidly across the skyline (hence was no sort of balloon). (From the "Fremtiden Drammen," south Norway.)

There were the elusive and mysterious "Foo Fighters," met by U.S. bomber planes flying from a base at Dijon, to operate over Nazi areas along the Rhine, near Strasbourg, in 1944. These "Foo Fighters" were also encountered by British war planes; but as I have said, I found the Right Hon. Clement Attlee singularly silent and entirely uncooperative when I asked him to explain why the Air Ministry in 1950 ignored my requests for information. At that time, the Air Ministry and the Royal Air Force had not imposed the ban on flying saucer information which they applied in 1953-1954, and still enforce with characteristic stupidity.

The reader's attention is also directed to another remarkable encounter of which details were given earlier. At sunset, on June 30, 1954, a pilot of the British Overseas Airways Stratocruiser sighted a mother space ship, with seven satellite discs. For eighty miles they flew on a parallel course with the airliner. The pilot and a woman stewardess were mystified by their inexplicable changes in shape and then *vanishing into nothingness* when, as they (the mysterious entities) apparently knew, U.S. Sabrejets, ordered out from their Goose Bay (Labrador) base, to intercept them, were about forty miles away.

Earlier in this chapter, I spoke of possible abductions by fourth-dimensional, or as it may have been, by third-dimensional saucer entities, of people, or even planes from the earth. Allied to this phenomenon is the mystery of what is called *teleportation* of people, or objects, or animals. The following incidents suggest that something unseen exerted a force from the sky:

1859: On May 29, at Nottingham, England, large hailstones nearly an inch in diameter fell *slowly*.
1873: On September 10, near Clermont-Ferrand, in the Puy-de-Dôme, near the mountainous Massif Central, in south-central France, stones over an inch in diameter, fell *slowly*, as if under unknown influence. They fell so slowly that no damage was caused. Some landed on roofs, but rebounded. It was noticed that as if they had lost their invisible control, the stones on the rebound fell faster than those whose fall was unbroken! (This phenomenon has recurred in France and England since.)

Here there seems to be at work contra-gravitational influence or force, possibly exerted by unseen visitants from space, or near the earth. Let a "rationalizer" object that, as a violent flash of lightning abstracts heat from the vapor in a cloud about to condense, and produces ice, or hailstones, a partial suspension of gravity-pull may accompany the phenomena of atmospheric electricity. (I have never heard a physicist advance this latter part of the theory.) If he attributes the slowly falling hail-stones to this, let him or her glance at the following:

On May 2, 1842, at Liverpool, England, when not a breath of air moved, on a sudden, clothes on lines shot upwards, and moved away *slowly*. Smoke from chimneys showed that above ground, the wind was southerly, but the clothes *moved away northwards*. On June 30, 1842, on a bright, clear day, women at Cupar Fife were hanging out wash. There was a sudden detonation and clothes on the lines shot upwards, some falling to the ground, but others sailed on out of sight. On May 4, 1910, from ten A.M. until noon, at Cantillana, Spain, stones shot upwards from the ground. The phenomenon was preceded by loud detonations. (Reports in the "Annals of Electricity," "London Times," and "London Daily Mail.") June 11, 1919, at Islip, near Northampton, England, a basketful of clothes suddenly shot upwards into the air, after a loud detonation. This time, the force was taken off, and the clothes fell back to the ground.

A similar mysterious incident is recorded near Marbleton, N. Y., in the fall of 1815:

"Men working in a field near Marbleton, N. Y., watched stones rise three to four feet from the ground, then move horizontally from thirty to sixty feet." ("Niles Weekly Register," November 4, 1815.)

In August, 1878, M. Adrian Arcelin was excavating at Solutré, Saône-et-Loire, France, a celebrated Neolithic site, when under a superb sky, *parfaitement clair*, was no trace of any wind, when a strong unknown force suddenly seized on the paper, *but touched nothing else*. M. Arcelin says that the dust under and around the paper was not in any way disturbed. The sheets of paper continued ascending until they were lost to sight in the sky. ("La Nature," 1888.)

A mysterious accident occurred to a fishing-vessel, on September 23, 1875. Something raised it into the sky and so far, that when it crashed back onto the sea, it sank to the bottom. There was no wind. A quarter of a mile away other vessels sent rescuers to the aid of the sailors who had been hurled into the sea; but, owing to the entire absence of wind, the rescuers could use only their oars. In the same year, on a cart from Schaffhausen, near Beringen, on the Rhine, October 2, a man with two companions was pushing Germany, when he heard a whirring sound and his right arm was perforated from front to back. No bullet or missile was found, and laborers at work in the field beside the road heard no shot.

1879: On Easter Sunday, in the commune Signy-le-Petit, in the Belgian Ardennes, an isolated house was hit by some force unknown, and suddenly its slate roof shot into the air, and then fell to the ground. There was no trace of wind. The *trouble inoui* (inexplicable accident) was so mysteriously selective that nothing in the environs of this house beyond a distance of 30 feet was disturbed. ("Le Courrier des Ardennes," 1879.)

Now the incident that startled Mrs. E. Harrelson, working in her farmhouse near Georgetown, South Carolina, on April 17, 1951:

"She heard overhead a noise like that of a plane, but no plane was anywhere in the sky. Then came a terrific crash. She rushed outside and across the way

was an untenanted house which had been unroofed.
Timbers and bricks were scattered over a wide area.
So loud was the noise, that people half a mile away
heard it. No plane could have crashed into that house
without itself being wrecked. U.S.A.F. officers at the
local base at Shaw call the incident 'fantastic.' "

Was some fourth-dimensional world type of invisible
flying saucer concerned here?

1880: Two people were in a field at East Kent, Ontario, when they heard a loud explosion, and saw
stones shoot upwards from the ground. They examined the spot, which was sixteen feet in diameter,
but found nothing to account for the phenomenon.
There was neither wind nor whirlwind at the time,
and no weapons or explosives anywhere around. (The
"Plaindealer," East Kent, Ont., Canada.)

Weird animals, of which no terrestrial species or counterpart exists, have been found in various parts of the
world, and in conditions that make one speculate whether
they have been teleported here from some world unknown
in space!

1883: In September there was found by Mr. Hoad,
of Adelaide, South Australia, who was wandering on
the bank of Brungle Creek, the headless trunk of a
pig-like, but unknown animal, which had an appendage
that curved inwards like a lobster's tail.
    On May 9, 1883, great excitement was caused at
Masterton, New Zealand, when there was at large an
unknown animal with curly hair, short legs, and broad
muzzle. Its species was unknown. One dog sent after it
was flayed alive by it, while other dogs ran away.
1886: In New Zealand, after a volcanic eruption on
June 10, there was seen in the mud near a grove of
acacias, the footprints of an unknown beast. The
local Maoris said they had never seen it, and that it
had antlers, but was an animal never seen before by
them or mentioned by their ancestors.

I summarize from various sources, including the well
known naturalist, Frank Buckland's "Land and Water," of
October 5, 1878, accounts of the appearance of a strange
beast in London in 1878:

On a quiet afternoon in October, 1878, there appeared in the streets of the West End of London, one Davy, a naturalist who had a job at the defunct London Aquarium. Davy was leading a remarkable animal which might have come out of some Mesozoic swamp. At his appearance all quiet vanished, and the streets were awhoop with shrieks of terror. Traffic was held up, and portly London "bobbies" ran grave dangers of having their waistbands burst in by the throngs of sightseers, one set pushing the other forward while the rear ranks, reeling and thrusting back, roared: "For God's sake, keep back, can't yer? It's the old devil, or one of his angels this bloke is a-leadin'!" Policemen, fetched at a run from other beats, recoiled aghast as they saw what caused the traffic hold-up. There pushed forward some Negroes, then in London performing in "Uncle Tom's Cabin," but even they, who were used to strange sights on Louisiana's plantations, recoiled and shoved each other back with screams of fright. Behind Davy trundled a monstrous beast, two feet long, two feet high, of remarkable symmetry, but no beauty or grace, covered with hair like wire, with a head like that of a boar, a curly tail like that of a boar; veritably a walking, living cube. His wicked face and eyes were Satanic! He looked like no animal even dreamt of in a nightmare by the most experienced and knowledgeable zoologist or paleontologist. He looked to have no abdomen, and his hindlegs were uncommonly close to his forelegs.

The London bobbies bade Davy move on with the utmost quickness, anywhere. "Where to?" asked the bewildered Davy. A policeman mentioned a not very respectable place, and invoking the name of a very distinguished personage, ordered Davy to take that devil away from the public sight, and be quick about it. All this time, fresh crowds pushed forward and so jammed around him, that Davy ran towards a station of the London Underground Metropolitan Steam Railroad, where as soon as he had run down the steps to the platform, a most diabolical uproar burst out. A train was standing, about to start, and Davy pushed his way, leading the monster into a compartment from which at once other passengers, at risk of life and limb, jumped out onto the track of the other platform. Up came the guard of the train. He took one look at the monster, reeled back, and with amazing oaths, ordered Davy to take himself and the unspeakable thing into the rear brake van.

"I'll lock yer in alone with 'im!" said the guard. "You can have the coach to yerself, *I* am riding as a passenger. How far are yer goin'?"

Davy told him.

"Thank God!" said the guard. "That's the next station. If you was goin' with '*im* to the Zoo at Regent's Park, yer'd empty the blessed place in a jiffy! And not a train would run on this line while you an 'im was dahn eer."

At the next station, another vast crowd assembled and, at a respectful distance, followed Davy to the doors of the house where he lodged. Hearing the uproar in the streets, Davy's landlord came to the door, saw the wicked animal, looked at him, and the animal looked at *him*. At one bound, the landlord shut the front door with a bang like rolling thunder, bolted it and ran upstairs to the top story, where he opened the window and looked down on Davy in the street below.

"Take 'im away! At once, d'ye hear? And don't return! This is a respectable house, and not like the place where you took that 'orrible beast from!"

Meantime, there was a traffic hold-up and crowds were rushing in from all parts of London. They followed Davy and the monster to the house of Frank Buckland, where that gentleman swore that the thing was a demon, looked like a gargoyle from some ancient cathedral, or a figure out of Dante's Inferno. What happened to the monster has been left in total obscurity. There was no Barnum around to put it into a dime museum. Davy said he had obtained the beast from a man named Leman, who had seen it with some peasants in the Pyrenees, in South France. Leman bought it from the peasants; but, as he could not speak their patois, he could not find out how they had come by it, or where they had found it.

Had this amazing beast been teleported from some unknown world in space? If so, should any future space-voyager from our earth ever land in that world, he would certainly have some remarkable fauna to report. A preview perhaps was the beast that forty men with nets were sent to capture, by the Melbourne Zoological Gardens in March, 1890. Its enormous tracks, indicating a length of some thirty feet, were all that was available for study.

And they showed nothing that could be connected with fauna on this earth. The animal had appeared at Euroe, Australia, and had terrorized people for miles around.

In February, 1855, a strange event startled five townships in South Devon, England. One morning, in the deep snow, strange animal footprints were seen on houses and walls. The tracks ranged from—and *over*—Topsham, Dawlish, Teignmouth and Exmouth, and covered a distance of 100 miles! It was to be inferred that the maker of them had moved very swiftly, having covered 100 miles in four hours.

Had he, or it, come from some type of flying saucer?

Such a suggestion is "fantastic" but so are the flying saucers! I summarize here from researches I have made a year or two before German bombers' incendiaries destroyed the British Museum's newspaper files, stored at Colindale, Hendon. The repository had been foolishly erected close to an R.A.F. airplane testing field and to munition factories. About 200 years of irreplaceable files of English country newspapers were lost.

The tracks were vast in number, and their discovery on the morning of February 16, 1855, evoked a sensation in the towns of Topsham, Lympstone, Exmouth, Teignmouth and Dawlish. The prints in the snow, and *vertically* on walls, were of the strangest sort. They were found in the most unexpected and inaccessible places: tops of houses, and narrow walls, in enclosed gardens, and courtyards shut in by high walls and fences. The marks seemed to have been made by a very strange biped who took eight inch steps. They were something like a donkey's shoe— that is, small—and from one and a half to two and a half inches across. The "shoe" was continuous, and as the snow in the center of the marks had remained entire, showing the outer crest of the foot, it was evidently convex.

The unknown being had approached and then retreated from house doors. It was a night, as they say, not fit for a dog to be abroad. Foot followed foot in a line. The mysterious thing passed only *once* down or across each garden or courtyard. In some cases, the tracks passed over the roofs of houses and haystacks, and high walls—fourteen feet high or higher—without displacing the snow on either side, or altering the distance between the feet. It had passed on as if vertical

walls were no hindrance. It covered 100 miles across
the sleeping countryside, going over commons and
across farms. Investigators who measured the tracks
for one mile found that there were exactly 8½ inches
between each impression. (Below, I give a copy of
these most eerie marks, made in February, 1855.)

It is singular that marks like these had been seen before,
thousands of miles away from South Devon, England, on
Kerguelen, or Desolation Island, on the fringe of the
Antarctic Ocean. This island is seldom visited, even by
whalers. Sir James Clark Ross, R.N., the Antarctic explorer, who was there in 1840, reported strange footsteps
like small horse-shoes. They were three inches long, and
two and a half inches broad, with a small, deeper depression on each side.

I venture to suggest they were made by no known or
unknown animal of this earth of ours. *But by whom?* If
this eerie entity could scale vertical walls, it would seem
to have had some means of defying gravity—as have the
elusive flying saucers. In any case, it seems to have feared
contact with human beings.

On April 16, 1954, a weird beast was seen by a policeman, S. Bishop, in Dumpton Park, Ramsgate, Kent, in
the early morning. He ran to a call box and summoned the
police. I give his account:

"The thing was covered with quills, had a long
snout and a short tail. It was as big as an Alsatian
dog, and had large claws. You might have thought it
was a walking fir-cone."

Police hunting it in the park were told that the mysterious animal had run off into the Kentish countryside.
Theories that it was a scaly ant-eater from the tropics are
not borne out. No zoo, circus or private collector reported
missing such a beast. Some assume that it had been
landed here from a space ship in the night. I myself offer

Strange tracks discovered in England, February 16, 1855.

no theory; but, in July, 1951, on the outskirts of the same town, Ramsgate, Kent, a beast with hedge-hog like spikes, the head of a cat, and a tail like a rat's, was caught by a naturalist who could not identify it with any species to be found in a zoo, or as a hybrid, or listed in zoological compilations. It remains a complete mystery, exactly like the origin of a monkey found in February, 1954, frozen to death in deep snow under the winning-post on the famous race-course at Epsom. No one had lost a monkey.

And was the queer thing found by the Rev. Joseph Overs, on August 10, 1954, on the beach of Canvey Island, off the lower Thames estuary, something teleported here from space—or just one of the denizens of the sea, still unknown to marine biologists, like the sea serpent? Or the mer-man!

"It looked to me like a sort of fish with staring eyes but with a big mouth underneath. What was strange, however, was that it had two *perfect feet,* each with five pink toes. A similar weird beast was washed up on the same beach in November, 1953. Length two and a half feet."

Have beings in human shape ever been teleported from, or landed on the earth from outer space?

The twelfth century monk, Gervase of Tilbury, tells of "The Green Children," who emerged from some caves or pits, in Suffolk, in such queer circumstances that one might conclude either that they had been teleported from some world in space, or from some terrestrial subterranean world! This story is also given by three other monastic chroniclers: William of Newburgh, Walsingham, and Giraldus Cambrensis.

Gervase titled it: "De Viridibes Pueris":

"There is a village in England, some four to five miles from the noble monastery of the blessed king and martyr, Edmund, near which may be seen certain strange and memorable antiquities, called in the English 'Wolfpittes.' (*N.B.* The modern Woolpit, seven miles from Bury St. Edmunds, Suffolk). They give their name to the adjacent village. There came a harvest-tide when the reapers were gathering in the corn. On a sudden, there crept out from these two pits a boy and a girl, green at every point of their body, and clad in garments of strange color and unknown texture. They wandered distraught about the field, until the harvesters took pity on them and brought them to the village, where many thronged to see them, marvelling at the strangeness of the occurrence. And for some days these children refused all food that was placed before them. But it happened that some beans were brought in from the fields, and the two children snatched at them greedily and sat in the pits, weeping bitterly; for they found the pods empty. Then one of the bystanders offered them only shelled beans, which they took gladly and ate forthwith. On this food they were nourished for some days, until they learnt to eat bread. At length, under the prevailing influence of our food, they slowly changed the color of their skin, and learned to speak English. Then, on the advice of wise folk, they received holy baptism; but the boy, who seemed the junior in age, lived for only a brief time thereafter, while his sister throve and lived on, differing in no wise from the girls of our own country. The story goeth that she later married a man at Lynn (King's Lynn, Norfolk?) where she is still said to be living, or was so said, up to a few years ago.

"These two strange children were often asked whence they came, and replied: 'We are folk of St. Martin's Land*; for he is the chief saint among us.

---

* "St. Martin's Land" is probably Merlin's land of "grammarye," or necromancy: a subterranean world, or twilight land, to which the "gods," or god-men were forced to descend after the submersion of Greater Atlantis. Hints of it are found in Amero-Indian myths and folk lore, from Patagonia to Alaska; and there are obscure references to it in the tradition told to Egede, the missionary, by Greenlanders who said that the first Greenlander came out of a subterranean world. The American soldier, John Cleve Symmes, actually petitioned both houses of a derisive Congress to grant him a ship, in 1823, to find the North polar opening to an inner sphere, or underground world "which was warm and fertile, and well stocked with fruits and vegetables."

Before merely dismissing Symmes as "a madman," as did le Comte de Volney of the Académie des Sciences, at Paris, in 1822, let it be recalled that no one has cleared up the mystery of the "marked reindeer," with clipped ears, shot in desolate Spitzbergen in 1876. The first statement on this point was made in 1705 by Nicolaus Witsen, a Dutchman, in his "Noort ooster gedeelte van Asia en Europa." He says that reindeer, far remote from any living man in the Arctic,

We know not where the land is, and remember only that one day we were feeding our father's flock in the field, when we heard a great noise like bells, as when at St. Edmund's, they all peal together, and suddenly we were rapt up in the spirit and found ourselves in your harvest-field. Among us no sun riseth, nor is there open sunshine, but such a twilight as here goes before the rising and setting of the sun. Yet a land of light is to be seen not far from us, but severed from us by a stream of great breadth."

It is difficult, at this stretch of time, to estimate on what basis of fact this story may rest. Obviously, a certain amount of Catholic hagiology has been imported into it. It might be a subject of speculation—many would call it fantasy!—whether the green skin might be that of Martians, living underground in their very cold planet, in whose skies the orb of the sun appears much smaller than it does in terrestrial skies. Or, have we here, as in the Vedic myths, some garbled memory of the lost Arctic continent of Hypea, whose disruption by a great cataclysm forced survivors to take to a life in tunnels and underground pits? Are similar Amerindian legends crystallized memories of this?

With reference to the phenomena of detonations, or strange noises preceding teleportation, note that these green children spoke of a "great noise" of tintinnabulation. Here we seem to be confronting phenomena of a fourth-dimensional world type, or supernormal, but well known in the annals of psychical research and occultism. The strange examples of teleportation set down below, suggest the creation of a vortex or whirlpool in matter, by what agency no one knows, into which the helpless victim is drawn. It is accompanied by amnesia which persists, should the victim or patient return to his or her usual life. But, one might speculate also whether this phenomenon

are found mysteriously marked in the ears and on the horns, and that he himself heard hunters, in Norway, who were well acquainted with the care of reindeer, state positively that, in and before 1700 A.D., they had shot reindeer in Spitzbergen—totally uninhabited—clipped in the ears. These Spitzbergen reindeer are smaller and plumper than other Arctic breeds.

One would like also to know more about these "Wolf pittes" at Woolpit, Suffolk, and whether there exist deep caves or subterraneans in this part of Suffolk.

can be created by external entities, such as might be found in a space ship, or fourth-dimensional flying saucer.

Gervase of Tilbury cites a teleportation of a non-living object:

> "Here again, is a still more marvelous testimony. In the county of Gloucester is a town called Bristol, of wealth and prosperous citizens, from whose port men sail for Ireland. It befell upon a time that a native of Bristol sailed to Ireland, leaving his wife and children at home. Then, after a long sea voyage, as he sailed to a far-off ocean, he chanced to sit, banqueting with the mariners about the hour of tierce (9 A.M.), and as he washed his knife over the ship's side, it suddenly slipped from his hands. At that same hour, at Bristol, the knife fell in through the roof-window of that same citizen, which men call a *dormer*, and stuck in the table that was set before his wife. The woman, marvelling at so strange a thing, was dumbfounded, and laying aside that well known knife, she learned long afterwards, on her husband's return, that this misfortune happened on the very day when she found the knife."

A few words on Gervase of Tilbury will not be out of place. All that is known of him is that he flourished *circa* 1200 A.D., in the reign of King John of England. He is said to have been related to the Earl of Salisbury. A wandering scholar and adventurer, he became a favorite at the court of Emperor Otto IV, under whose patronage he wrote the *Otta Imperiala*, full of quaint and very interesting table talk, folklore and tidbits of history and geography. In fact, an early encyclopaedia.

Gervase speaks, as do Irish monks, of a cloud or space ship, seen over a churchyard—perhaps in Kent, at Gravesend, on the estuary of the Thames, when the folk were coming from mass. A "man" came down from the space ship but "died stifled in our gross air, as a shipwrecked mariner would be in the sea." The space ship sailed away, leaving her anchor flukes hitched either onto the churchdoor, or a massive tomb-stone. "The iron bands of the door of that church were forged from the anchor the cloud ship let down, and are there for all men to see." It is now impossible to say what actually did occur. Two or three of these space-ship visitations seem to have occurred during the thousand years prior to our thirteenth century. And much else must have happened after the fall of the

Roman Empire, that went unrecorded, or the records of which vanished in the vandalism of those times.

I shall tell below of a very eerie modern case of apparently frustrated or inhibited teleportation in this same city of Bristol, in the age of railroads. Here are other cases of possible teleportation—only the few permitted by the space at my disposal:

January 5, 1900: Sherman Church, a young fellow employed in the Augusta Mills, at Battle Creek, Michigan, has mysteriously vanished. He was seated in the company's office when he arose and ran into the mill. He has not been seen since. The mill has been taken almost to pieces by searchers, and the river, woods, and country scoured, but to no avail. No one saw Church leave town, nor was there any known reason for his doing so. ("Chicago Tribune," January 5, 1900.)

April 15, 1851: In December, 1850, a mysterious stranger was found wandering in a village near Frankfurt-on-Oder, in Brandenburg, Prussia. No one knows how he got there. He knew very little German. Taken to Frankfurt, he said his name was Joseph Vorin, and that he had come from Laxaria, in Sakria, which is far from Europe "beyond vast oceans." (Possibly by "oceans" is meant outer space.) ("Athenaeum," London, April 15, 1851.)

August, 1869: Thirteen children mysteriously vanished in Cork, Ireland. In the same month, Brussels, Belgium, was agitated about the numbers of missing children. In both cases there was no suggestion of kidnapping—no ransom notes or other signs.

April 23, 1885: Isaac Martin, a young farmer of Salem, Virginia, went into a field to work, and disappeared. Other people in this region have mysteriously vanished.

1888: Five "wild men," and a "wild girl," speaking unknown tongues, appeared in Connecticut on January 1.

July and August, 1892: In Montreal, so many people mysteriously vanished that every other day, the newspapers headlined the events with: "Another Missing Man." Similar mysterious disappearances had occurred in the same city in July, 1883.

1895: While detectives were investigating the disappearance of a little girl named Rooney, in Belfast (August 3), a little boy, named Webb, vanished . . .

followed by another child, and by a third. On September tenth and twelfth, two more small boys vanished in Belfast.

1920: Eight small girls, all under twelve, mysteriously vanish in Belfast. The people are in a commotion.

August 13, 1912: Five men vanish unaccountably from Buffalo, N. Y., in one week.

January 10, 1905, and following days: A man who spoke in a language none could understand, and whose manner was "wild" and strange, was arrested by a metropolitan policeman, in a London street. Detectives from Scotland Yard said he carried a book in which he appeared to have made sketches of things he had seen along the roads. In the book were writings of which linguists told Scotland Yard: "We do not know what language they are written in: it is not Turkish, Bohemian (Czech), Russian, Polish, Arabic, Persian or Hebrew."

September 18: "Le Matin" of Paris reports that a young man, arrested in a Paris street, and charged with vagrancy, speaks a tongue no linguist understands. In vain have Orientalists and experts in European or African tongues spoken to him; but, by the language of signs, he has made known that he comes from 'Lisbian.' He says the Lisbian word for chair is "eisar"; table, "lotoba," and "sonar" means nose; God was "Odir," house was "sacar."

1906: On October 15, a young woman was arrested in Paris, charged with picking pockets. She answered in an unknown language, which no expert in European or Asiatic tongues understood.

1926: In early November, a whole series of mysterious disappearances of people—eight in three days— in Southend, Essex: a mother and two small children; girls aged fifteen and sixteen.

Another mystery that has a suggestion of teleportation about it: On the evening of April 3, 1817, a strange girl appeared at the door of a cottage near Brislington, Bristol. She spoke an unknown tongue, and signed that she wanted food. Later, a Bristol magistrate, Samuel Worrall, took her to his home at Knowle Park, as she was a very "prepossessing young woman." (Whether Worrall was animated by the same feelings as those of a London archdeacon who, in 1920, attracted the notice of the London police by what *they* regarded as his suspiciously benevolent interest in pretty young women, we will leave the cynics to investigate.) Worrall's protégé wrote in characters said to look like "frying pans, combs, and bird cages." Experts at Oxford University could not identify them. Mrs. Worrall, no doubt with entirely disinterested reasons, shipped the girl out to America, and paid her passage at least *one way*. In Philadelphia, the girl gave public exhibitions of her mysterious writing. Thereafter she dropped out of sight.

Some eleven years later there came through the gate of the old walls of Nuremberg, Germany, a strange boy who appeared unacquainted with the most ordinary objects and experiences of human beings. He snatched with delight at the pretty flame of a burning candle and was scorched. A certain Professor Daumer, who took him to his house, found him very intelligent. The boy soon learnt to speak German, though with a queer accent. Later on, he said he had been shut up in a dark room, and tended by a man who taught him only two German sentences. Eye-witnesses, who saw the boy soon after he entered Nuremberg, said his color was too healthy for him to have been confined for any length of time. On December 14, 1833, five years later, he ran out of a park at Anspach, Bavaria, crying: "I have been stabbed!" and soon died. No weapons were found and no other footprints than his own in the newly fallen snow. The autopsy showed that his heart had been pierced by something that had cut through his diaphragm, penetrating heart and liver. Doctors agreed that the wound could not have been self-inflicted. There are suggestions of amnesia about this strange affair—which *may* point towards teleportation, perhaps from some other world in space!

Herr von Feuerbach, who had interested himself in this mysterious boy from the first, wrote:

> "He showed such complete deficiency in words and ideas, such perfect ignorance of the commonest things and appearances of nature, such horror of all customs, conveniences, and necessities of civilized life, and, moreover, such extraordinary peculiarities in his social, mental and physical disposition, that one might feel oneself driven to believe him to be a citizen of another planet, transferred by some miracle to our own."

His name?
Kaspar Hauser, one of the greatest enigmas of history.

A final incident.

At four-thirty on December 9, 1873, the Night Superintendent, T. Harker, of the Bristol and Exeter Railway, at Temple Meads joint station, was sitting in his office, poking up the coal fire into a blaze. Outside a nipping wind blew from the nor'east. The down express from Derby and the North to Bristol, and the connecting express from Paddington, London, were not due for an hour. The station was all in shadows. The few flickering gas lamps but dimly lit up the dark spaces from the bleak aisle of iron pillars. The sort of early morning not fit for a dog to be abroad.

On a sudden, the silence was rent by a scream of "Murder! Murder!"

Down the platform, on bare feet, frantically bounded a woman, dishevelled, wildly excited, clad only in a Victorian night-dress. Behind her ran a man, also in nightdress, but with a smoking pistol in his hand. Both kept glancing anxiously behind them.

The woman stopped at the door of Harker's office and beat with her fists upon the panels. Knocking over his office chair, the startled Harker opened the door.

The woman screamed at him: "They will murder us! They have followed us onto this station. I demand that you search the waiting rooms."

Harker shouted and two porters raced up, rubbing the sleep out of their eyes.

"Stay here in my office," he said to the man and woman, "whilst these men and I make a search."

Harker and the porters hunted all around the big bleak station, but found no one.

Returning to his office, he found the man so agitated that he stammered badly and Harker could not understand a word he said. Concluding that the two were either drunk or mad, Harker sent a porter to fetch a town policeman. The sequel was heard next day in Bristol Police Court, and the "London Times," of December 11, 1873, headed the story:

"Extraordinary Hallucination. At Bristol Police Court yesterday (December 9, 1873), Thomas B. Cumpston and his wife, Mrs. Annie Martha Cumpston, of Virginia Road, Leeds, Yorkshire, were brought up before the magistrates for being disorderly at the Victoria Hotel, Bristol, and letting off firearms. It is said by the landlady of the hotel, Mrs. Tongue, that the defendants took an apartment at the hotel, on Monday evening. They retired to rest at about 12 o'clock. About 4 A.M., she was awakened by loud screams and shouts in their bedroom, succeeded by reports of firearms. She went down and found that they had both leapt from their bedroom into the yard, twelve feet below. They then both made their way to the railroad station opposite.

"Mr. T. Harker, night superintendent of the Bristol and Exeter Railway, said the Cumpstons rushed into his office partly dressed, and crying out, 'Murder!' They were in a terrible state of excitement. They told me they had escaped from a den of rogues and thieves, and they had had to defend themselves. They were under the impression that someone was following them, and that made me search the waiting-room to see that no one was there. Upon my sending for a policeman, Mr. Cumpston was searched and a revolver and three knives were found on him.*

"Asked by the magistrates what they had to say, Cumpston, who has an impediment in his speech, said that he and his wife had been staying at Clifton, two miles away; but, intending to proceed to Weston-super-Mare in the morning, they came to Bristol and engaged a room at the Victoria Hotel, being near the railway station. They were alarmed at about 4 A.M. by terrible noises they could not explain, and were badly frightened. The bed seemed to open and he heard all sorts of strange things. The floor, too, opened and they heard voices. They were so terrified that they opened their bedroom window and leapt out.

"Mrs. Cumpston gave her version of the affair. She said: 'We heard terrible noises at 4 A.M. The floor seemed to be giving way. It certainly opened. My husband fell down some distance, and I tried to get him up. What we said was repeated every time we spoke!' Being very much frightened, she asked her husband to fire off his pistol, which he did, into the ceiling. The noises continuing, they got out of the window, but she did not know how. When they got outside, she asked her husband to fire off his pistol again. Then they ran up to the railway station.

"She told the Bench that she did not hear the

---

* It is curious that a *respectable English* Victorian, in 1873, should arrive in Bristol carrying a *revolver and three* knives! Had he experienced similar adventures *prior to* 1873?

noises so plainly as her husband. Ultimately, a Mr. Butt telegraphed to come from Gloucester, attended the Court and told the magistrates that the couple occupied a very good position in Leeds. He offered to take proper charge of them if they were handed over to him, which was ultimately done, the defendants being discharged from custody. No explanation can be given of this strange affair, and the belief is that it was the husband's hallucination."

The "Bristol Post" added more details:

"As Cumpston was about to be dragged into the opening in the floor, his wife says she dragged him back. In Court, Cumpston's excitement was still so intense that he could not clearly express himself. Mrs. Cumpston also said that, earlier in the evening, they had both been alarmed by loud sounds, but the landlady reassured them. At three or four in the morning, the sounds were heard again. They jumped out on the floor which was giving way under them. Voices, repeating their exclamations were heard, or their own voices echoed strangely. Then, according to what she saw, or thought she saw, the floor opened wide. Her husband was falling into the opening, and she dragged him back. The landlady was called, and she testified that the sounds had been heard, but she was unable to describe them clearly. Policemen said they went to the Victoria Hotel, examined the bedroom, but found nothing to justify the extraordinary behavior of the Cumpstons. They suggested it was a case of collective hallucination."

Of course, it was nothing of the kind! I draw notice here, as in other cases, to the strange noises preceding and accompanying the phenomenon. If the discreet and business-like landlady did not let her own tongue run about these noises, her reasons would be obvious. It would hardly be a good advertisement for the hotel to let people say it was "haunted."

The very mysterious phenomenon of teleportation is well known to students of the occult and in the annals of psychical research. Those who have experienced it—often young children—show amnesia. They have no recollection, afterwards, of what occurred in the long or short interval when they were mysteriously missing. Teleportation might be defined as the act of opening a vortex in matter and bringing it from one form through another. In some of its very mysterious aspects it reaches from the chemico-physical world into the unseen.

It is possible that, in this phenomenon, a physical body, either animate or inanimate, is reduced to its "etheric state" by the "condensing form," and the being or object is transported to a point in the vast universe. Some of these aeroforms of the non-terrestrial, fourth-dimensional or, if one prefers, "intra-dimensional" types, appear to have the amazing power of passing themselves and their saucer-discs from one plane to another, including that of our three-dimensional earth! One example of this is the incident of the Goose Bay, Labrador, saucer fleet with carrier ship, described in earlier pages.

We have no proof that among the mysterious visitants to our skies, there may not be three-dimensional beings. According to some speculations there may be an underground sentient life on Mars, whose climate must be much more severe than that of the earth, and whose evolutionary age may be considerably older. In the very far past, that red planet may have experienced cataclysms which removed her orbit farther than our common sun.*

In January, 1950, a Japanese astronomer, Sadeki, of Toyko University, reported observing a great explosion on Mars. The eruption was calculated to have devastated about 10,000 miles of its surface, and was accompanied by terrific earthquakes. If the surface of Mars has life forms only of a low type, then no sentient beings like ours were affected. But under the surface there may exist a subterranean life of highly developed beings. It may be more than a coincidence that, as Canadian scientists at Shirley's Bay station, Ottawa, observed in March, 1954, flurries in saucer sightings occur when Mars comes nearest us, at intervals of two years 2 months.

On July 2, 1954, Mars was less than 40 million miles from the earth. Before and after midnight, it shone redly in the southern skies of England. The mean distance of Mars from the earth is about 48.6 million miles, but it may reach an apogee of 63 million miles. After examining more than 500 colored photographs of Mars then taken, astronomers at Johannesburg said that the planet seems to have changed. They would give no details until 50,000 more photos, taken at Johannesburg and Bloem-

---

* One may ponder about the implications of the terrific cataclysm which, Bode's Law implies, shattered a planet that once revolved in an orbit between *Mars and Jupiter.*

fontein observatories, have been collated. Dr. Slipher of the Lowell Observatory at Flagstaff, Arizona, hazarded the opinion that the observations *might* finally settle the question of whether life exists on Mars. Some astronomers suggest waiting until 1956, when Mars will be 5 million miles nearer the earth.

Its surface is known to have both green areas and desert wastes, across which sweep dust storms. Some scientists believe they know what that dust contains. It is generally accepted that little or no oxygen exists in the planet's atmosphere; nor hydrogen nor helium. But there is carbon dioxide and nitrogen, the bases of plant life. The planet has bluish clouds, believed to consist of ice crystals. Some think that Mars has mountain ranges, others not; and no lakes or sheets of water, because they are not reflected. There is controversy as to whether or no Mars is a dying planet, far gone in evolution. The American astronomer, Dr. Dean McLaughlin, thinks Mars may become a habitable world, and that it is now where the earth was about 4,000 million years ago. Heat comes from Mars' *underground!*

If it be correct that the oxygen in the Martian atmosphere is less than one-thousandth part of the terrestrial volume of oxygen, and that spectographic analysis of the light reflected from Mars' surface shows that that planet's atmosphere is mainly nitrogen with a percentage of carbon dioxide, then coupled with a Martian atmospheric pressure about one-fifteenth of that on the earth, these factors would seem to call for a pressure-suit and helmet with oxygenators, in the case of future voyagers from earth who may try to land on Mars.

Moscow Radio told the world, on August 16, 1954, that nuclear fuels, or atomic fission power will "soon" enable men to reach Mars and other planets. Whether this rash assertion was or was not made, it struck the Viennese physicist, Professor Hans Thirring (as it had many thoughtful people in Great Britain), that as he stated at the International Astronautical Congress, held at Innsbruck, in August, 1954, there is grave doubt if Governments can or will spend billions of dollars on making the dream of interplanetary flight possible. And the problem of first establishing an intermediate space vehicle between the earth and the moon has not, he said, been in any way eased or altered by the development of power from fissioning the atom.

Undeterred by the difficulties of the Kenealy-Heaviside layer of ions in our upper stratosphere, Harvard University announced plans in June, 1954, to attempt to get radar echoes from Mars, to determine that planet's exact distance from the earth. Both Australian and U.S. observatories have "bounced" radar echoes off the Moon; but our satellite is only some 239,000 miles away, compared with Mars' mean of 48.6 million miles. Officially, astronomers have little to postulate about Mars, but *some* of them appear to have "off the record" views.

I extract the following from my log:

May 26, 1954: Russian astronomers plan to measure the temperature of the soil on Mars, on July 1, when the red planet will be 40 million miles from the earth.

June 5, 1954: Professor Nikolai Barabashov, a Russian astronomer, says that large areas of the planet Venus are covered by water, as was the earth 300 million years ago, when organisms began to evolve, and life first appeared. He thinks that "life may develop on Venus, any time now."

June 11, 1954: Dr. George Anderson, president of the Victoria (Australia) branch of the British Astronomical Association, dogmatically and on principle denies the existence of flying saucers, and asserts that "talk of them is nonsense." Anderson, at Melbourne Rotary lunch, is very dogmatic, too, about biotic conditions on all the solar planets, including Mars. "No life exists on other planets. There is no possibility of it." More justifiably, however, Anderson is skeptical about predictions that man will ever conquer other planets. Less justifiably, he asserts that flying saucers "cannot come here from other worlds."

Author's Comment: Anderson, who says or hints that saucers may be just planes, meteors, "newspapers blowing about the sky," or a fashion or hallucination "like the Loch Ness monster," may also take little notice of my assurance as an Englishman who has toured Loch Ness recently, that the "Loch Ness monster" has been seen and even photographed by reputable eye-witnesses, who are neither liars, hoaxers nor hallucinated. I very carefully investigated the Loch Ness mystery and obtained from local people their own story of what they saw there. But, as to the possibility of life and intelligent life, too, on other planets in the solar system, neither Anderson nor anyone else is at present in a position to pronounce so dogmatically as he does. My reader should study what is said in this book of mine on the possibility, *inter alia*, of intelligent life existing *below the surface of Mars*. Life is very adaptable, and because the conditions on other planets may not be viable for human beings, who is to say—not even Anderson can!—whether sentient life long ago adapted itself to conditions on certain planets of the solar system. Dr. Anderson is, like myself, not a young man, and he should bear in mind that arrogance and dogmatism do not go well with advanced years.

June 13, 1954: Harold Rothman, evidently taking a leaf out of the book of Richard de Touche-Skadding, founder of Moon Metals and Minerals, Inc., of New York State, has filed at Phoenix, Arizona, a claim to 100,000 acres of the moon. He says he is "foresighted." Well, at least the old time Spanish, Portuguese and English-Elizabethan and Stuart adventurers waited till *someone* had got to the American Indies before putting in their claims. Alas, the poor old buccaneering guys did not understand the art of publicity. In *those* spacious days, you ran some risk of finding your legs clapped into bilboes and stocks, or your ears tastefully nailed to pillories, did you make such claims.

August 8, 1954: The BBC, TV newsreel gives the story of an astronomer (name not stated) who says that Mars, seen through big telescopes in the U.S., shows signs of being *inhabited*. The astronomer also says he saw, from an aircraft, flying above the clouds, three saucers. The moon, too, is exciting speculation. Hardly a month goes by without *new features* on it being noted. In 1954, Mars had very peculiar weather, more than usual clouds. The polar snow-caps are larger, and the canals now *show blue*. This indicates more water in them, and *may* suggest that entities have landed on Mars and may be *reactivating the canals!* They appear to be renewing an ancient Martian canal system! It looks as if, on Mars and the Moon, mysterious beings from outer space may be *contemplating an invasion of the earth*. In England people are asking, as they have done in the U.S.A.: Are the authorities gradually preparing the public for some startling announcement?

Of our own moon, we appear to know not a *great* deal more than we do of distant Mars. It is usually said to be a dead or lifeless world, although one or two of the less official or conventional astronomers and selenographers have concluded that there are signs of some very lowly types of vegetation on the slopes of some of the craters, whose form is so singularly unlike what we call a crater on the earth. Is our moon so lifeless?

From the year 1794 onwards, bright and unexplained lights have been seen on the dark part of the gibbous moon. Also what might be signals in craters, often in the north-west quadrant; moving flakes of lights from other craters to that called Plato; lights flashing on and off intermittently; also a light on the dark part of the moon that might be a reflection from a moving mirror. These have caused certain people to wonder if cosmic visitants, or as we say today, flying saucers or space ships may use the moon as a cosmic way-station, in trips to the earth. Some, in the U.S.A., have located this way-station on the dark side of the Moon, whose only part—a mere edge—is occasionally revealed to our astronomers by "libration." They assume a Lunar base from which the saucers or space ships have a mechanism to transmit a "master pulse wave," or kind of "mental ray," with which the satellite discs, visiting our terrestrial atmosphere, synchronize. With this master pulse wave the aeroforms can convert from their own order of dense or invisible matter, to ours, at will.

I venture no opinion on this fantasy or theory, which can neither be proved nor disproved. And enterprising Americans, in New York and Arizona, have set up companies and staked claims to minerals and gems on the moon—and also in Mars and Venus! The specific gravity of the lunar crust being about that of a diamond, they feel *certain* that virgin gold and gems will be picked up by the first space-man landing from the earth.

Others speculate on military possibilities concerning them. Dr. R. Shepherd, chairman of the British Interplanetary Society, recently said:

"Military operations on the Moon may be possible . . . people will be attracted, covetous aggressors, with immense ambitions to race transportation warfare to the Moon first . . . but even the devil would never have the idea to dirty the beautiful Moon with human blood."

However, these gold-hungry and world-dominating gentlemen may find, if they land on our moon, that their first visit is to be their last.

They may then regret listening to the advice of some roaring late twentieth-century newspaper magnate: "Go up, young man! Up to the moon, and get on them thar golden lunar hills fust, or bust!"

The ingenious idea of going into the depths of the Sahara (but it had better not be within range of the fierce and matriarchal Touaregs of the Tibesti mountains!) to fire projectiles at the moon and planets, that will "uncover secrets of the universe," occurred in the summer of 1953 to Dr. Fritz Zwicky, astrophysicist of the California Institute of Technology. These were to be discharged from balloons, controlled by electronic devices, some twenty miles above the earth. The American Government refuses permission, owing to the risk to the territory below.

In England, France and the U.S.A., between 1950 and 1954, flying saucers have been seen to drop substances from the skies which could not be analyzed, since the elusive stuff quickly vanished into nothingness. But the 1856 incident below belongs to a class of phenomena that have never been explained satisfactorily.

March, 1856: The "Courier Journal," of Louisville, Kentucky, reprints a queer "Fortean" incident happening in March, 1856: "A rain of knitting needles fell during a severe storm in the night, and in the morning, thousands of these needles were found at the western edge of Harrodsburg, Kentucky." *Note:* There were no reports of any needle factory that, *anywhere,* had been demolished in a storm!

The Swedish Academy of Science takes an excerpt from its Transactions of *1808:* "A two-hour long procession of numerous reddish objects, shaped like hat-crowns, passed in the sky over Skeninge, Sweden, from four to six P.M., on May 16, 1808. They caused the sun to glow red. Some of them fell to the ground, leaving a gelatinous substance that vanished in five minutes." (*Vide* Chaps. 6, 8, 12 and 13, and pp. 311-14 of my "Flying Saucers on the Attack.")

June, 1953: A policeman saw a six foot globe alight in a field in a Pennsylvania village, and when he touched it, it generated into a mass of gelatin. (*Vide* references above.)

July 23, 1953: Mysterious *yellow* fireballs have been several times seen in a *cañon* of the Kaweah River, in the Sequoia National Park, California. The local ranger sent out squads, but found no traces of fire or explosion. Lights had been seen in this region on three previous nights, and the yellow fireballs were seen on two following nights, but there have been no further reports of them.

December 6, 1953: Two girls at Crymnach, South Wales, saw a queer thing spinning in the sky at the back of their house. They searched in a nearby·quarry and found a jelly or colloidal substance, as large as a dinner plate, which melted and left no trace.

What was the unknown stationary object seen on the radarscope of the liner "Mauretania," which deflected the U.S. liner "United States" from its course, though the latter ship saw nothing on her own radar. Had the mysterious object submerged or vanished into the sky?

I have already drawn attention to mysterious lights seen off The Wash, near Hunstanton, Norfolk, England, in 1952, and to very mysterious objects seen both on the surface of the ocean and under it, by ships in the nineteenth and the early decades of the present century— some emitting sounds like working machinery, but not of terrestrial origin. (*Vide* Chap. IX of my book, "Flying Saucers on the Attack.") :

N.B. Radar beams reflect a *solid object.* The time difference between transmission and the return of the reflecting ray is used to calculate the distance of the reflected object. Rays follow the curvature of the earth, but *do not penetrate water.*

Who or what dropped the mysterious object described below onto a ploughfield, near Bexley, Kent? Is it a "marker" from some flying saucer? And why the curious lack of curiosity—real or apparent—of the London and country newspapers? The only photograph was official and secret:

May 29, 1954: Albert Billing, a farmer, ploughed up on his field at Bunker's Hill farm, Bexley, Kent, England, a strange object of solid iron, which he at first took for an unexploded 500 pound German bomb. But when the bomb disposal experts of the British Army's Royal Engineers' Corps examined it, they said it was *no bomb at all.* It was cylindrical in shape, two feet six inches long, and a foot in diameter, pointed at one end, blunt at the other, and weighing five hundredweights (*cwt.*). "I have never seen such an object before," said a Royal Engineers captain. "It is a solid mass of iron and made a crater where it fell on the ground. It must have been dropped from the air, since it made a 'splash crater' in the field."

Author's Comment: I live three miles from this farm, and on one occasion (*Vide* Chap. I, pp. 11-12 in my "Flying Saucers on the Attack") saw a globular saucer over the sky in this very region. During the Second World War, on more than one occasion, I found strips of tin foil, or similar substance, scattered over the fields and in the woods; but this was after heavy night raids and may have been dropped by German bombers to confuse the radar posts on the ground.

I doubt very much if this strange object was dropped by any air raider. *N.B.* It is significant that not one British newspaper has reproduced the photograph taken of this mysterious object. Why? Someone in the British War Office is probably alive to the fact that flying saucer phenomena are real and portentous.

Compare this "Bunker's Hill farm mystery" with the incident below:

August 7, 1954: A mysterious object resembling a three-foot long bomb was seen in the mud of the Ouse, close to the south quay of King's Lynn, Norfolk. Police removed it to their station yard, but could not say whether or not it was a "live bomb." There is no indication of its origin, and the British Army's disposal unit has been notified.

Is *this*, also, a "marker," and has, or will some mysterious space ship, or flying saucer come over to look for it?

Was the mysterious object on the radarscope of the British liner "Mauretania," a flying saucer or a space ship that had alighted on the Atlantic?

June 1, 1954: Fifty huge icebergs strung between the latitudes of New York and Newfoundland, force the liner "Queen Elizabeth" onto track B, a diversion of thirty miles out of her normal course. The U.S. liner "United States" has a mysterious experience: At 40° North Latitude, and 50° West Longitude, in the Atlantic, she is warned by the British Cunard liner "Mauretania" that the latter has seen, for some hours, right on the track of the "United States" liner, a stationary object. Commodore John Anderson, master of the "United States" liner, at once orders a change of course twenty-five miles south, but is puzzled to find nothing indicated on his own radarscope.

Another singular feature in the drama of the flying saucers is the way birds and animals, unlike modern man, in whom the growth of intellectualism has weakened other faculties, react to strange things in the air, or on the ground:

October 2, 1948: The flying-boat, "Australia," on both her Tasman Sea crossings to and from New Zealand and Australia, flew through a vast cloud of strange brown insects. It took her three minutes to regain clear air. The insects were at 2,000 feet above the sea, 100 miles from the Australian coast. On a second trip in the morning, the flying-boat was 200 miles out from Sydney, over the sea, when at a height of 5,000 feet, she again met the tremendous swarm. The pilot opened the cockpit window and tried to catch some of the insects for identification, but failed.

October 9, 1948: Millions of mysterious black insects swarm over Sydney (Australia) and suburbs. Hundreds of people are stung; the pests get into eyes and ears, and settle on clothes. When killed, they leave a dirty mark behind. So many of them invaded the railroad station, that they drove the North Sydney stationmaster from his office. Newly painted buildings have been ruined by them, and so thickly did they swarm on a golf links, that players had to quit their games and seek refuge in the club-house.

April, 1954: Half an hour before a violent earthquake, its epicenter in the Pindus mountains, 130 miles northwest of Athens, rocked central Greece, storks were seen flying around in agitation. It may be noted that, in 1938, in Poland, a stork was seen to remove squawking and protesting nestlings from a tree a few hours before the tree was struck by a thunderbolt. Birds have a peculiar sensitivity to changes in electrical tension, and this may explain why, in Oregon, pigeons were seen to be wildly agitated when flying saucers were overhead. During the Nazi daylight raids on Dover, in 1940-44, the agitation of sea-gulls often gave the first warning of enemy planes approaching.

I summarize other curious entomological and piscatory incidents, which occurred in June, July and August, 1954:

Damage of £3,000,000 to fruit trees in the German Palatinate caused by hordes of caterpillars, which also invaded houses. At Passy, near Paris, destructive white ants eat through woodwork. Their queen produces 4,000 eggs a day. They have trailed all across France, 250 miles as the crow flies. One theory is that they came from South or Central America.

Thousands of dead fish floating in the Chelmer River, England. No one knows what caused their death. (N.B. There had been in southern and midland England, in 1953, and again in Yorkshire, July, 1954, mysterious siphoning of rivers and streams like that in Canada, in 1952, when a flying saucer was seen by four people, hosing water from Sawbill Lake, Ontario.)

Out of 7,940 pedigreed homing pigeons released at Milford Haven, only thirty reach their lofts. The mystery is not explained by high winds. Electromagnetic disorientation is a likelier explanation.

Millions of gnats swarm on lines over long railroad bridge, the Storstrom, Denmark. Train held up for ninety minutes.

Miami, Fla. newspapers report the worst mosquito plague for years. Insects appear to be becoming immune to insecticides. Atom bomb explosions are believed to have disturbed the equilibrium of insects life. New strains are being "mutated."

Waves of pests invade Texas.

Plagues of flying ants stampede people on buses at Bexley, Kent. At Birmingham, England, they drive golfers off the course. Flies unusually "pestiferous" in south, south-east and west of England.

Fish in the Seine at Paris die at alarming rate.

Carl Warburton, in his "Buffaloes," says that just before an earth tremor, every bird became silent. In Madang, New Guinea, and at Bugia, a station on the Papuan coast, every bird falls silent at least twenty seconds before human beings feel the first violent tremor.

What was the explanation of the oddity below? Had it anything to do with the fact that flying saucers, in the

nineteenth and twentieth centuries, have been seen by
ships in the Atlantic, the North Pacific, and the Indian
Ocean both alighting on and ascending from the sea?
Who really knows?

Overpowering stench, as we have noted, was said to
have come from a flying saucer "space entity," who landed
on a hill-top at West Virginia in September, 1952.

October 15, 1948: A nauseating stench, of unknown
origin, floated into San Francisco from the ocean,
and wild rumors that an enemy was projecting a gas
attack caused women to dash into the streets with
children, others to jam the police telephones. No
one knows where the reek came from. One theory is
that a submarine earthquake opened a fissure in the
ocean-bed and released a petroleum bubble. The
stench spread over an area of thirty miles of coast-
line, and was more pungent at upper levels. Workers
in top floors rushed to the streets when the stench
became intolerable.

Old Robert Burton wrote in his "Anatomy of Melan-
choly":

"Meteors rain stones, frogs, mice in Norway, which
they call Lammer (as Munster writes). Seen by people
to descend and fall like flocculent showers, and like
so many locusts, to consume all that is green. Leo
Afer says that in Fez, Barbary (North Africa), locusts appear all of a sudden in the fields, and also at
Arles, France, in 1553, when the like happened, and
all fruits and grass were devoured. . . . Could not
imagine whence they came, if not from heaven.
(They suddenly darken the sky)."

Were these mutants from outer space? Such phenomena
have been noted before Burton, and have recurred since.

There was something strange about what was called
"a severe electric storm" that set fire to twenty-six houses
at Washington, D.C., on May 4, 1954. Fire brigades answered more than a thousand alarms. Tornado warnings
were given in the states of Maryland and Virginia. Equally
mysterious were outbreaks of food poisoning all over
England, in May and June, 1954. At one case, London,
forty-nine nurses were taken ill, and no analysts could
determine the cause.

How explain the following incident? I recorded other such cases occurring in the eighteenth century in England and Scotland, in my "Flying Saucers on the Attack." We seem little nearer to a solution than were our eighteenth-century forefathers. One might wonder if some hostile space ship were demonstrating against the earth, fantastic or absurd as such a speculation may sound:

July 5, 1954: A boy of eleven, named David Parslow, was cycling home from Sunday school at Ridgway, Somerset, when out of a glowering sky, there suddenly appeared a strange globe of fire, as big as a football, said Mrs. E. Caple. It splintered windows, burned out electric ovens, and its searing glare compelled people to screen their eyes. David was hurled to the ground, where he lay paralyzed in legs and arms, and he had to be helped home. A large hole was rent in the ground. Red marks, shaped like forked lightning, appeared on his waist, shoulder and back. He suffered from shock for days.

Of course, it might have been a thunderbolt; but in America there have, as my correspondence shows, been cases where balls like these played round a room, danced freakishly around people, and then vanished out of the window. Their behavior induced a belief that they were under some invisible control.

As old John Lydgate said 514 years ago:

> "Straunge thynges ther bee,
> On lond, in sea."

He might have added . . . "eke, in ye skyes!"

And that may have been what a U.S. Air Force pilot thought after an experience with an "Etherian," fourth-dimensional space-world or intra-dimensional saucer of very dense matter, on September 2, 1952:

U.S. Air Force pilot, Captain William Maitland, flying a jet fighter plane, says he flew "right through a spot" where the radarscope showed an unexplained material object. He said: "I saw nothing but empty space." He added: "I believe it is the first time a U.S. Air Force interceptor actually tracked down and flew through what some observers said were mysterious

extra-terrestrial flying craft, called flying saucers."
Two Sabrejets had been summoned, after night radar
crews of the Civil Aviation Aeronautics reported
tracking a number of unexplainable objects over
Chicago. The jets passed right over the spot where
radar reported reflections of tangible and material
objects. But Captain Maitland and the pilot of the
other interceptor saw "only empty air."

It may be stated that is by no means the first (nor will
it be the last) time that planes sent up to track such
mysterious objects detected as spots on the radar see
nothing.

STRANGE STORIES OF COLOSSAL
SPACE SHIPS

IN THE STRANGE DRAMA of the flying saucers, the elusive
or "god-like" and indifferent satellite discs have been
more often reported than the colossal space ships. One
of the latter, in 1949, was computed at an air and naval
base on the eastern coast of the U.S.A., using radar,
theodolite-telescope and mathematical calculations, to
have been a *mile long!*

Usually, these colossal space ships remain far aloft,
but sometimes, they appear to descend close to the earth,
as in the tragic affair of January 7, 1948, when pilot
Thomas Mantell, flying a chaser plane, was blasted out
of the sky. The cosmic machine he encountered was of
tremendous size, according to his last radio message. It
may have smashed up his plane with a heat ray or some
other lethal radiation.

As Mantell's message was being sent to his base at
Godman, near Fort Knox, Kentucky, the fatal emanation
was being directed at him:

"I see the thing . . . almost 70 yards across . . . at 2,800 degrees Fahrenheit, the girders of the bridge I'm very close to it." (*Silence*)

The following sightings suggest observations of something more than satellite or controlled discoidal aeroforms—something like vast carriers or space ships:

1952: Space ship very high in sky seen over Denham, Bucks, Eng. (August 28), at 3 P.M., in act of releasing three satellite discs which fly off in different directions. Same or similar object seen over Sweden, a few hours later, also releasing satellites which flew off at terrific speed. Ten Royal Air Force officers see a large unknown object very high over an airdrome in south England. At Göteborg, Sweden, same day, September 21, a large, noiseless, glittering object, of high speed, with a phosphorescent tail. September 28: Danish Royal Air Force officers see out of operations room at Karup, Jutland, "large and unique flying object," while Operation "Mainbrace" is on. Saucers seen all over Denmark that day.

1954: January to February. An extraordinary unknown object seen high over beach at St. Kilda, near Melbourne, Australia. At eleven A.M., same object, like a large sheet of aluminum, rocked from side to side, and flashed in sunshine. Each flash was accompanied by an enveloping purple halo. It did not seem to give off light of its own, emitted no vapor, and looked like a large silver butterfly. Speed computed at 1,800 miles an hour; altitude, 30,000 feet; and must have been *over 300 feet wide*. Hamilton, Australia, reported sighting a dazzlingly bright orange thing, like a double saucer, the top one inverted. First seen at 9:45 P.M. It left a vapor trail lasting twenty minutes.

On January 25th, the British Air Ministry warns all personnel *not* to talk of flying saucers.

Amazing object like a large planet, moving swiftly, vertically, then sideways, seen between 2:30 and 3:15 A.M., over Adelaide, Australia. Yellow-white, shading to deep orange. Man and wife see a bright point of light circle the space ship at high speed. Two days before, a strange object with a corrugated top, seen flashing crimson lights low on horizon at Sale, Australia. As they watched, the space ship turned from crimson to misty green, moved up and down and vanished. At 7:40 P.M., the same day, February 10, pilot Booth in an Australian National Airways air liner, saw dead ahead, high in sky, a very large unknown object moving erratically. He could not get near it. *N.B.* He was 100 miles north of Adelaide, Australia.

I now give a remarkable sighting of my own, over north Kent, extracted from my diary, entry made the same day:

July 23, 1954: At 5:10 A.M., I was awakened by the drone of very high-flying R.A.F. planes engaged in summer maneuvers. Sat up, as I could not sleep. My house stands on a low hill and my bedroom windows command a view of about ten miles. At 5:25 A.M., when the planes were no longer within earshot, I chanced to look out of the windows and was startled to see a strange, large object in the southwest sky. It seemed to be on fire from end to end, was shaped like an airship rounded at both ends, and was flying about thirty degrees above the skyline, which was barred by low rain clouds. In the east, the sun was shining. The object, flying on a horizontal course, had about twice the speed of a jet plane. It was clearly silhouetted against the clouds and the low hills towards Chislehurst, Kent. The strange object appeared to have no windows or ports, and at that distance of fifteen miles I could see no indication of anything within it. It made no attempt to seek cloud cover. It had come from the direction of Chatham and the lower Thames estuary, and its course might take it over Staines, toward Middlesex and Herts. It was certainly no plane, or rocket, or balloon of any sort. It was visible for thirty seconds, until the trees in a local park cut off my view. I rushed for my binoculars, but by that time it had passed southwest out of my view. At that time in the morning, it is possible that policemen, postoffice mail van drivers, or railroad men would have been out. But so fiery red was it that it could not have escaped observation. Its altitude was not more than 800 feet. As Biggin Hill, Royal Air Force base is only a few miles away, if the observers saw it on their radarscopes, they might conclude, since they would know that seasonal maneuvers were on, that the object had something to do with the R.A.F. planes. But it was certainly *not* a flare dropped from a plane.

I think this may have been a non-terrestrial space ship. In this same region early one autumn morning in 1950, I sighted a satellite object like a glowing sphere.

Here appears to be evidence of what I have mentioned before: that such non-terrestrial objects may be taking clever advantage of terrestrial air flights and normal military operations with which they may be and are confused, and thus escape detection. In any case, if this space ship were registered on a radar, the radar men have official orders to say nothing to anyone outside.

I at once sent off a report of my sighting to the "London Daily Mail" and the "London News-Chronicle," which gave no acknowledgment. If my report were not "filed" in the wastebasket, and the editors rang up the Air Ministry, their naïveté must be greater than any efficient newspaper should possess, in view of the official policy of censoring flying saucer "alarms."

The report following may be of a space ship, seen over Idaho. I summarize from various western American newspapers:

August 9, 1953: Mysterious lights had previously been reported after dark at Moscow, Idaho, by the ground observer corps. Air Force jets had interpreted them as reflections of town lights. But observations and photographs taken between 9:23 P.M. and 11:37 P.M., on August 9 and further observations on the next night, from 12:30 A.M. to 5 A.M. do not support this conclusion. On the night of August 9, a mysterious disc-shaped object, dropped down to 1,000 feet and moved southeast at about twenty miles an hour. It appeared to be about 200 feet in diameter, and the pinkish-white light emanating from it was too sharp to be a reflection. At 5 A.M., on August 10, a soundless "flash explosion" came from this, or a similar object, then 1,500 feet up. In daylight, the object was seen to be shiny and metallic. Five photos taken by the chief ground observer, Mr. L. E. Towner, show the object varying in shape—a wedge, an oval, a rectangle, a globe, and a cylinder tapering at one end. Mr. Towner made careful calculations and concluded that the mysterious silent object must have been of *tremendous size.*

Ontario, Canada, seems to have been surveyed by a gigantic space ship, three months later:

October 31, 1953: Oscar Plewes, of Lambeth, Ontario, Canada, was repairing a television aerial when, about 1,000 feet overhead, he was startled to see a strange object whose front part was V-shaped and brilliantly lit. "Its size was monstrous," he says. "Why, it was bigger than a B-36 bomber! It left no vapor trail and vanished in two seconds. I should say it was travelling at 500 miles an hour."

Another startling report may be interpreted in two very different ways: (1) that our earth has satellites previously unknown to astronomers; or (2) that our earth is being, as it were, patrolled between the moon and us by interplanetary vehicles. Less probable is any theory that either Russia or America has been able to launch into space a satellite of the Forrestal type, which both nations are known to be now working on. It is improbable that this could have been done by either side without the secret services of the other learning about it. Nor could *all* the newspapers on two continents, in their frantic competition for "scoops," be kept in blinkers about something so revolutionary.

January 14, 1954: New York newspapers state that Dr. Clyde Tombaugh of Lowell Observatory, is searching the skies for a group of tiny moons believed to be circling the earth at altitudes of from 10,000 to 240,000 miles. He is using the new Schmidt telescope. These little satellites are from one foot to 120 feet in diameter. The new telescope could photograph a forty-two foot object 100,000 miles away, and a four foot object 10,000 miles away. The U.S. Army Ordnance Corps is interested, because for one thing, the discovery would assist in estimates of the cost of establishing stations out in space. Of course, it might also enable skeptics to suggest that flying saucers are merely small lunar satellites!

April 3, 1954: Dr. Lincoln La Paz, meteoritics expert and selenographer of the University of New Maxico, is said to be anticipating the discovery of two new satellites of the Moon, which move at high speed around the earth, and have not been photographed by astronomical cameras, owing to their great velocity.

May 24, 1954: It is stated that astronomers at the White Sands proving ground, New Mexico, have been alerted to watch for *two artificial satellites* said to be circling the earth in space. It is not known that either the U.S. or Russia has succeeded in launching a satellite vehicle between the orbit of the earth and the moon. Certain quarters in the U.S. say that these satellite vehicles are controlled by flying saucers on the moon, and that they may be advance bases for a landing on the earth by saucers within three months or three years!

Author's Comment: Obviously, a case of "Wait and See!"

July 22, 1954: V. Dobronavov, of the Committee of Cosmic Radiation of the Central Air Club of the Soviet Union, predicts that Russia will have an artificial satellite over the earth by 1964. He also thinks that within thirty years, three men in a space ship will reach the moon. He adds that these dates are conservative. "Russia may achieve it earlier still. The U.S.," he asserts, "is working on a space platform for interplanetary travel for atomic purposes. The Russian satellite will be a rocket that will move around the earth, and three types of engines are being planned to carry ships to the Moon. Up to sixteen miles, turbo-jets will be used to attain 621 miles an hour; then the jets will be automatically detached and air-engines will take over, at a speed of a mile per second! They, too, would then be detached, and liquid jet engines go into action. (*From the Soviet magazine,* "*Technics for Youth.*")

In Australia, in April, 1954, what looked like a vast space ship roared down from the sky to survey a freight train, about an hour after dawn! The overture to this Cosmic Opera of the Valkyries of Space had been seen and heard two months before. The following extract is from the Sydney Sun:

February 18, 1954: A queer object streaked with a roar over Alice Springs, Central Australia, at 4:30 A.M. It was neither a jet nor any other type of terrestrial plane, says the Australian civil aviation traffic control. Only a month earlier the local newspaper, "Centralian Advocate," had published a local photograph of a saucer, black, and over 150 feet in diameter, seen hovering over Mt. Gillen. It whizzed off at terrific speed and *its size was enormous.* The picture showed that the thing was circular in shape and had heavy veins running to the rim of the circumference.

In March, what may have been a space ship surveyed an American radar station at Noah Bay, on the west coast:

March 3, 1954: At noon, in bright sunshine, a thing like a silver spot hovered motionless, then seemed to travel with the moon, which was visible, over the radar station at Noah Bay, Washington. The mysterious object was far beyond the range of the radar elevator finder. It had been seen at least five times in 1952 and 1953.

Nothing in sensational Hollywood film fantasy can throw into the shade an incident which might well have culminated in tragedy. It excites two questions: (1) where, in the name of nightmare, did this colossal aeroform come from? (2) What sort of entities were on board, and what motive had they beyond possible curiosity, or a desire to warn or astound in this grotesque demonstration?

April 28, 1954: Two Australian railroadmen have a terrifying experience with a "swooping, screaming flying saucer" which rushed straight down from the sky at their locomotive, forty-five miles west of Geelong, Victoria, at 7:20 A.M. Its size was "gigantic." The engineer is Ted Smith (26), and the fireman Colin Beacon (23). Both, skilled and dependable men, have reported their experience to the Council for Scientific and Industrial Research.

Says Mr. Smith: "I nearly keeled out of the cab of the engine when I saw a huge, round, dark mass plunging straight down at my train. It screamed down and then suddenly raced up towards the sky. The adventure lasted four minutes and was amazing and terrifying. I could see no windows or doors in it. Trees in the background looked like matchsticks against its vast bulk. *It could have been a quarter of a mile in diameter!*

"I called Colin, my fireman, and we both saw it stand still in the air, like a huge monster hovering over us, and unlike any possible aircraft. . . . It was a beautifully clear morning, and no possibility of any illusion. It came within 350 feet of us, and I felt that it was driven; but the way it careened round the sky, you would have thought it was driven by an amateur.

"It may sound silly, but it must have been something from another planet! After plunging about the sky, it rose higher and higher and went out of sight."

Mr. Beacon said the object looked dark blue.

Summarizing the report in the Melbourne *Argus*, the engineer (engine-driver) Smith declared: "Its size was just colossal. For the four minutes in which we saw it over our engine, it partly obscured the sun, but all the time the light was clear. I feel definitely that the weird thing *was* piloted! It was not a clearly lined or defined object, for it was somewhat covered in a haze—perhaps caused by its speed or design. It was *not* like any aircraft I've seen or read about . . . more like something out of a dream."

(The *Argus* added that the Royal Australian Air Force intelligence section would investigate the report from the two railroadmen.)

May 10, 1954: The Australian railroad engineer Ted Smith, and his fireman Colin Beacon, firmly adhere to their report of their encounter with a vast flying saucer on April 28, 1954. They are both skilled and reliable men and, for the doubtful benefit of skeptics, one may add that no engineer on a railroad, or fireman, any more than an Air Force pilot in a cockpit, would be allowed to remain in the very responsible position in the cabin of a locomotive unless they were very well mentally balanced. They have convinced a hard-boiled reporter of the Melbourne *Argus* of the objectivity of what they saw.

There is reason to suppose that flying saucers have attacked British and U.S. jet planes and jet air liners. Was the above a reconnaissance in a cosmic campaign against our *ground* transport? It is easy to dismiss such a supposition as nonsense, but other evidence given in this book suggest that such easy dismissals may be dangerous.

I cite from a report in a Cornish newspaper:

May 25, 1954: For the second time in three months a mysterious object, shaped like a fountain-pen, flashed across the sky in West Cornwall, England, at 9:30 P.M. Hundreds saw it and say it was about 5,000 feet high. Some heard it emit a hissing noise and saw it jet an orange flame at the tail. Others reported that a deep blue glow surrounded the object, which was black. A woman at St. Ives, Cornwall, said its speed was terrific, that it emitted no sound, lit up the sky and earth, and radiated a blue luminiscence. The course of the object was horizontal and parallel with the ground.

Author's Note: If the object was actually at a great height, its size would have been immense. It may have been a "mother space ship" rather than a satellite disc, or saucer.

Was this, too, a space ship seen in the skies near Boston, Mass.:

June 1, 1954: The pilot of a Trans-World Airliner from Paris, France (Capt. C. J. Kratovil) saw a mysterious object in the sky ten miles north of Boston. Jet planes went up to chase it, but abandoned the pursuit when there came the usual official brushoff that it was just a weather balloon of the U.S.A.F. *But,* as Capt. Kratovil says: "It is the first time I ever saw a weather balloon *travelling against the wind.* The thing was large, white and discoidal, and I had a good look at it, although it kept vanishing into cloud."

Washington, D.C., has again (June, 1954), had flying saucers over this city of the Pentagon. The visitants appear to have "teased the big shots there, as on the night of August 15, 1952," writes an American engineer friend of mine.

He adds: "I and others have seen in the skies of California a very big ball—a space ship—of about 400 yards diameter, and twice in May and June, 1954, a big space ship has been seen high up over the Canadian border."

But what was the strange space ship—a "mother ship" with six satellites, circling round it—seen by the pilot of a British stratoliner (Capt. James R. Howard), eleven members of the crew, the stewardess, the co-pilot, and about forty of the fifty-one passengers, when at sunset, June 30, 1954, the plane was flying between New York and Goose Bay, Labrador?

The airliner was at 18,000 feet, 150 nautical miles southwest of Goose Bay; the time was in the evening, under a clear, serene sky; and the mysterious objects were seen for half an hour, from five miles away, for 80-90 miles, flying at about 274 miles an hour on a parallel course. Against the evening light, the objects appeared dark. Mr. Boyd, the Canadian co-pilot, at once radioed the station at Goose Bay, and was told that the radar there had picked up a large number of dark objects on the screen.

No other plane but the stratocruiser was in the sky at the time. Two U.S. Air Force Sabrejets were sent up to investigate the formation. Probably owing to the American and British Air Force bans on such information to the public, I can find no report of what, *if anything,* the U.S. jets found.

Half the passengers were asleep, and nobody on board had a camera.

Captain Howard, on his arrival at London Airport, gave the press remarkable details which seem to import that the space, or mother ship, may have been a fourth-dimensional aeroform:

"I am sure they were *not* birds. Their speed was too great for that. The central object was of *large size,* and six smaller objects circled round it. The large object *appeared to alter its shape constantly.* We called it 'the flying jelly fish' for that reason. The six satellites seemed to keep station round the big object, much as fighter planes would when acting as escort to a big bomber or a passenger airliner. At first, Boyd and I thought the central big machine might be a delta, or swept-back-wing bomber plane. But it changed its shape several times—one time appearing as a dart, another time like a dumb-bell or mushroom, and also like a sphere with a projection. It was difficult to assess the dimensions of these mysterious objects, since there was nothing in the sky against which to measure them. They flew parallel with us for 80-90 miles, but did not approach nearer than five miles."

It was added that the six satellite discs flew around, either ahead of or in front of the space ship. But when a U.S. interceptor jet, sent out from Goose Bay, radioed to the stratocruiser that he was closing in, almost as if the mysterious entities heard the call, the satellites returned to the mother ship and they all faded away rapidly. The airliner pilot had no doubt that the objects were solid, and under intelligent control.

Might this have any connection with the fact that the red planet Mars was then nearer to the earth's orbit than at any time since 1939?

Subsequently, the British Air Minister asked the pilot of the stratocruiser to report to him. Of course, nothing has been heard of this, or will be.

On July 1, 1954, another mysterious incident occurred, which I summarize from a report in the "London News-Chronicle":

At 12:37 P.M., twenty-five miles southwest of Bournemouth, on the shores of the English Channel, Captain Marciano Veiga, flying a plane to London Airport, saw floating in the sea what looked like a large white plane. He went down about 3,000 feet for a closer look, saw the object again, then lost it in the haze at the time of a solar eclipse. He radioed a warning to the Ministry of Civil Aviation control station at Uxbridge, and Royal Air Force planes and naval helicopters and lifeboats were sent to the spot, along with five British Navy frigates. They searched the area until 4:45., but found nothing.

This incident was officially explained, or explained away, as probably an optical illusion induced by haze, and the partial solar eclipse.

But *was* it?

Veiga says he distinctly saw the mysterious object floating on the sea, and that it was of "giant" size.

A similar mystery was recorded on the evening of June 26, 1954, in the sky over the Forest of Dean, on the west bank of the Severn estuary. A man at Littledean saw an object fall from the sky. He warned police and firemen that a plane had crashed. A wide area was searched but nothing was found, and no plane was reported missing.

All one can say is that such incidents will vanish into secret official files. Will higher authority, someday, take the public, its paymaster, into its confidence—and tell what it knows, or guesses—*if*, of course, it knows or guesses anything. Our masters might be museum archaeologists in the way they have of ignoring inconvenient phenomena that do not fit in with *official* scientists' views and the preconceptions to which they cling. But the Time Spirit will not stay its course to oblige these official and military gentlemen.

A final word: it may be noted that the stratocruiser pilot was startled by the alteration in the shape of the central space ship round which the satellites circled. This phenomenon of mutant shape seems strangely to underline the theories of Dr. Meade Layne, of the Borderland Sciences Research Associates of San Diego, California. He wrote to me, in June, 1954:

"The aeroforms are MUTANTS. They come from a world of the etheric, fourth-dimensional type, a *real* world, not one of discarnate beings or spooks, or a world of the so-called 'dead,' but of another order of matter than ours. These aeroforms can and do change size, shape, color, mode of action, and become transparent, or nearly so—while under observation. The matter of which they are composed is not matter as we know it, but of the etheric prototype . . . etheric steel, etheric copper, etheric aluminium."

We stand on the threshold of a new and revolutionary age—by which adjective one connotes not war, politics, imperialism, economics, or other politico-ideological concepts—although it may comprehend all of them—but a transformation of scientific values and mental and physical concepts. Physics, as we know it, will be forced to take account of metaphysics, the supernormal, the parapsychological, to achieve a truer understanding of the amazing cosmos. But, like all unlearning and jettisoning of obsolete ideas, the process is likely to be as painful as it is inevitable.

It looks as if a space ship passed over Eire, in August, 1954:

August 2, 1954: A strange bluish-white object travelling horizontally, from which trails of flaming pieces fell from each side, was seen by P. D. McCormack, of the School of Cosmic Studies of the Dublin, Eire Institute. He said it passed over the Dublin Mountains at a speed of not less than 1,000 miles an hour. "As a scientist, I have never seen the like of it before."

I have the report following from Mr. Roy Safire, of 629 South Woods Avenue, Los Angeles, California. He has a four-inch refracting telescope with clock-driver and camera attachment:

"I wish very much to tell you of a mysterious object I have seen twice. When I first saw it through my telescope I took it for an ordinary jet plane. But on February 18, 1954, at about 11 P.M., I saw an elliptical cylinder accelerating at a tremendous speed, heading west and then almost instantaneously shifting true north. I could not determine its dimensions at the great height at which I saw it, but by calculating its speed at the number of feet it moved out of view of my telescope, I should say its speed was about 1,200 miles an hour."

Mr. Safire wants me to publish a map showing where saucers have been sighted. Why, bless me, the difficulty would be to draw up a chart showing where flying saucers have *not* been seen; for the sightings are both legion and ubiquitous!

Did Kansas see a flying saucer forty-one years ago? The report below sent me by the observer seems to import as much. Flying saucers, like angels, may be met with "unawares":

1913: One evening at Winfield, Kansas, U.S. (day and month not stated), at 9:10 P.M., the full moon halfway up the sky and no clouds—Mr. W. L. Shelley was walking home from church, with his parents, uncle, aunt and two cousins, when, as they glanced up at the moon, they were startled to see a strange object "sailing along in the sky," in a north-south direction. It did not appear to move very fast, but was not in sight for more than a minute. The body was black, perhaps 100 feet long, and appeared to have some superstructure. Its altitude might have been about 3,000 feet. Mr. Shelley's uncle thought the object might have been "some large tropical (*sic*) birds," but no wing movements were to be seen.

(*N.B.* Height and dimensions of any object in the sky are not easily estimated without instruments and experience in aeronautical observations. But, apart from the improbability of tropical birds being seen so far north as Kansas, Mr. Shelley and his relations appear to have sighted a type of "black space ship" seen before and after the year 1913.)

I am sometimes asked if there exist today large topographically unmapped regions in this vast continent. I have been told that, even in the eastern state, Maine and others, there are forested areas little known and seldom entered.

My friend, Frederick G. Hehr, an engineer and traveller who resides at Santa Monica, Calif., writes:

"The U.S.A. has been pretty thoroughly mapped from the air, where ground mapping was lacking, and that is still the case over much territory. The Air Force has done most of it as training exercises. There are, of course, many regions here in the West where no scientist or accredited stuffed shirt has ever set foot. For example, there is a tremendous strip from Wyoming and Idaho, south into Mexico; also between the Rockies in Colorado; in the center of Utah; through New Mexico and Arizona, widening into southern California, where are thousands of square miles in which only Indians, prospectors and cowboys have ever set foot.

"I heard a story of a ten-year-old boy who lost himself in western Colorado, while herding sheep, and who came out in Utah seven or eight years later." (*N.B.* As the crow flies, the boy might have wandered over a region from 300 to 350 miles wide. *Author.*)

"This boy was said to have lost his language and all vestiges of civilization on his trek. It was a feat deemed impossible because the country is so wild, dry and hot in summer, fearfully cold in winter.

"But stories of 'large mansions of unknown origin,' etc., etc., are just stories. Weather and the termites and other insects would make short work of them. Even in the deserts, one never finds dead wood of any kind. The termites get at it before it can rot.

"There are a few *fey* locations . . . where there might be inter-mountain dépôts for space ships, one being not very far from the state of Washington, and others in the sierras of British Columbia.

"True, there are a few queer sculptured cliffs, and forgotten heads of stone, and other prehistoric remnants, but most of them are so old and weathered that it takes a very sharp eye and a particular light to see them. One is here in Soledad Canyon, visible under the first rays of the sun. It is a colossal female head carved out of a great cliff, and may be the memorial of some very ancient race.

"The satellite discs have a drive, I think, utilizing magnetic 'currents' found round the planets. The big space ships obviously use a reaction drive. The satellites are probably not flown across space. In many respects these aeroforms tally with the most advanced flying ships ever developed in Atlantis. I know of one place which might be a space ship port, and it is located in California. I suspect there are others in western Canada, Mexico, on the sierras, and high *mesas,* or tablelands in South America and Central Asia. In North Carolina, there is a mountain massif that is 'queer,' and has been avoided by the Indians for centuries.

"My opinion is that the saucers look for 'markers' scattered all over the world in far past ages. Some of these 'markers' must have grown dim. They are in straight lines and about fifty miles apart. One was found in Oregon, when some guy set up an assay office over the spot and was nearly shot because his assays differed widely from those taken outside.

"No, I do not think that flying saucers are 'etheric.' If they were, they would not be visible. I think they are totally shielded by a force field against mass and gravity. This may explain their brilliance and mathematical form and perfect finish. Others who have seen some of them at slow speed have noted a material formation with lack of this utter perfection. In my opinion, the saucers are left-overs from one of the Atlantean civilizations and there may be a few from a Lemurian civilization."

MYSTERY OF THE MARTIAN "DEATH CEILING"

WHY HAVE THE SAUCERS COME TO EARTH in apparently increasing numbers and larger formations, in the last ten years?

I wish I could accept with complete assurance the rather complacent views expressed in various quarters in England and the U.S.A. In these views all saucers are here to help us in an age of confusion, when man, or *some* men seem bent on blowing this planet to fragments with diabolical cobalt, and hydrogen and strontium bombs. It may very well be, as my friend Dr. Meade Layne (founder and director of the Borderland Sciences Research Association of San Diego, California) contends, that the fourth-dimensional type of flying saucers, which hail from a *real* and etheric world in space, are here to perform the thankless task of saving us from our own folly. Possibly they *are*. But an accumulation of data in the last eight years has forced me to believe that *other* mysterious visitants are far from friendly, and their aims and intentions, and ethical code are *not* ours. Some seem to hail from a three-dimensional world akin to our own.

Let me cite two opinions on whose validity the reader must decide for himself:

January 19, 1954: The Melbourne (Australia) "Argus" publishes a reader's story that, "at a séance in England, in 1950, the spirit of a pilot killed in a crash, said that space ships came to the earth from the planet Saturn, and were manned by 'little men.' These were conducting intense scientific research, in order to harness the hidden powers of the universe for knowledge and progress. These Saturnians, said the pilot, did not understand that the earth was now using these great forces for destruction. The pilot urged great caution in approaching these Saturnian space ships, if they landed on the earth, or great damage might be caused."

June 2, 1954: Lord Dowding, British Air Chief Marshal, head of the British Fighter Command in the "Battle of Britain," in 1940, tells a conference of spiritualists at Herne Bay, Kent, England, that: "I believe people on other planets are operating through flying saucers to help our world in its present crisis."

June 17, 1954: A medium at a séance, in Melbourne, Australia, said that saucers were from planets outside our solar system, and have been attracted here by man's explosions of atomic and hydrogen bombs, and the breaking of the sound barrier. They come to warn man that he must stop these mad experiments. They will establish some form of contact with the earth. The lost continent of Atlantis, in its far day, attained a high scientific standard and had started using blast forces which destroyed them, exactly as aeons earlier, another terrestrial civilization had destroyed itself.

This time it will not be permitted. The thing will be halted in time. The breaking of the sound barrier by suprasonic planes penetrates into another plane or sphere, such spheres being related to each other analogically, as are the skins of an onion. Man's attempt to penetrate beyond the terrestrial world, and its vibrationary rate into other planes or spheres is madness. He could not exist in them. Saucers have destroyed terrestrial planes which pursued them.

Of course, séance revelations are regarded by many people with suspicion since subjective phenomena may intrude where no fraud is intended. For that reason I have ignored such testimony, and I have had querulous letters from people in protest. I reply that the *facts* are already fantastic enough without importing other "extraneous" elements into them.

Among the—as I believe—*hostile* visitants, is the weird aeroform, shaped like a long cigar, surrounded by a ring so singularly like Saturn within his rings. This visitant, to which I have several times referred, has been seen between 1952 and 1954 over England, Sweden, California and Ohio, apparently "quizzing" the surroundings. Some quarters in California, where it was seen in daylight releasing a satellite disc, suggest that it comes from the constellation of Orion, which is 3¼ light years distant from earth. It would then be a fourth-dimensional entity.

What proof anyone may have for such an assertion I do not know. My own fallible opinion is that the world from which the visitant came may be akin to our own order of matter. But *what* world one has not the faintest notion. In fact, one may say: "God only knows!"

I have had other reports of the appearance of this probably hostile type of saucer:

December 5, 1953: Strange cigar-shaped object seen twice over Flanders, Belgium in daylight. Altitude estimated as six miles.

December 11, 1953: At 2 P.M., a cigar-shaped, gleaming object glided over Wensleydale, Yorks, England, moved slowly, had no wings, and was not, apparently, very large. Sky clear. Object soundless, and seen for six minutes. At 4:15 P.M., same or similar object was seen at another place in Yorkshire, when it ascended rapidly.

March 17, 1954: A cigar-shaped, flying saucer flew very high over Malaya. On the other side of the world at Preston, England, spectators at a football match saw a flying saucer heading west.

August 25, 1954: Three people say they saw over the river Seine, near Evreux, northwest of Paris, a flying saucer which, as a satellite, was linked to a huge cigar-shaped object. (*Daily Mail*)

September 17, 1954: For forty minutes, the Italian Air Force radar station at Pratica di Mare, forty-four miles southwest of Rome, tracked a strange cigar-shaped object flying at a height of about 3,000 feet along the western shores of Italy. The thing was shaped like a cylinder cut in half, with something like a large antenna placed amidships. From its tapered rear trailed luminous smoke. Technicians at Ciampino airport say that at one time the object dropped towards the earth, and then ascended in a northwest direction at tremendous speed. It was held on the radarscope for nearly an hour. On one side it was silver, on the other red. Thousands saw it and the police telephone lines were congested with excited reports.

Author's Comment: Elsewhere, in this book, I report my sighting of a similar object, at 5:25 A.M., on July 23, 1954, in the skies of North Kent. I have also stated how two national dailies and the War Office treated my report.

It may be noted that this strange visitant is one of the eerily silent type. Not the faintest clue can be got as to *what* is on board and manning it: human, or humanoid! But, I have some reason to believe that it uses a heat ray of some type, which has caused serious fires, both in England, and in Oregon and California.

Below, I set down a number of incidents whose overall pattern suggests aggression, or attempts to terrorize, on the part of some of these strange visitants:

September 19, 1952: At 10:52 A.M., as a Meteor jet was descending at a height of 5,000 feet, under a clear sky over Topcliffe airdrome, Yorkshire, men standing on the ground were startled to see, about 10,000 feet above the jet, a bright silvery object, five miles astern of the jet, and travelling at a slower speed on the same course. The Meteor turned towards Dishforth, and the strange object began to descend with a slow pendulum motion like a falling "sycamore leaf." The jet was coming in to land, and the saucer seemed to be following it. After about four seconds, it ceased its pendulum motion from right to left, and hung in the air, rotating about its own axis and flashing in the sunshine. Then it accelerated, and at an incredeble speed, turned and vanished to the southeast. A signaller said it had a halo, but was a solid object with no marks on it. At the time, "Operation Mainbrace" was on, and the British Air Ministry set up an investigation into the report that a saucer had been seen "shooting over Yorkshire faster than a falling star."

In July, 1953, it was stated in certain circles in Paris, France, that one General S., who is the French representative in N.A.T.O., was on a routine flight in a French army plane, when he was startled to see a strange "turret-shaped object" fly at a tremendous speed over a military airfield in Paris. The French Minister of the Air ordered a secret investigation.

This is what General S. reported:

"I was up 6,000 feet and my plane was doing about 250 miles an hour when, on a sudden, an object about the shape and size of a small ship's turret flashed towards me. It was black-grey in color, and shot by only a few yards from my plane wings. Its speed was tremendous, but I was able to keep it in view. In amazement, I followed the course of this dark object till it disappeared. What in God's name was it?"

September 13, 1953: Men repairing a road vehicle in the Pennsylvania mountains saw a strange thing hover over them for fifteen minutes. They said it had a rotating turret-top, and went back and forth over a village. It was also seen on a radarscope. (*Newspaper reports.*)

December 4, 1953: A discoidal saucer hovered ten yards in front of a parked car on a road in Norway. The saucer had previously chased the car which had two passengers, for seven miles. (*Oestlandets Blad.*)

December 30, 1953: The journal, "Outspan," South Africa, reports that a saucer followed a car on a road at Johannesburg.

January 9, 1954: An orange light was seen moving about thirty feet above the tree tops near Warrenton, Virginia, in undulating fashion. The impression of observers was that the strange object may have been searching for something, or sending back visual or television reports to some unseen flying saucer.

The correspondent also reports that, at midnight, on November 9, 1953, several people near Omaha, Nebraska, saw high in the sky (the planet Venus being clearly visible) an object like a cylinder, bright red in color, and flashing lights on and off. In a few seconds, a number of other lights, flashing like stars,

Flying Saucers seen over Taormina, Sicily, spring of 1955.
(*United Press Photo*)

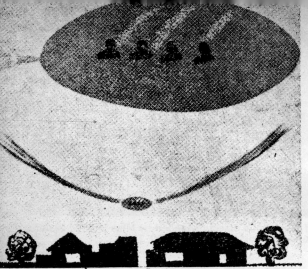

Sketch of Saucer seen over East Malvern, Victoria, Australia, on May 31, 1954. Observers were David Reese and five friends. Mr. Reese, who made the sketch, says: "I could distinctly see inside it, dark shapes like busts." (Enlargement at top of sketch.)

Strange unidentified objects seen in the sky over Helsinki, Finland, early in September, 1954, and published in the *Helsingin Sanomat*. Unless the lower object is some type of weather balloon, it has a remarkable similarity to the doughnut-shaped Flying Saucers seen over Washington, D.C.

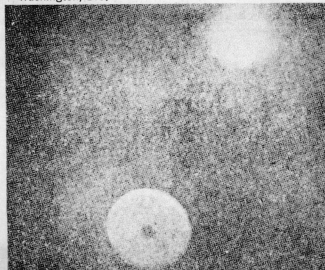

A photo of mysterious objects snapped by Miss Mildred Maier of Chicago during the solar eclipse, June 30, 1954.

Flying Saucer or unidentified light in the sky photographed by Mr. K. M. Gibbons in September, 1954, over Nelson, New Zealand. Mr. Gibbons says that he saw three such objects.

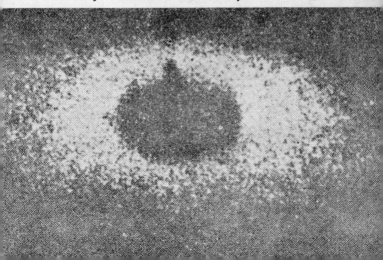

This unretouched photo of an unknown black object leaving a trail behind it was taken near Grenoble, in southeastern France, on September 24, 1954.

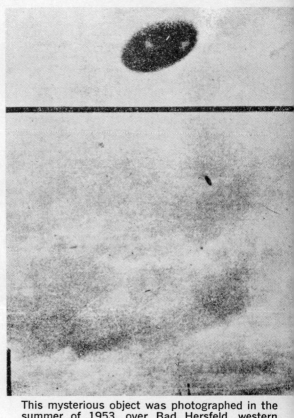

This mysterious object was photographed in the summer of 1953, over Bad Hersfeld, western Germany. The top picture shows the lower disk enlarged about 35 times. As will be noticed, it appears to have a cupola near the center and another protuberance near the right rim.

A telephoto picture taken on September 9, 1954, at Nelson, New Zealand, when three disks were seen hovering in close formation at about 450 feet altitude. They were visible from five to seven minutes.

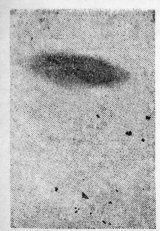

A Flying Saucer photographed in California in the summer of 1953.

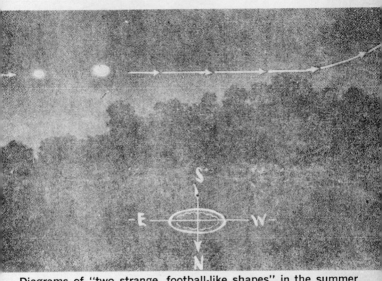

Diagrams of "two strange, football-like shapes" in the summer of 1952, seen by George Charney, Chicago *Daily News* art director. "They were like nothing I had ever seen," he noted.

A discoidal Saucer, reflecting the sun, which appeared when the negative of a photo taken by Mr. Marvin Tjornham of Minneapolis, during the solar eclipse of June, 1954, was developed.

Two strange cosmic airfoils of Flying Saucer or space ship type which appeared when the negative of a motion picture taken by Mr. Johnnie Bjornulf of Fredrikstadt, Norway, during the solar eclipse of June, 1954, was developed. The picture was taken from an airplane, the wing of which is seen at bottom, right. The strange objects are seen at the top left of the photo.

clustered around the cylinder which was visible for six minutes. The cylinder seemed to be in line with Venus and the earth, and slightly to the apparent right or eastern limb of Venus.

March 1, 1954: A well known American mystic warns that flying saucers from the constellation of Orion, many light years from earth, are hostile and bent on destruction.

March 2, 1954: A British Tudor freight plane went out of control in a cloud near Paris, France. The mystery has not been cleared up why these Tudor planes and airliners have repeatedly come to disaster while thousands of airliners have passed without mishap through clouds and air turbulence.

March 29-April 20, 1954: Among the unconfirmable stories are the following:

A test pilot's plane was stopped and then raised in the air by a "magnetic radiation device" of a saucer. An unnamed astronomer from the famous Palomar, California, Observatory, alleges that its files contain many saucer photos. A cameraman in a plane took a picture of an unidentified object which shows a fan at its rear which radiates bands of light, or bars like blades shuttling across the fan. The photograph also shows a sort of conning-tower and ports, on the rim of a disc. Desvergers, the Florida scoutmaster*, shot at by a saucer, on August 19, 1952, is in hospital suffering from a mysterious skin disease. A jet plane crashed near an unidentified flying object; and on the radarscope at a ground station, another jet plane was seen to merge into and be swallowed up by an unidentified aerial object. An unnamed American scientist showed photos and documents, at a conference, indicating that some of the saucers hail from Jupiter, are human in appearance, very advanced in science, and have eliminated war and disease. They are friendly to the earth, and question the intentions of cigar-shaped types of Saucers.

---

* A correspondent living at Arlington, Virginia, informed me, on July 15, 1954, that the "Scoutmaster has admitted to him, having dreamed this incident up," and his purpose in the hoax was "to hit the spotlight of newspaper publicity." *If* so, and I am unable either to confirm or deny it, as the Florida police were called on to investigate the story, the Scoutmaster must have run a serious risk of a prosecution, on a charge of creating public mischief.

I summarize certain incidents occurring between April and August, 1954. Many of these may suggest external interference of sinister flying saucer origin. Proof cannot, of course, be expected at present.

A new type of fighter jet plane, the "Mystère," suddenly exploded near Paris, France, when the test pilot, Col. Romanoff, was trying to push it beyond 837 miles an hour.

At Carlton, near Nottingham, England, a mysterious noise in the night is followed by ringing of untouched electric bells, sudden flashing on of electric lights, rattling of windows, ringing of fire and police alarms, splitting of the end-wall of a house from top to bottom, and mine subsidence. Panic was caused. (No jets were up and no earthquake reported). The American Air Secretary finds that his plane, in daylight, is followed for thirty minutes by a saucer keeping a hundred feet below. He ordered his plane to close in on the object, which at once vanished at fantastic speed. (Said not to be the first time he has been so "tagged"). A "huge apparition" blazing with light, zoomed down from the sky in Somerset, England. It hovered for a few minutes, then slowly vanished from sight at an even keel. Seen by a man and a woman. At 1 P.M., July 14, a Victor atom-bomber, on a test flight, suddenly dives and its tail drops off. It crashes on a runway near Bedford, in a typical mushroom shape pall of smoke. Structural defects offered as explanation.

But note the following incident which happened *on the same day*, in the adjoining county.

In full daylight, at Great Easton, near Market Harborough, Leicester, thirty-three miles northwest of Bedford, a farmer, Mr. H. C. Craythorne, was amazed to see a large saucer travelling behind a jet plane, which it gradually overtook. The saucer was discoidal, transparent, and gained on the jet. The saucer was very high above the jet. (Is there any connection with the incident above, seeing that all such high-speed jets are a stage towards future terrestrial interplanetary flight?)

July 22, 1954: Police, farmers and shepherds search for two R.A.F. Sabrejets missing between Crewe and Linton-on-Ouse, Yorks, after taking part in "Exercise Dividend." The classic explanation is given: "Returning to Linton-on-Ouse, they ran out of fuel."

(*N.B.* To "shortage of fuel" was also attributed accidents on January 11, 1954, and December 16, 1953, to a British R.A.F. plane and a U.S. Sabrejet, flying over Darmstadt, Germany, and the eastern English midlands. The pilots of both were forced to bail out. The fate of the American pilot remains unknown. Another Sabrejet crashed at Cadmor, Yorks, and the pilot bailed out at a height of eight miles.)

August 3, 1954: An Air France Constellation airliner had completed its transatlantic run, and was about to land at Idlewild International Airport, New York, when a driving rainstorm is said to have caused the pilot to circle the airport for ninety minutes. Then he is said to have signalled the control towers that he was running out of fuel, and must try an emergency landing elsewhere. The airliner dived at a sharp angle through the rain scuds and narrowly missed a farmhouse. Shearing off treetops and skidding across a sodden field, it smashed through a barn and came to a standstill. The area was near Preston, Connecticut, 100 miles from Idlewild Airport. The right wing caught fire in the air and there was an explosion as the plane came down, but luckily no one was killed.

Author's Comment: There was a series of strange accidents to commercial planes taking off or coming in to land at the Newark, New Jersey airport in 1953. So serious was the loss of life that public protests forced the authorities to close this airport. All that was said was that "for some reason unknown the planes went out of control and suddenly crashed." It is also odd that "running out of fuel" was the reason advanced for crashes and force-landings of British and American jets in England and western Germany on January 11, 1954, and December 16, 1953.

Two mysteries that remain to be cleared up: *One*—the cause of hundreds of disasters to American, British and Danish jet planes, some of so strange a character as to suggest a cause external to the mechanism and the skill and experience of the pilots. Of course, it is known that once the pilot passes the sonic barrier, he cannot manually control his plane, power controls becoming necessary at such high speeds. The force needed to maneuver the plane is beyond normal physical strength. But on May 13, 1954, a power control failed in a Vickers-Swift jet fighter of the R.A.F., possibly owing to a failure in an electrical circuit. The pilot was killed, and all Swift jets were grounded. There have been hundreds of cases where the cause has never been determined, and the circumstances induce a suspicion that some hostile space ship or large saucer might have been around at the time.

The other mystery is the cause of the repetition of the disasters to the British Comet jet airliners in May, 1953, when they were put again into the air after being grounded in January, 1954.

Many people, by no means crackpots, or fantaisistes, perceive in these mysterious aeronautical incidents possible external and *non-terrestrial* jet airliners.

I summarize disasters occurring between January and June, 1954:

R.A.F. Meteor jet explodes and strews wreckage over Poulders Green, Kent. Pilot, gallantly remaining at controls, is killed. Vampire jet cuts out at 15,800 feet and falls on plowed field at Old Lackenby, Yorks. Pilot killed. Royal Danish Air Force grounds all its Thunderjets and Sabrejets after numerous disasters. British Undersecretary for Air says that 507 R.A.F. jets crashed in 1952-1954 with great loss of life (112). Some crashes caused by engine-disintegration. Six-engined Stratojet, U.S. B-47, crashes at Townsend, Georgia, immediately after take-off. Four men lost. Skilled chief test pilot, Ed Griffiths, crashed in field and was killed at Rugby, England, only a few miles from his starting-point. He was testing new Royal Navy propeller-jet, torpedo-carrying Wyvern, and had only time to radio his position before his sudden crash. Canberra jet bomber explodes in air over suburbs of Doncaster, Yorks. Crew of two killed. On the same day, a few miles away, at Six Mile Bottom, Newmarket, a second Canberra crashes, the crew of three missing. The bodies of two pilots were found in a Vampire jet wreckage at Lewes, Sussex.

We now come to the still unsolved mystery of the disasters to the British Comet jet airliners which crashed in May, 1953, were grounded, and again crashed after being returned to the air, in January, 1954. I have hinted above that there might be a "death ceiling" set up by hostile flying saucers, against terrestrial aeronautical machines that are advancing towards future flight to the moon and, ultimately, *perhaps*, beyond.

April 9, 1954: Two weeks after the removal of the flight ban on the B.O.A.C. Comet jet airliners, the Comet jet airliner *G-Alyp,* took off from Naples, at 7 P.M., for South Africa. Her last radio message said: "Over Naples. Still climbing." That was the last heard or seen of her. It is believed that she fell right out of the clouds, at a height of about six miles, over Stromboli (volcanic island), into the Mediterranean, at a location 340 miles southeast of the similar unexplained disaster to the Comet airliner of the same line, on January 10, 1954. All fourteen passengers and seven of the crew were killed. The British government immediately reimposed the ban.

Italian air pilots report seeing bodies floating in the sea among flotsam like white fabric and orange boxes. No evidence of sabotage. It was later proposed that a well known British test-pilot should fly a Comet jet airliner up to 35,000 feet high and see what happens. All Comets, subsequently ordered to be grounded, had strict orders to fly home below the height of 30,000 feet. The normal Comet cruising height was 45,000 feet.

March 20, 1954: A TV underwater camera used in a British Royal Navy ship searching for parts of the wreck of the Comet jet airliner off Elba, Italy, showed on the screen a beautiful statue of an ancient Greek woman, with swept-back hair, lying in an ancient wreck. Nearby were ancient urns. No attempt made to salvage the statue.

It has been admitted by the Parliamentary Secretary to the British Ministry of Transport and Civil Aviation, that at a depth of 500 fathoms no salvage is possible. Sir Miles Thomas, head of the B.O.A.C., owners of these airliners, thinks the answer to the mystery will ultimately be found. "But," he told the press on September 23, 1954, "the Comets are not likely to come back into service in a short period of time." Tests for pressurization defects as possible causes would have to be made.

June 11, 1954: London Daily Mail. A refuelling tanker at Rome might have put too great a pressure into the tanks of the Comet jet airliners. At the lowered atmospheric pressures at high altitudes, the tanks may have burst from within, spraying fuel oil into the engines and cabins. (*N.B.* Before the final disaster occurred, armor plate had been fitted around the airliner's four engines to shield oil tanks and passenger cabins from possibility of flying fragments and explosions or fires, should the jet turbine engines fail. Also, more than fifty modifications had been made to the fleet of seven Comet jet airliners of the B.O.A.C. A test flight of the toughest character had also been made over London at the height of 40,000 feet, at which the disaster later occurred. Only after these precautions had an official safety certificate been given to the Comets).

Since then all has gone silent!

I am aware that aeronautical experts believe that the only "death ceiling," in the case of these turbo-jet liners (*Vide, supra,* incident dated April 9, 1954), is that arising when extremely hot turbines are too near the fuel tanks. At a certain altitude, reduced atmospheric pressure will cause fuel oil to boil. Then the inner structure becomes saturated with explosive gases which may ignite on contact with a hot surface. (It was to obviate such explosions that, in the larger U.S. turbo-jet planes, the turbines were slung beneath the wings.) But, in view of modifications made to the Comet jet airliners *before* the final disasters, one may most devoutly hope that *nothing* may occur to invalidate *this theory, too.*

However, in July, 1954, the investigators ruled out faulty refuelling and sabotage as probable causes of the disasters. Nor is it believed that the calculations of jet-propulsion and high-speed flying are faulty. Meantime, on July 15, 1954, the U.S. 25-ton Boeing 707, counterpart of the British Comet jet airliner, made a maiden flight at Seattle lasting eighty-four minutes.

On October 19-23, 1954, the Court of Inquiry into the Comet disasters over Italy reported. Sir Lionel Heald, Queens Counsel, cited the conclusions of Sir Arnold Hall, director of the British Royal Aircraft Establishment at Farnborough, that the disaster to the G-Alyp, whose wreckage had been examined, was probably caused by metal fatigue in a roof panel (containing a radio-direction-finding aerial) of the pressurized cabin. There was no engine fault. No wreckage of the other Comet jet airliner, G-Ally, had been located.

Sir Arnold Hall told the court that the airliner G-Alyp appeared to have broken up in the air into six main pieces, and that the first break occured in the top center of the fuselage. Simultaneously, the rear and front of the fuselage fell away downwards and the center rapidly disintegrated. A powerful force threw the passenger seats forward, then back again.

Dr. Fornari, Italian pathologist, said the victims showed signs of sudden explosive decompression, occurring within a fraction of a second, while they were still alive. All were dead when they hit the water. He added: "I have never come across anything like this."

On October 22, Sir Arnold Hall said he did not think that cracks caused the accident in a direct sense; and the maintenance engineer, Mr. G. Corfield of B.O.A.C. (British Overseas Airways Co.), which owned the Comets, said that neither he nor his company knew of such cracks. Hall added that it appeared that when the liner burst, a failure ran through a manufacturing crack. He then made a comment to which the British newspapers which still, in the main, dismiss flying-saucer phenomena as largely psychological aberrations, or misinterpretation of probably terrestrial secret devices, have paid little or no attention.

Sir Arnold said:

> "I think flying saucers and mechanical gremlins are *very* remote as causes of these disasters. As to planes having been shot down by a machine from the planet Mars, unless they use ammunition very different from our own, I should have expected to find some evidence of that in the wreckage."

My respectful comment is this: Such "ammunition," if used, might very likely be of very different sorts from ours. What trace of what we may call a "death ray" would be found, had it struck these Comet jets, flying at or above 35,000 feet? I draw attention, elsewhere in this book, to the mysterious recent breakages of car windscreens. Neither metal fatigue nor plastic defects can be convincingly adduced as the cause of these fissurings— and *very* peculiar they are. Suppose that hostile and elusive non-terrestrial operators work on *other substances,* as they may have worked on the glass?

Consider the following, which has been denied by a spokesman of the British Air Ministry:

May 2, 1953: A British Comet jet airliner caught fire in the air, disintegrated and crashed, immediately after it had taken off from an airdrome at Calcutta. Wreckage was strewn over an area of five and a half miles. An investigator, Mr. J. H. Lett, sent out by the British Ministry of Civil Aviation, said that lightning had *not* struck the airliner, nor had it come into collision with any other plane, nor was there the slightest evidence of faulty materials or workmanship —*BUT* . . . he found that it broke up in the air after striking some heavy and unknown body!

THE SHADOW OF THE UNSEEN

In 1953 AND 1954, mysterious incidents and phenomena recorded in England and the U.S.A. have suggested to some minds interference by cosmic entities of some world in space. The phenomena may be experiments or demonstrations of their powers to affect our air and, more recently, land transport and essential matériel of our economic and industrial civilization.

There have been mysterious explosions whose cause is difficult to find. The second and third incidents below, remind one of the mysterious white object of large size, seen floating in the sea off Bournemouth, England.

October 23, 1953: At 3:30 P.M., a violent explosion was heard all over the county of London, to the south and west. It was like the crash of a V-2 World War rocket. The explosion was also heard in the City of London. The police were overwhelmed with telephone calls, but neither they nor the Fire Service could explain it, nor the Ministry of Air, which said that it was "neither a hydrogen bomb nor a flying saucer." Any theory that it was caused by a plane passing the sonic barrier was denied by the Royal Air Force, and by the only private airplane company which, at the time, had a high-speed aircraft up.

May 25, 1954: A mysterious "double bang" rattled windows in towns twenty-five miles apart on the Sussex coast. The explosion came from out at sea but it was not from a wartime mine, and its cause could not be determined.

June 2, 1954: The whole of the waterfront of Sydney, Australia was rocked by a mysterious explosion at 5:30 A.M. Thousands of people were awakened. Police failed to discover the cause of what some people said seemed to be of subterranean origin. Every power-house and factory was investigated. A local observatory found no tremor reading on its seismographs. Though the explosion seemed to fill the whole sky with thunder, there was no electrical storm. No damage could be traced.

October 6, 1953: Dreadful explosions shook the "ghost town" of Boroloola, on the Gulf of Carpentaria, N. Australia, thousands of miles from any center of white population. There was a rumble travelling east, at terrific speed, at 4:50 P.M. No jets or suprasonic planes were up; the "abos" (aborigines) were badly frightened by the "debil-debil" noise. Baffled officials cannot explain the phenomenon.

Nor has any explanation been given of the mysterious noise heard by Augustine Courtauld, the explorer, in 1931, when he spent five months alone on the Greenland ice-cap. For forty-five days, from March 21 to May 5, when a rescue party reached him, he was penned up in his hut alone in darkness, imprisoned by snow.

He said in London, on December 29, 1931:

"One day, while I was at the ice station, I heard a terrifying noise. It was like a tube train coming down a tunnel and getting nearer and nearer, and it ended in a great crash overhead. I could think of nothing to account for it. . . . The first time I went outside, I found that nothing had happened. That made it all the more mysterious. It was not a case of nerves, for other people have noticed this phenomenon. Scientists say it is caused by a settling of masses of snow. It was most terrifying."

One comment: if this mysterious sound was the result of settling snow masses, how came it that its crescendo of commotion was heard as "a great crash overhead"?

Similarly inexplicable was the sudden musical droning reported the same year by Bertram Thomas, from the "Empty Quarter" of Arabia Felix. The sound resembled a ship's foghorn, and lasted two minutes and ended abruptly.

It occurred in the afternoon from the rear of a slanting cliff. Mr. Thomas investigated and found no funnel-shaped gorge with rushing wind that might have produced such a sound. And he rejects "singing sands" as the explanation for a sound of such volume. These sonic mysteries are at their most enigmatic on the *gentilars,* or dunes north of Trujillo, Peru. There, at night, are heard sounds like the beating of drums from underground. All around are ancient *huacas,* or pre-Incaic burial grounds. I know a French traveller who heard these sounds again in 1931. He scouts any explanation of underground water or singing sands.

And who knows what caused the strange wail, like a fire siren that, at 3 A.M., and again at 4 A.M., on February 26, 1938, woke the people of Dorchester, England, and which neither the police nor the fire department could explain?

It is theorized in some quarters of the United States that cosmic phenomena involving differential "etheric" stresses encountered by our solar system on its vast voyage through space, may set up explosions. Whether this be so or not, who can explain the following mysteries?

August 19, 1954: A mysterious double explosion in the sky alarmed people in Trowbridge, England. No jets known to have been up.

June 12, 1954: An unexplained explosion blew up Washington's WTOP, TV transmitter, putting the station off the air for many hours.

September 16, 1954: A mysterious "bang" heard by a conductor on a train passing through the Severn Tunnel of the Western Region Railway, England, caused the tunnel to be closed for an hour at night. Inspectors could not discover the cause.

September 16, 1954: A train was approaching Liverpool, England, when with a loud explosion, the carriage window shattered, and a fireman, Oswald Taylor, of Warrington, collapsed, covered with blood. He died of severe head injuries. Detectives found a steel object on the line, but there is no proof that the mystery was linked with it. The mysterious force broke a foot-wide gap in the window.

Strange "whirlwinds" have also been recorded.

I have received from Mr. P. F. Sharp, of "Abbots Leigh," Knutsford, England, interesting data which have gone unrecorded elsewhere. Some are a reminder of the official bureaucratic censorship which is being more and more subtly clamped down on saucer news in Great Britain, in its free and liberal-minded press. In Australia the press "splashes" news of sightings of mysterious objects in the Australian skies. Mr. Sharp has kept a diary from which I extract the following incidents:

August 16, 1952: In the afternoon, I was sitting on the beach at Chapel St. Leonards, England, when on a sudden, people a few yards from me were hurled off their deck-chairs. One man was almost flung into the sea. Papers and hats went high in the air. One man said it was almost as if an unseen arm had picked him up and dropped him down. I put it down as a "localized whirlwind," but when I read your article in a magazine about a boat that was suddenly and unaccountably hurled into the air off the beach at Seattle, Washington, I think that if we had not been too startled to look up to the sky, we might, perhaps, have seen a saucer.

Author's Comment: It is just as likely that Mr. Sharp would have seen nothing at all, since the possible source of the interrupted teleportation might either have been fourth-dimensional and invisible, or too far off to be seen by the eye.

February 27, 1954: A whirlwind at Perth, Scotland, flung a new car with its driver right across a road into a tree.

Fire phenomena, too, including the strange *red* fire balls (not meteors), rushing down from the sky, in western U.S.A., and spraying red jets of flame at about 150 feet above the ground, and a weird cylinder of blazing light seen, over the Cotswold Hills, England.

December 13, 1932: Crew of drifter "Reality," of Brightlingsea, Essex, notice in a haul of scallops, off the French coast, a hard fragment that burst into flames. The skipper was forced to turn the ship to the wind to fight the fire. Water merely added fuel to the flames, which streamed from this singular, wedge-shaped amber substance. (Was it thermite—or something from a saucer?)

February 1, 1948: Three fields on a farm near Hoddesdon, Herts burned for six months. No one could explain the cause. It was not from a German incendiary.

October 10, 1953: A red-blue, burning thing falls from

the sky near Morningside, California and burns up a pavement in three seconds.

December 2, 1953: Sheet of flame over Birmingham, England, 3,000 feet high. It disintegrates and small pieces burn out.

January 7, 1954: Blinding glare in sky, followed by terrific explosion, over Dieppe, France. Something falls into sea. Observers report that a strange shining disc had flashed from the sky into the sea. Captain of trawler says he saw at the time an enormous bowl of fire in the sky streak towards Dieppe.

In the summer of 1954, mysterious lights at sea, off the south and west English coasts, called out lifeboats. These found nothing, but mysterious fires broke out in lighthouses:

March 19, 1954: At night, fire suddenly broke out in the Lizard Lighthouse, Cornwall. It started in the engine-room at a time when the assistant-keeper, John Billett, was alone. "There was a sudden burst of flame around No. 2 engine and then all the channellings right around the room were ablaze." Next door were tanks with 5,000 gallons of oil, and in the engine-room 40-gallons of oil were in each engine-base. The town fire-brigade had to be called in.

(*Author's Note:* Two days before, March 17, 1954, the Skerryvore Lighthouse, sixty miles out in the Atlantic, of Argyllshire, Scotland, was destroyed by fire.)

Along with action against air and land transports, are we seeing "action" on the sea by saucer entities?

Some very mysterious phenomena were associated with the great fires in October, 1871, in Chicago, and in the state of Wisconsin. Ignatius Donnelly, a leading political figure of the 1890's, attributed these great fires to a brush with the tails of Biela's comet. One might also justifiably speculate whether, in fact, *something else was at work:* say, a heat-ray projected from some hostile space ship!

I summarize what occurred:

After a period of drought, on October 8, 1871, at 9:30 P.M., in points hundreds of miles apart in Wisconsin, Michigan and Illinois, devastating fires suddenly broke out. *Whirling flames seemed to come out of the sky.* From great clouds came a rain of fire and sand. Balls of fire unrolled and shot forth flaming streams.

In the week before and after the Great Fire of Chicago, vast areas of forest and prairies were ablaze. In the Chicago fire the heat melted "fire-proof" building stone, fused iron, glass and granite. Fantastic flames of blue and red and green played along the cornices of buildings. Nothing was left half-burned. The heat-blast was remarkable. An iron pole, 200 feet from any building, was fused by *heat*."

I compare this with a note from my own flying saucer case-book, in which is recorded a similar mystery:

July 24, 1947: A timber trestle bridge on steel girders across the Salmon River, Oregon, was found on fire from end to end. Though to fuse the steel required a temperature produced only in an electrical furnace, at 2800 degrees Farhenheit, the girders of the bridge *melted* in the open. A few days before, when flying saucers had been seen overhead, mysterious fires broke out in Oregon forests. Rangers called in F.B.I. agents, because they were baffled to account for the fires.

August 21, 1953: Mysterious fires on a night of torrential rain broke out on two farms and, simultaneously in a youth's hostel four miles away at Winchcombe, England. In the hostel, and also on the farm, *29 bicycles and steel tractors* were destroyed. The cause of both fires is a mystery. Exactly a month earlier, a strange cylinder of white light, from which red balls of fire were dropped, was seen by four people on the Cotswold Hills, some eighteen miles south of the location of the cylinder-phenomenon, and in the same Cotswold region.

On the night of the Great Chicago Fire—as Mr. Stephen Calvert of Benton, Wisconsin, reminds me—there occurred, in that state, the worst fire in Wisconsin's history. I cite a report in a Chicago newspaper of October 10, 1871:

"At a place south of Peshtigo, Wisconsin, a farmer named Griffin describes what he saw on the night of the great Chicago fire, in the Sugar bush region of Wisconsin. 'I heard the roar of an advancing tornado, ran out of my farmhouse and saw, overhead, a *tre-*

mendous black balloon-like thing whirling toward us through the air over the tops of distant trees. When it was over us, it seemed to explode with a terrific noise, jetting out fire on all sides. In one second, my house was in flames.' "

In this fire at Peshtigo, about 1,500 people were killed and more than two billion trees were burnt.

In passing, I may say that a phenomenon identical with the mysterious white pillar, or cylinder of light—but not dropping balls of fire—was seen on March 23, 1763, west of Lausanne, Switzerland, and reported by a professor of the Académie Royale des Sciences, at Paris.

There was also something very peculiar about the fire on the British-troop-ship, "Empire Windrush," off Algiers, on March 28, 1954. The mystery has never been solved. There was a sudden flash in the engine-room and the resulting fire made a holocaust of the liner:

At the public inquiry by the Wrecks Commissioner, in London, June 22 and 24, 1954, a letter was read which stated that a junior engineer, Leslie Pendleton, who lost his life when the liner sank off Algiers, said the "Empire Windrush" was a "hell of a ship." The chief officer said that four-fifths of the ship was ablaze an hour and a half after the fire started. No fire-door would hold back the flames. "Something seemed to have engulfed the engine-room at one go, and it sounded as if a tank had discharged all its contents. There was more than a mere leakage of oil." The engineer, Mr. Jack Tozer, said that neither he nor the chief engineer could get very far into the engine-room, and no torch would pierce the black smoke. It sounded as if oil drums—of which there were seventeen—containing from five to forty gallons each, had exploded in the engine room. During the voyage, none of the main engines had overheated. He agreed with the suggestion of the counsel for the shipowners that, at Port Said, Egyptian fitters and laborers, who went aboard the ship might have secretly introduced inflammable material into the engine-room. But there is *no proof* of sabotage.

July 27, 1954: Mr. J. V. N. Smith, chairman of the Ministry of Transport inquiry, said he could not determine the cause of the fire in the "Windrush," which was undoubtedly a ship fit to be at sea. Sabotage, electrical failures, explosion in the main engine or generator, or smoking in the engine-room were discounted as possible causes. (*Summarized from official reports.*)

Here are other incidents of a peculiar nature.

In May and July, 1954: A farmwoman, Mrs. White, of Shiphay, England, hears her three-year-old daughter suddenly scream: "Ma, the house is on fire!" She rushes in from the yard to find that although there were no fires in the grates, both the kitchen and the dining room were ablaze. Mystery unsolved.

Nightworkers see over Monmouthshire, a fiery disc trailing flames.

Mysterious explosion in the 38,000-ton American aircraft-carrier, "Bennington," after twenty jets had been launched. Explosion kills ninety-one men. The commander, Capt. McRaborn, says the cause is a riddle. There was nothing explosive in the area where blasts occurred.

Something like a flaming jet falls into the sea off Brest, France, but no plane had been seen aloft. British R.A.F. cannot clear the mystery.

Strange lights, seen three miles off Seaford Head, Sussex, at noon, cause lifeboats to put out in heavy seas. Nothing found.

The mysterious phenomena of ice falling from the sky, in England and the United States, has been officially but unconvincingly ascribed to the jettisoning of ice by pilots. This ice is supposed to form from the air intakes of jet planes, or from defective de-icing mechanisms, although in the latter case, the ice is dissipated into spray before reaching the ground.

There have been cases, as at Stebbing, an Essex village, where the so-called ice was not ice at all, but some unknown, translucent material of the sort dropped from saucers over western and southern France. In the Stebbing incident, the local police, by order of the Air Ministry, took possession of the substance. To this day, they have not told the public what it was—if, indeed, the analysts knew!

There happened an incident, in May, 1954, in which the new phenomenon of a *roaring sound from the sky* was again accompanied by the fall of some object:

June 7, 1952: A lump of ice as big as a bucket crashed through the roof of a bungalow at Downend, Bristol. No plane could possibly have dropped this ice.
May 5, 1954: Over Victoria Road, in London, at 11:10 A.M., a roaring sound was heard in the sky, followed by a crash that sent roof slates to the ground and hurled books across an attic. But no falling object was found, nor ice. A woman says she heard something in the sky before and after the mysterious crash. British Air Ministry baffled.

The fissuring of motor car windshields in England, the United States and Australia, is another phenomenon which may have a cosmic origin. It was first noticed in the summer of 1950, and has lasted into 1954. I summarize incidents which would fill a fair-sized book:

1952: (England) For the second time, a car on the Evesham Road, near Stratford-on-Avon has its windshield mysteriously shattered.
Summer, 1953: Side window of a truck, parked in Grasmere Road, Gloucester, suddenly shattered by what look like small beads.
January 15, 1954: (Australia) Windshields of cars on 2,000 foot high plateau of Pentland Hills, Victoria, shatter or are mysteriously pierced. Same thing happens on Bacchus Moor. Police record such incidents weekly.
February 23: Missile Mile, Esher Common, Surrey, has hundreds of these incidents, in which a supernormal element appears at times. Phenomenon also reported at Newbury, and on Kingston by-pass road, Surrey.
   Over Esher Common, a pilot, Douglas Gilbert, 1,000 feet up in an R.A.F. plane, finds his compass glass burst in center and fly up in his face. Fissure is in dead center. Another pilot, over same common, sees a mysterious silver disc or saucer in the air; a third pilot finds his compass needle *weaving wildly on the dial.*
March-April, 1954: (United States) Thousands of cars on road between Bellingham and Seattle find screens inexplicably shattered. Mayor Pomeroy of Seattle says that a powder found on glass may have been dispersed by winds. As in England, the phenomenon occurs in isolated regions remote from war in-

dustry factories. Glass so shattered of both plastic *and* ordinary type. In Oregon, tiny black specks falling from the sky are found to have electrical charges. No scientific explanation yet offered.

If this mysterious disintegration should spread from glass to metals and other industrial materials, the consequences might be very grave. One theory—not proved— is that meson particles, or cosmic or hydrogen bomb radiations, may react on chemical constituents in the atmosphere to produce glass-shattering effects.

In Washington, on the American west coast, it is said that a sooty deposit on fissured wind-screens has been found to be temporarily charged with an energy of "magnetic," or electro-magnetic type. But why has not this deposit been observed in England or Australia? Why, too, in England, are locations of the phenomenon so apparently *selective?* No one knows.

Here are other windshield incidents, from April to June, 1954:

At Buffalo, N. Y., windshields are mysteriously pierced; in Toronto and Ottawa, Canada, plate-glass windows of shops are found holed in the center. Toronto people complain of stuff falling from the sky and stinging and burning their skins, forcing them to run for shelter. At Cincinnati, in the United States, when car-screens were pierced, a woman says she saw fall from the sky, small "granitic pellets" that sizzled, hissed and burned as they hit the ground.

Author's Comment: Had these pellets an electro-thermal charge?

What was called "water dropping from a clear sky," holed a windshield at Key West, Florida. Police and detectives at the industrial town of Kokomo, Indiana, were baffled by minute holes pierced in sixty plate glass windows. Behind the minute holes is a small crater. Phenomenon started in September, 1952, and broke out again in May, 1954. Similar incidents at Peru, twenty miles from Kokomo. (Theory starts that flying-saucer enemies are experimenting on silicon in glass, and may later attempt to produce "fatigue," or "disease" in metals.)

The two following incidents resemble poltergeist activities:

April 28, 1954: Mrs. R. McCort, of Neward, Ohio, heard her three-year-old daughter calling: "Mamma, someone is throwing stones at the car." She went outside into the yard, and looking upwards, saw "a cylindrical mass of particles falling nearly vertically downwards, at high speed, and striking the car's windshield. She and her husband, an engineer, found quarter-inch indentations in the windshield, and on the car's hood slivers of glass the size of peas.

April 29, 1954: At Jacksonville, Fla., housewives complain of holes of mysterious origin in newly laundered clothing.

A Canadian physicist advances an ingenious theory to explain these phenomena. But it fails to account for the peculiar selectivity of the location and the objects affected; and for the curious periodicity of the incidents:

April 30, 1954: At Fort William, Ontario, Canada, Trevor W. Page, mining instructor, has examined a piece of metal a sixteenth of an inch wide, found embedded in a car windshield. The metal contained iron with a trace of nickel, such as is found in meteorites. Briant W. Pocock of the Isotope Bureau of the Michigan State Highway Department's research laboratory, theorizes that hydrofluoric acid, borne by air currents from hydrogen bomb blasts in the Pacific, may cause windshield pitting. Mr. Pocock points out that this acid, used for etching glass, is the only known substance having a *direct* chemical effect on glass. It need not be radioactive. He thinks that the slant of wind-screens and the forward motion of cars tend to attract the acid particles.

In June, 1954, the windshield of a car on the Sutton Road, nine miles northeast of Esber Common, England, suddenly shattered with a loud report. Three days later, the same thing happened at Denham, Bucks. Up to May, 1954, three hundred of these mysterious incidents had happened in various parts of England. Car-makers say that, as the glass is toughened by great heat, changes in temperature would not affect it.

Nor, as the report below shows, could the organizers of a Motor Show in London solve the mystery:

"A special test of a windshield made at a Motor Show, in London, showed that, when a special ma-

chine twisted a shield 1½ inches in each direction
every day, only on the last day of the show was the
glass fractured.

Summer, 1954: A lump of quartz has been found in
Colorado, synchronizing with the fissuring of windshields on automobiles near Seattle, Washington. The
quartz has in it a number of "burnt holes." For some
reason American official authorities have pronounced
that "MUM" shall be the word about this phenomenon. "Mum," too, says the British Air Ministry
about the stuff that fell from the skies over Essex in
November, 1950.

It is possible that cosmic ray particles, whose velocity
is immense, may release hydrogen into our atmosphere,
and create intense heat which penetrates and powders
the glass. If so, the heat effect appears to be of short
duration. In the state of Washington, a sooty or graphite-
like substance has been found on the punctured car-
screens. This carbon substance appears to have a positive
electrical charge of very short duration. Whether radioactivity in the atmosphere produces these singular
byproducts we do not know. Unless the effects spread to
other substances, such as silicon, semi-metals, and metals,
there need be no cause for alarm. *But,* if it does, one
may wonder if some of these elusive saucer entities are
trying experiments on our industrial civilization!

As I write these lines, I have a report of an extraordinary incident in California:

Burning chunks of metal, ranging in size from a
dime to a half-dollar, red-hot and lined with something like asbestos, have been found (August 28,
1954), over a 250 feet stretch of highway, at Woodside, California. Later, a woman motorist found the
road ablaze. Firemen found scores of small pieces of
flaming metal in the road-surface, and bubbling
where the bits had embedded themselves. The pieces
were still hot twenty minutes later.

The metal appeared to be cast, and irregularly
shaped, a quarter of an inch thick. Some of its edges
seemed milled, or worked on a lathe. It is supposed
that they come from a cylindrical object, for the bits
are concave. Fire-chief Vulpiano said the asbestos-
like lining of the metal bits had been charred. The
road surface is studded with shallow holes, as if hit

by shrapnel. The only plane in the area was there three hours before the fire occurred.

Two days later, an absurd "explanation" came from some genius: that a bucket of hot tar had fallen on the road and set it on fire!
(*Summarized from the "San Francisco Call-Bulletin," and other sources.*)

Another phenomenon seems to be connected with the mysterious red fire balls (not meteorites) which rush from the sky towards the ground and dissipate in a red spray, some 150 feet from the ground.

January 13, 1954: At 5 A.M., men in the control tower at Selfridge Air Base, saw what seemed to be red and green flares dropping half a mile away. At 5:10 A.M., a naval station saw a flare fall into the Detroit River. Flares in the sky were reported all the way from Michigan and Wisconsin to New York. In New York State, hundreds saw a red ball in the sky. Was this a meteorite?

The question may be answered in Scotch fashion by another: Whoever saw meteorites taking two hours to travel to Troy, N.Y., from Michigan, reverse direction of flight at Marietta, Ohio, and then return to the original eastern course?

Up to the end of May, 1954, the U.S. Air Force had received no object or particle of unknown substance falling from the skies, and no detailed photos of unidentified flying objects. It is still, however, unable to explain ten per cent of sightings out of 1,700 saucer reports in 1952, 429 in 1953, and 87 up to April, 1954.

In an earlier chapter, I spoke of the mysterious prints in the snow seen a century ago, in south Devon, after a blizzard. What, or who left their *giant* prints in the snow during the night of February 7, 1954, in the Isle of Wright, described in a letter from a friend living on the island?

"Last night, February 7, 1954, people at Colwell Bay and Totland Bay were greatly puzzled by giant footmarks in the snow. Coastguards at the Needles traced a track of these weird footsteps right to the edge of a cliff where they disappeared. They have been traced over a tennis court belonging to a holiday summer camp. They are 22 inches long and 12 inches wide, and taper to the heel; and there are five distinct toe-marks"

Had this entity with the presumably naked unshod feet, indicating a being of uncommon stature, and one apparently oblivious of frost bite, any connection with a space ship, or a larger than usual satellite disc? Whence did he go from the edge of the cliff?

Below, a number of oddities and unexplained phenomena:

September 26, 1950: The sun over Edinburgh was a deep *indigo-blue*, and the moon that night was *blue*. The cause? A forest fire at Alberta, Canada, 4,000 miles away, according to the astronomer at Edinburgh Observatory. Can he explain his explanation? *(Summer, 1951):* Soldiers all over England collapse on parade, as if struck by a death ray! *(April 7, 1954):* Pure petrol suddenly starts gushing into the cellar of a hotel at Rushden, North Hants. *(July 10, 1954):* The Loch Ness monster, with head and three humps, sighted by a waitress, Maggie Macdonald. *(N.B.* The monster is *not* necessarily a byproduct of Scottish distilleries.) *(July 22, 1954):* Freak wave, eight feet high, sweeps Tor Bay. No explanation. There were, it is said, twelve of these waves. No ships were near, nor was it a tidal wave, as there was a lee wind and slack water. At Brixham, on the opposite side of Tor Bay, no waves of this type were seen. (Was it a submarine quake, or had a saucer or space ship fallen into the English Channel?)

There have been singular interruptions to radio transmission from airliners, in two cases accompanied by disasters, which cannot be convincingly attributed to normal "fading," or ionization.

Consider the following incidents:

July 31, 1954: A mysterious radio message that a U.S. airliner with seventy-two people aboard had fallen into the North Sea, between Amsterdam and Dundee caused a vain sea-air search by British and Netherlands services. It was the second false warning of this type. *(N.B.* Recall my account earlier, of the space ship I saw over North Kent, at 5:25 A.M., on July 23, 1954.)

August 23, 1954: Five minutes' flying time from Schihpol airdrome, Amsterdam, the traffic men lost radio contact with incoming 4-engine K.L.M. (Royal Dutch Airlines) airliner, on last lap of trip from New York. She vanished with twenty-one people aboard. Burning wreckage was found seventeen miles out at sea, and the body of a five-year-old boy from Woodbury, Connecticut. The last radio contact was at 12:32 P.M. About this time, people near Amsterdam, thirty-eight miles east, heard a dull aerial explosion.

Author's Comment: The circumstances surrounding the loss of the K.L.M. airliner may be compared with the "five-minute radio mystery" of the "Lancastrian Star Dust" airliner over Chile, on *August 2, 1947*. It is singular that both these disasters occurred *in the month of August*, at seven years' interval. Is this more than a coincidence?

September 5, 1954: Two minutes after its take-off, at 3 A.M., from Shannon Airport, Eire, the airliner, "The Flying Dutchman" (K.L.M. Royal Dutch Airlines), crashed on the waters of the Shannon. The captain and flight personnel say the weather was clear and the take-off normal. The airliner's radio contact with the airport was suddenly broken off. There were scenes of panic after the crash. Twenty-eight passengers were fatally gassed by petrol fumes. The President of the K.L.M. is baffled. He says that the instruments showed that the airliner "was at the correct height, but did not rise."

Consider the following series of accidents to jet planes in England, Denmark and the United States, difficult to explain as mistakes of personnel or mechanical defects:

June 21, 1954: American six-engined Stratocruiser jet bomber exploded in flight and crashed near Townsend, Georgia, just after the takeoff. All the crew were killed.

August 23, 1954: Two U.S. Sabrejets in flight over England disintegrate in the air, one at Old Buckenham, the other at Canterbury. Both pilots killed.

August 25, 1954: After being grounded for four months, the Vickers Swift jet fighters were put back in the air. But the pilot experienced trouble at high altitude, bailed out at 10,000 feet and landed safely at Newmarket. The abandoned jet crashed into a wood near Thaxted, Essex.

When these jets were put back into the air, the Royal Air Force announced that they had traced the previous crash, in May, to a failure in the electrical power control system. This "had been rectified."

On August 25, the Air Ministry official spokesman did not advance any theory of the accident, so reminiscent of what happened to the British Comet *jet* airliners when *they* were put back into the air. The official said, with a sapiency resounding like a runaway brewery truck over a steel suspension bridge: "No reason yet to reground this type of jet."

No, sir! Just keep on till the next mysterious crash, sparing no public money. After all, does not the taxpayer exist merely to justify official "wisdom"?

These Supermarine Swift jets are faster than sound. The British Royal Air Force has lost four of them in 1953-54.

September 9, 1954: Two R.A.F. Meteor jets crashed in the air over Norfolk, and fell in flames at the village of Neatishead. The pilots bailed out.

In England, in 1954, a number of curious incidents occurred which might induce speculations by some *fantaisistes* whether certain entities, contemplating a landing, might be testing their powers on our ground and rail transport. Bear in mind the crucial importance to any army of efficient transport.

At Chalfont St. Giles, and at Leigh-on-Sea, Essex, and possibly in other places in Great Britain not so far reported to me, there have been unexplained noises which seem to come from underground.

These noises were first heard in September, 1953. They became very audible around Christmas, 1953. The sound was described as a persistent humming of deep vibration and regular pulsation. On occasions it kept people awake at night, when the sounds intensified to a noise like a plane "revving" up its engines, or a motor truck climbing a hill.

There are airdromes and bases of both the British and American Air Forces in this region. But neither the air authorities, nor the police could throw any light on the sources of the noises. Factories and engineering operations were eliminated as sources.

From a correspondent who lives about eight miles from this region, I have had a very interesting story of local flying-saucer incidents. One occurred only four miles from Chalfont St. Giles, the location of the mysterious subterranean phenomena. By his special request I may not give his name. He says:

"I am moved to give you an account of a most singular object I saw a few weeks ago, this Spring, 1954. I was walking along a rough lane leading from Bovingdon towards my house at Boxmoor, Herts. The night was clear and still, the time 10:30 P.M., and I was deep in thought about some personal worries.

"On a sudden, it penetrated my mind that I could see, cast on the ground, the shadows of overhanging trees. For a moment I supposed, rather confusedly, that the moon had come out from behind a cloud. Then, just as confusedly, I realized that there were no clouds, and something said to me, as if the words had been spoken: 'There is no moon tonight!'

"I looked up and saw in the sky an intense white light, probing downwards through the branches of an oak under which I was passing. The branches appeared jet black against the intense light.

"Hurrying forward into the open, I saw a brilliant light motionless in the sky above me. I now had a clear and uninterrupted view of it. I watched it for half a minute. It did not move at all, but hung there like a single lamp, high in the roof of a lofty warehouse. But, of course, there was nothing that it hung from. There was no sound of any aircraft.

"I am certain it hung in the same place as when I had looked up through the oak, and the shadows were stationary. So I think it was motionless for at least a minute.

"How high it was I am unable to say; nor can I give any impression of its size; but it was almost vertically above me. Its altitude might have been about five hundred feet, and its diameter about twenty feet. The intensity of the light it projected was like that from an electric welding-arc. It hurt my eyes to look at it.

"About thirty seconds passed. Then the light seemed to give a convulsive jerk. A kind of bulge or blister sprang out of the left side. I could now see that the thing was a globe. The blister was not as bright as the main body.

"A moment later the light vanished. Where it had hung, there was nothing! I could see the stars and the sheen of the Milky Way. It seemed to me as if something had violently given way—as if there had been an explosion—a recoil as from some blow or impulse.

"It may be that some solid object sprang away and that the thrust and speed of its movement produced a violent distortion. True, I saw no such solid object released. There was no sound at any time. Perhaps the object was surrounded by a sort of field of light or energy, and the object used that energy for its propulsion, and reacted against the pull of gravity.

"Whatever the thing was, it swept my mind clear of everything else. I knew instinctively, that it was alien, that it came from very far away, perhaps some world incredibly remote. Not only that, but I felt I was being watched by it, that it knew I was there. Of course, such intuitive impressions are of uncertain value."

My correspondent's eerie story suggests that the weird phenomenon was of fourth-dimensional nature.

He mentioned two other phenomena of the flying saucer type that he had witnessed:

"One was a steady orange light moving north over the sky of Herts, *against* a westerly breeze—and at night. Hence, it could not have been a weather balloon. It seemed to float along, quite unlike the hard, defined lines of a plane. I think it was about three miles high. I looked away to see where I was walking, and when I looked up again, it had vanished. It did not reappear. This was in the summer of 1953."

My correspondent's second sighting leaves me with the impression that certain of these flying saucer entities may be cleverly masking their operations to synchronize with terrestrial operations such as air force maneuvers:

"One evening in the late summer or early autumn of 1952, at about 9:30 P.M., I saw a light descend vertically from a very great height until my view was obstructed by trees on high ground. The light descended about two miles northeast of Chalfont St. Giles. The spot would be in a steep and rather secluded valley, about a mile from the nearest highway. Far overhead, a stream of very high-flying airplanes were on sub-stratosphere maneuvers, so high that there was only a faint mutter of sound and dim vapor trails. I assumed that the light must be a flare dropped by one of these planes, but for the fact that it descended too swiftly to be a flare. It was a big object, and struck me as rather dangerous to have been dropped over populated country. Next day, no newspapers local or national, spoke of a crash, and I lost interest.

"Suppose the phenomenon I then saw came from some kind of saucer? It would have been masking itself by the maneuvers. The ground defense might interpret any radarscope record of it as something else. The thing could have landed without any suspicion of its being non-terrestrial in origin. I did not report what I saw to the authorities, since it seems to be official policy to hinder or veto free discussion."

My correspondent adds that he knows of no caves or quarries in the Chilterns. Some faults are caused by chemical action between the clay and chalk, seen as deep dells in the woods. There is, too, the well known subterranean steam, "Misbourne," which, local folklore says, rises to the surface when war threatens. Some underground cavities revealed themselves, in the spring of 1954, in the new town of Hemel Hempstead, when some new apartments collapsed into them.

"I believe we are watching an inevitable and tremendous historical process," writes my correspondent. "Sooner or later, the space ships will come, in their own time. They may not choose to use methods involving indiscriminate slaughter, but their 'enlightened plan' may be to confront us with that which will prevent, not provoke useless resistance. If anything can be done, it must be done *now*. But one cannot see our rulers admitting, even privately, that their power politics may be a thing of the past."

In another communication, he wrote me of information he had got from a lady in the neighborhood. Worried by the strange underground noises she heard, she had sought explanations from the local authorities. She was told that they had none. The noises did *not* come from road work or pumping operations, or factory machinery. Examinations of "victims," by a London specialist, have disposed of the "noises in the head" theory.

My correspondent adds:

"One difficulty is that only certain people hear the sounds. I, myself, could hear only a very faint throbbing; but, on the afternoon I called, Mrs. Craig told me it was not anywhere near as loud as it can be. She has very acute hearing, as also has the other lady, Mrs. Fielding. The mysterious sound is not high-pitched. Mrs. Craig describes it as resembling the sound of 'giant wheels turning.' Sometimes it seems to go up and down the walls of her rooms. But the actual direction of the sound varies and seems to be unaffected by wind-direction. The bungalow in between hers and Mrs. Fielding's does not appear to get the sound at all; but the floor of this bungalow is laid on solid concrete, unlike the other two. Both ladies are normal, charming, commonsensical young women.

"Mrs. Craig wonders if it might come from some planet trying to signal us. She says that she has recently heard of similar underground noises on Anglesey Island, in North Wales, 'where there are no heavy industries!' Mrs. Fielding is inclined to think there is a *beam* effect, as if the sound were alternately beamed on one, then on the other bungalow. Both ladies agree that the sound has diminished. There is some confirmation of this, because the sound was formerly heard at a place a mile away towards Chenies, but not of late. There is also *one* record of its having been heard at a point in between.

"I send a rough sketch map, from which you may see that it *appears* that there may be a definite line of movement of these strange sounds.

"Now comes an interesting new fact. There is said recently to have been an epidemic of windshield splintering on the crossroad here. (This has been described earlier.) A few months ago, a windshield was splintered on a car that had been garaged for the night. Both ladies feel that some officials may know more about this mystery than they are prepared to say. (It is likely that they know nothing! *Author*).

"A local bit of folk lore is that the bungalows are on the site of an ancient Danish encampment, and that a hollow or cave is underneath the site. . . . You are right—shadows we pursue, and elusive shadows— but every shadow must be cast by *something!* I think there are many false trails, some of them chance— some perhaps *intentional*."

At the end of July, 1954, my Chilterns correspondent personally explored the region where he had seen the strange light disappear in the Spring. What he tells may suggest the "fantastic theory," referred to before, that these visitants from outer space (there is nothing whatever to link them with Mars or Venus, or any other planet in our solar system) may long ago have established contacts with elusive people of this earth. There is nothing inherently impossible, improbable though it may be.

The annals of old Rome, as preserved by Titus Livius and Julius Obsequens, contain nine accounts of mysterious aeronautical craft in the skies over Praeneste (B.C. 216); Hadria, in the Gulf of Venice (B.C. 213); Fregellae, (B.C. 295); Lanuvium (B.C. 168); Campania (B.C. 98); Aenarie, Bay of Naples (B.C. 90); Latium (B.C. 42); Rome (B.C. 41); Umbria (B.C. 16). I say nothing about the records of similar phenomena in the monastic chronicles of England from the Anglo-Saxon Chronicle onwards.

My correspondent proceeds:

"Why should some of these mysterious space ships glow fiery red, as if from friction with our atmosphere, from which their interiors may be insulated? Maybe that is why you saw no open ports. Why are others *black?* Could the space ship you saw have been not the actual object, but one enveloped in this glow, or force-field? Could it be that the power which drives these space ships surrounds them with radiation which may cause the atmosphere round them to glow gaseously?

"One might also wonder if this force-field is the shield that guards them from, or deflects meteors or meteorites they encounter in their voyages in space. Was what you saw the glow, or radiation still switched on? If some space ships are black to the view, it might suggest that the radiation can be switched on and off.

"Yet another possibility crosses my mind: There appear to be two types of these space ships which may belong to rival powers, who in such cases when we see them, may be at 'battle stations.' I imagine such battles and attendant maneuvers would cover enormous distances and speeds. It is a strange thought that we, on our planet, may be the prize for which they fight or contend! . . .

"I have now been to the valley where I thought the lights must have landed, but with negative results. There are a number of bottoms or dells hidden among dense trees and woods well off the beaten track. But if any of them concealed a secret, it concealed it from me, too. The soil of the valley is the chalk and clay usual in the Chilterns, with some gravel deposits on the crest of the south-west slope. The river Chess, a shallow stream about ten feet wide, runs along the bottom. One of the deils I examined appeared to be a disused gravel-pit. Of course, it was impossible for me to pinpoint the light, and I shall widen my search. There are hundreds of these dells in the Chilterns.

"As to possible caves, a similar local legend at Hemel Hempstead was found to be true. Another large cavity, now being filled near Tring, Herts, is said to have a chamber at its bottom 'big enough to turn a wagon and horses in it.' "

I again asked my correspondent *where* he thought the mysterious light may have landed.
He wrote:

"I am inclined to think now that the more likely place . . . would be on *very private property!* A mile or so nearer Chalfont from the valley stand many large houses on their own grounds. There must still be a lot of money about, for all these places are beautifully kept. For me to be seen loitering in the lanes and fields there might draw on me the notice of the police, and suspicions of 'loitering with intent.' I do not, of course, suggest any conspiracy. It is merely the normal thing in a wealthy neighborhood. *But what perfect cover if the occupants of any of these houses happen to be—'in the know'—shall I say?*"

I at once advised my correspondent to keep his own counsel, and not to frequent that, or any similar locality, lest mysterious intermediaries might "bump him off," adding to the other mysteries, that of a vanished man! For in view of what he says below, and the reports of the ladies, these mysterious noises *might* indicate a beam-ray put on the region by some unseen space ship. It might also suggest the "reactivation" of some stretch of the *very* ancient and mysterious tunnels well known to students of the Atlantean riddle.

I do *not* connect the very peculiar nature of these sounds with any secret construction of underground hydrogen bomb shelters which the nations in Europe and America are, as this book shows, known to have constructed, or to be constructing.

My correspondent refers again to the Chalfont sonic "mystery":

"After several visits to the Chalfont area, I can say, with fair certainty that I *do* hear the sound, but only faintly. I hear a sound in various parts of that area which I certainly do not hear elsewhere, and it is always the same sound, and distinguishable from other sounds. Mrs. Craig told me that although its volume varies, the pitch never alters.

"It sounds to me like a very heavy machine working a long way off, and it has a regular pulse of vibration, which suggests either that the machine passes through a regular phase of vibration, or else there is a regular periodic build-up of sound waves. The unchanging pitch indicates that the machine always runs at the same speed. I know of no normal machine which could do this, day and night for months. (There was one break: when the sounds stopped for about a week before Whitsun, and started on Whit-Monday night.)

"One cannot tell the direction of the sound. It is simply there. One may lose it by moving a short distance from a point where it is audible. Go back to that point, and the sound is still there. Another odd feature is that although Mrs. Craig, in particular, and several other folk have searched for miles in every direction, on foot and by car, no one has ever succeeded in getting closer to the cause of it.

"It seems completely elusive. One can go away from it, but not apparently approach it beyond a certain limit. Either it must be *very* deep below the surface, or else—a wild surmise—it might be located in a fourth dimension! As a matter of fact, I do not get the impression that it is subterranean in origin. More like an effect of 'over the hills and faraway.' It is an oddly disturbing sound. It is harsh, daunting, and chilling.

"I have listened for it at Bovingdon, near Hemel Hempstead, in the still of night, but definitely, it is *not* there. There must be some reason for its being heard in the Chalfont area.

"Near the bungalows are two large dells, close to a lane. I managed to enter one, but saw nothing very much. And the sound did not appear any louder there. I could not enter the other dell, because of the perpendicular sides bordering on the lane. Also, both dells are on private ground, limiting one's movement.

"This lane itself is one of the points where the mysterious sound is audible. It is in a small valley.

Going over a footpath up a slope, I lost the sound at the top. Returning down the slope, I got it again.

"Mrs. Craig sometimes hears it very loudly, as if, she says: 'It was going up and down the walls of the room'; but, even then, the sound always appears to come from outside . . . from over there.'

"Keep your binoculars handy! If one space ship came over the North Kent course, so may another. They seem to me more and more indifferent whether one sees them or not. I suppose they don't think much of our jets!"

Another indication of possible mysterious operations on the perimeter of greater London, of the same kind as in the Chilterns and Chalfont St. Giles areas, reached me on July 6, 1954, from another correspondent—this time in Essex. He indicated that a phenomenon similar to the Chalfont mystery had been heard at Leigh-on-Sea, near Southend, about sixty miles east by south of the Chilterns, and east of London:

"I live at Leigh-on-Sea, Essex, on the top floor of one of a block of flats, self-contained and of brick and concrete construction. For the past twelve months, 1953-54, my wife and I have been hearing a strange noise, intermittent, but continuing for fairly long periods. It is a combination of buzzing and grating sounds. The description of rumbling trucks, such as you mention about the Chalfont St. Giles sounds, would fit very well. Strangely enough, the noise is not apparent earlier than about 11-11:30 P.M. On occasions it is extremely loud.

"My wife at first thought the noise might have arisen from work on the railroad line nearby. But there is no evidence of such work being done there. Again, we surmised the noise might come from the oil refineries, but there are none near enough for their operations to be heard.

"What is to me a rather curious feature is the fact that when, on occasion, I have gone out in the expectation of hearing the noise more clearly or being better able to judge the direction it comes from, I have been unable to hear it at all. The sound is too loud and strange to come, as has been suggested, from some neighbor's electrical, or other appliance. And the sound is most audible during the night, when such appliances would not be in use."

There are reasons why I am unable to give the name and address of this correspondent.

In regard to the British Railways incidents below, "experts," or science news reporters may deem that no other than normal causation was at work—and dismiss other theories as "manifest nonsense." But those for whom flying saucers cannot be so dismissed may take comfort in the fact that they cannot yet be hanged for deeming otherwise:

June 11 and 18, 1954: Twice in one week, coaches of the same boat-train of the London-Midland region railroads parked in Allerton sidings near Liverpool, were found on fire. Railroad detectives are baffled.

Four days before this mystery, ten locomotives on a crowded traffic line serving the Eastern region railroads suddenly failed and brought services to a standstill during the evening rush hours. Engineers were puzzled. They found no mechanical defect, and could suggest only the theory—not acceptable to every railroad engineer—that the injector feeds had failed, owing to use of unsoftened water from tanks.

The location of the Chalfont mystery is only thirty-eight miles, as the crow flies, from this Eastern regional railroad! I am left *wondering!*

The incidents following may, or may not have some connection with these railroad fires. I have reason to feel that the type of mysterious saucer here involved is definitely hostile, being known to have caused disastrous fires in both Oregon and California, as well as in England:

Summer, 1952: A sinister, cigar-shaped, non-terrestrial object was seen over Denham, Bucks (not far from the Chalfont region), by ten people, at 3 P.M. They saw it in the act of releasing two satellite discs which, at high speed, flew off in opposite directions. A few hours later, the same or an identical flying saucer, was seen releasing a satellite disc over Sweden, on the other side of the North Sea. About the same time as the mysterious fires occurred on British Railways, June, 1954, a strange, solid iron object weighing more than two and a half tons was found by a Kent farmer. It had left a crater in his field. British Royal Engineers who photographed the object said it was not a part of any bomb—British or German.

Was this Kent object a "marker" left by a flying saucer from some unknown world in space? If so, what purpose was it meant to serve?

I here set down some extracts from my saucer case-book:

If a hostile cosmic power—and let us hope this is mere fantasy of the science-fiction sort—had a general staff planning aggressive tactics against the earth, it might act in England, from hidden centers in hilly and wooded regions around London. (The same tactics would be used in the case of *all* the world's great capitals: New York, Paris, Moscow, Berlin, Melbourne, Rio de Janeiro, Buenos Aires, and so on).

First: We find the air traffic attacked. Great Britain has had to ground all her jet airliners after a series of strange and still unexplained disasters. Hardly had she done so, before an airliner belonging to Pakistan, India, failed on a flight from Cairo to London, and exactly as in the other cases, but with better fortune, was forced to make an emergency landing.

Second: Ground air transport. The railroads may now be attacked, or have been attacked in experimental fashion. What next? Power lines and generating stations, atomic piles, shipping, etc.

Proof? None! And it would be impossible for anyone to warn authority, for this would incur the risk of having his sanity impugned.

All he can do, all anyone can do, is to hold his tongue and quietly investigate—as I myself am doing. From my continued and close observation of phenomena, in the British Isles, in Europe, in the U.S.A., and in Australia, a most disturbing pattern has been slowly built up.

Who can wonder that both in England and the United States, there are folk who look up to the skies in apprehension:

"WILL THESE SPACE SHIPS LAND ON OUR EARTH? *WHEN* WILL THEY LAND?"

One warning, and I repeat it: It is folly to suppose that these mysterious entities, whencesoever they come, are here only to aid us, or serve us.

No! They are here on business of their own. And their ethics and code of morality are likely *not* to be ours! It would be utter folly for any sane man at this moment to do more than quietly investigate. It is likely to be extremely difficult to discover *anything* evidential or conclusive. Yarns about telepathic contacts with alleged men from Venus, or any other planet, must be treated skeptically. Telepathy is a parapsychological fact, but no scientist has any reason to accept the allegations that telepathy is under control like a telephone line, which is all such yarns imply. The serious observer and investigator of these saucer phenomena has his, or her task made the more difficult by the telepathy reports which tend to cover the whole subject with ridicule and derision. All one can do is watch, wait, weigh, collate and synthesize.

Another unexplained and mysterious phenomenon *not* connected with the explosion of wartime mines. Strange roaring noises were heard out at sea off the coast of Hunstanton, Norfolk, November, 1950. The Air Ministry has not yet arrived at an explanation. No planes had crashed in the sea there.

I have had a letter from Mr. F. P. Sharp of Knutsford, Cheshire, which may have some relevance:

August 12, 1954: "At 10 P.M., I and my friend, "Nobby" Clark, saw flashes of light out at sea—not lightning or gun-fire. We put it down to illuminations from Hunstanton, on the other side of the Wash, England. When I studied the map I concluded that the lights did *not* come from the land."

August 13, 1954: "Saw a thing like a ball of fire, or shooting star, heading towards where we saw the mysterious lights the night before."

On May 25, 1954, similar phenomena were reported off the Sussex coast:

A mysterious "double bang" rattled windows in towns twenty miles apart on the Sussex coast. It came from out at sea. Cause unknown; not wartime mines.

Summing up these phenomena a disturbing pattern seems to emerge. In it are the *Mutants,* as one may call the discoidal and other aeroforms associated with fourth-dimensional world space-ships. I suspect there are also some three-dimensional aeroforms emanating from some world in space, whose matter *is akin* to our own.

In the latter category may be put the sinister fusiform,

or cigar-shaped flying saucer, which is surrounded by a
Saturnian ring. Such saucers have been seen to send off
satellite discs over Denham, Bucks, England, eastern
Sweden and the United States.

In the summer of 1954, these have been again observed,
apparently surveying the skies over Washington, D.C.,
exactly as they did in squadrons on August nights in
1952. Some of my American correspondents call it
"buzzing the Capitol, and giving the brass hats the razz-
berry."

The following item from the "London Daily Mail," July
5, 1954, suggests that Berlin is undergoing such a survey:

"Berlin is seeing saucers regularly. Allied officials
there are investigating the appearance of mysterious
flying objects over the city. German eyewitnesses
claim that a formation of three fast-moving objects
can regularly be seen whenever the sky over Berlin
is clear. The objects, described as 'small and disc-like,'
are said to appear between 10 and 11 P.M., at extremely high altitudes. American experts have inter-
rogated dozens of people, and a long flying-saucer
questionnaire is being drawn up to be filled out by
people who claim to have seen the objects."

It may be noted that, here again, there seems to be
a cover tactic. These visitants choose to appear in circumstances where they may be mistaken for something terrestrial: in this case, Soviet planes.

But the phenomena are world-wide. All the world's
great capitals are probably being surveyed by these mysterious visitants. I do not doubt that if one could obtain
such information, one would find that Moscow and Pekin,
too, are under saucer scrutiny.

When will the curtain go up on this tremendous drama?

Probably the answer is: when THEY choose, and not
otherwise; for THEY are clearly indifferent to what we
think, or feel.

Before we pass from this mysterious, or if one likes,
fantastic subject of mysterious subterranean noises, one
may ask: just *what* was the strange "something" that *came
out of the ground* at, or near Amiens, in northern France,
in the year 1769?

I cite a letter from Paris to London, in that year:

"One has a surprising account from Amiens, received in Paris, of a man and his wife and four horses

being killed while at work in the harvest field, by something which came out of the earth, and of which no trace was found afterwards; but only the smoaking (*sic*) hole from whence it issued. Two or three other people were struck down, but not much hurt. The surgeons have inspected the bodies of those who were killed, but did not discover the least wound, but only a considerable swelling and great deformity of the features. The woman, who was young and handsome, appeared a very shocking spectacle."

There are no volcanoes in France. And, in that year 1769, no earthquakes were reported.

Was the mysterious something anything like the phenomenon of the white light seen to descend from the sky at 9:30 P.M., in late summer or early autumn 1952, and vanish into the ground in a wooded hollow in the Chilterns?

The appearance of flying saucers similar to the comets in ancient Rome and again in the Middle Ages, has revived speculations and fears of death and judgment. Romans saw strange things in the sky and considered them portents from Saturn or Jupiter: "A thing like a bow stretched over the forum of Rome and the Temple of Saturn" (B.C. 173). "At Capua, the sky was all on fire and one saw figures there like ships," (B.C. 216). "In the sky over Hadria, Gulf of Venice, the strange spectacle of men in white robes standing round an altar" (B.C. 213).

In 1186, in England, "a cross of marvelous size in the sky, on which the monks and laity of the abbey of Dunstable saw Jesus Christ, fastened with nails and blood flowing, but not to the ground." (*Gesta Regis Henrici Secundum*). Time after time, from the twelfth to the sixteenth century in many countries of Western Europe and England, crosses red or white were seen in the sky.

It may be that, in times of confusion, violent emotions, or acute fears do, as W. H. Hudson said of a hacienda on the Uruguayan pampas, photograph themselves in the sky or on the landscape, and a strange visual image is seen. But it is not necessary therefrom, to conclude that they establish or confirm any religious dogmas or cults. Let those who conclude that these portents or phenomena, cosmic or otherwise, demonstrate some religious belief of their own, consider the ancient Romans. The latter had just as much ground for deeming a strange thing in the sky to have been sent by Jupiter or Saturn, as Christians have for concluding that flying saucers or space ships are the heralds and advance guards of the heavenly hosts in the march of Millennium. What they really proclaim is our profound ignorance of the strange powers of the mind of man.

An American lady advises me of a scientific "Paul" in the Middle West, whose vision of a flying saucer was for him like the apostle's on the road to Damascus. From "an atheist, he became a devout Christian." Names are not given to me:

> "An American scientist, up to June, 1953, working on a phase of the atomic bomb was, in that month, converted to the Christian faith. Prior to this he had been an atheist. Sitting in his automobile one day waiting for the traffic lights to change, he had a sudden visitation from an 'angel,' or a young man from another plane. From a ball of fire that enveloped his car, the 'angel' emerged and told this scientist that Christ was coming soon. The scientist is now a preacher."

Apart from the obvious question, who else, held by the traffic lights, saw this "red ball from the skies," one may suggest that all such experiences are subjective and reflect the impact paranormal or parapsychological, of tendencies created by, or arising from the disorientations following upon two insane world wars, with a third one coming.

I have another interesting letter from a lady living in a London suburb.

Her letter reminds me of a singular incident recorded in the medieval chronicle of Benedict of Peterborough. The phenomenon he spoke of has puzzled modern meteorologists who have tried to analyze it. It is really outside their category since it involves parapsychology.

In 1186 A.D., wrote Benedict, at:

> "the ninth hour of the day (2-3 P.M.), on August 9, 1186, at the village of Dunstable, the sky suddenly opened and the laity and clergy of the abbey saw a cross of marvelous size, on which appeared Jesus Christ fastened on with nails. His blood flowed to the earth. This vision lasted from 2 P.M. until midnight."

My correspondent tells of a similar phenomenon which she saw at Bath, Somerset, forty-six years ago, at a time when I myself was living in Gloucester, about thirty-five miles north:

"One day in the summer of 1908 (it may have been 1909 or 1910), I was out shopping in Bath, Somerset, with my sister. There was a severe thunderstorm and we had to take shelter for about an hour in the corridor of the Guild Hall. The claps of thunder were terrific; I have never heard the like. We came out into old Bond Street when the sun was shining. We saw people kneeling in the streets. Up in the sky, towards Wilson Street, there were inky black clouds with an enormous crucifix in the center and pink clouds above, and what looked to us like angel faces and wings. It was awe-inspiring and beautiful. There was an account of it in the papers of Bath at the time."

Note that the lady saw people on their knees in the streets. Was this a "photo"-parapsychological phenomenon, an imprint on the clouds of the acute fears and religious emotions of people agitated by the violent electrical storm?

Obviously this belongs in a category quite outside meteorology or physics.

Consider the following similar "photo-parapsychological" phenomena:

August 16, 1934: Reichbenbach, Prussia. It is reported that a swastika (the Nazi symbol) was clearly formed by white clouds in the sky over Reichenbach, on the day President von Hindenburg was buried. It was visible for some time. Large numbers of people saw it.

May 7, 1944: During an air raid alert at Ipswich, England, many people saw in the northern sky a perfect cross silhouetted against a blue-turquoise cloud. Some people declare they even saw there the figure of Christ with bowed head and crossed feet. The image formation lasted fifteen minutes. The Rev. H. Green, whose church was said to have been crammed to the doors, said the phenomenon was "God's call to the nation, and an omen of victory." He denounced a Londoner, who had written about it skeptically, as a vulgar scoffer.

Was this phenomenon caused by searchlights reflecting the image of an outdoor Calvary onto the sky? There may have been no such a thing as a Calvary in Ipswich. On the other hand, what particular "call" came "from the sky to man" when the swastika was seen over Reichenbach, Prussia?

Phenomena in a different category, relating to the flying-saucer mystery, seem to be linked with our Moon. To judge from the incidents recorded in various sources; including the records of the Royal Society of England in the eighteenth century, the moon may serve as a stop-over for non-terrestrial space ships.

What are the strange rays beamed out towards the earth by our Moon? Are these harmful to flying-saucer and space-ship entities? If so, have they devised means to insulate themselves against this harmful radiation? It seems likely that they have!

The late Sir James Jeans believed that the Moon radiated a harmful green ray. And, as the police have reason to know, insanity appears to have some connection with lunar phases. It is well known, too, to any who have lived in the West Indies, that one who sleeps exposed to the lunar rays may experience unpleasant effects. Lieutenant Burton, many years ago, said:

> "Many a careless Negro, after sleeping under the light of a full moon in the tropics, has risen to find that one half his face is by no means the same color as the other. Nor does this strange metamorphosis fade away with the moon. Many months must pass before both sides of that dark face are the same color once more."

It is likely that future moon-voyagers from our earth will have to reckon with this radiation. Not for nothing is insanity called *lunacy!*

The question still to be resolved, in view of the persistent elusiveness, or indifference of the space entities towards us earth-dwellers is:

Whence do they come?

They *may* come from some world on which human life, as we know it, would be impossible. Would life anything like ours be possible on a waterless, or near-waterless planet? Yet, in Arizona, where rain may not fall once a year, a rodent, the *jaculus jerboa,* synthesizes water by chemical action within its own body! It does so by combining hydrogen and oxygen, drawn from metallic oxides. And the Saharan explorer, Ossendowski, reports a species of large black beetle, which synthesizes water from elements in the atmosphere.

It seems, at least *a priori,* unlikely that in an infinite

cosmos of worlds without end that such a chemico-physical synthesis would occur only on our own earth.

I would like at this point to cite a number of other mysteries, some of which appear to be associated with flying-saucer activities:

August 13, 1954: In an area of two square miles near Chiangi airport, Singapore, every man, woman and child has found *his and her eyes raining tears!* The phenomenon is not confined to the outdoors, but occurs indoors as well. Doctors are baffled. No cause can be found for it. The British R.A.F. deny that planes have anything to do with the mysterious lachrymation. What is it? Are saucers or space ships, far aloft, engaged on mysterious experiments? *If* so, for what purpose?

August 16, 1954: In the Breckland area of England, snakes are behaving queerly. They enter houses, and those species which are oviparous are laying eggs in the houses.

Here follows a phenomenon occurring both in Great Britain and in the United States, which I think has been wrongly attributed to saponaceous detergents in brooks and streams. Rather, flying-saucer activities, involving the siphoning of water from lakes and streams in Canada and England, may be the amazing explanation. This raises the question: (1) Are certain types of saucers using terrestrial water as a source of propulsion; (2) Are some sending "tanks" to siphon water for transportation to unknown arid or waterless worlds in space?

August 16, 1954: At noon, people along the Thames between Twickenham and Putney saw strange, globe-shaped objects racing across the sky in thousands. Dr. Marshall Hardy, an angler, said the objects were merely detergents and soap-suds which had reached the Thames from factories and houses, and had been whipped up by the wind.

Hardy will have to explain, or explain away, the following incidents:

April 10, 1953: At Grafton, West Virginia, the water department could not account for the mysterious loss of water during the night, from their reservoirs. Three times the water-level dropped several inches, as

though a fire hydrant had been turned on full-cock.
The police were baffled. Later, a saponaceous-appear-
ing scum was found in a river in the region. The
scum—which analysis showed was not a soap or
detergent-matter—turned black in a glass, and in a
warm room.

October 15, 17, 18 and 20, 1953: A similar whitish
substance or bubbling scum was found in widely
separated rivers and fishing-streams and lakes in
England, often remote from towns and factories,
houses or laudries. Analysis indicated no soap or
detergent origin.

August 28, 1954: The Wharfedale (England) Rural
Council cannot solve the mystery of the loss of a
million gallons of water at a local reservoir. Meters
and mains have been tested and have been found in
order.

I may again refer to the fact that on July 2, 1950,
men working in the mines of the Steep Rock Iron Company, of northern Ontario, saw a flying saucer over the
lake nearby. In it were small beings, said to be under
four feet, covered in a sort of armor. They were hosing
water from the lake into a hatch on top of their disc.
Local fishermen found a fluorescent green scum on the
water. Dead fish floated on the surface where the green
scum had been left.

One may suggest a solution to this mystery: Have the
people of West Virginia and those of the English counties
seen flying saucers in their region?

Has the following incident any connection with the
number of mysterious fires in Oregon, in July, 1947; in
California, in 1950; and in England, in the summer of
1953? In every case mysterious objects had been previously reported in the skies. Investigation showed no
evidence of human arson.

Phenomena of this sort go back to the eleventh century
in England, when towns, and villages and woods, and
standing crops were destroyed by "wyld fire," falling
from the skies twice in 1067. Gaimar recorded a strange
object that descended from the sky, produced a conflagra-
tion and then *returned into the sky!* As it did so, it rotated. Says Gaimar, in his "Lestorie des Engles Solum."

"Coming from Normandy, some people in a ship
perished in the sea in the English Channel. . . . A
fire flamed and burned fiercely in the air. It came

near the earth, and for a little time quite illuminated it. After, it revolved, ascended on high, and then descended into the bottom of the sea. In several places, it burned woods and plains. In Northumberland, this fire showed itself in two seasons of the year."

Lycosthenes (Greek name assumed by the German professor Conrad Wolffhart), writing in 1567, recalled having seen at Erfurt, Prussia, in 1520 A.D.:

"A wonderful burning beam of light of great size. It suddenly appeared in the sky, fell on the ground and destroyed many places. It then revolved, turned round and ascended into the sky, where it put on a circular form."

Then there is the mysterious fire that, on September 13, 1954, killed an infant in a harvest field near Babworth, England:

"The eighteen-months-old baby, Peter Halickij, was placed in his push-chair by his father, who built an enclosure of bales of straw to keep the baby out of mischief while he was working. Suddenly the whole enclosure burst into flames. When the father and other harvest workers rushed up, the great heat forced them back. When they did reach him, the poor baby was dead." (*London News-Chronicle.*)

Let my readers compare the above incidents, separated by 887 and 434 years, and make their own deductions. Again, one would ask: Had any saucer or mysterious sky phenomena been previously observed in this quiet rural region of Babworth?

Far north in Alaska, a lonely range of mountains encircles Lake Iliamna. Nearby is an airfield. The following was cabled to Seattle, Washington, September, 1954:

"What causes the mysterious brilliant light in these mountains forty-five miles from the Iliamna airfield? Several nights the airfield sentries have been startled by a light of tremendous brilliance suddenly shining in the mountains. Commissioner Holdsworth, of the Territorial Mines Commission, says it is not any emanation from uranium mines. The Alaskan Indians say it is 'chacyuk' (ghosts). Two planes have crashed in the area."

Has this light anything to do with a hostile and elusive flying saucer? Who *yet* knows?

I end this chapter of mysteries with a strange story of the aftermath of Hiroshima. It has been theorized, in the United States, that one of the reasons for the flying-saucer eruption is that they have been drawn here by blast effects in the ethers of space from atomic and hydrogen bombing:

"A respectable business man, Rotarian, and member of the Buddhist community, one Tabamura, had a dream which, when he woke he told his startled wife. A stranger, who identified himself by name and address, said he had been killed in Hiroshima, nine years ago. The ghost pleaded that Tabamura disinter his body from a grave in the Hatchobori area, in the epicenter of the atomic blast. 'Only my skeleton remains, but the traffic gives me no rest in death.' Tabamura went to the police, who would have repulsed him with jeers had he not been so reputable. They agreed to check on the details given by the ghost in the dream, and found that there was a missing victim of the name and address given. Three laborers dug at the indicated spot and found a male skeleton." (*Collated from Tokyo newspapers and the Melbourne Herald, of September 12 and 13, 1954*).

Before I close this chapter, I return to the mysterious and disquieting phenomena of the breaking of glass in cars, and falling of mysterious objects from the skies in the United States. Concerning the stuff that fell onto, and set a road on fire in California, my friend, Mr. Ed. Worthley of Denison, Texas, visited the place and, at my request, reported what he found.

"Those pellets which set the asphalt road afire, near San Mateo, California, have been analyzed as *pig iron*."

Well, at least *pig iron* is manufactured and not meteoric! But one may still be puzzled how *pig iron* could have generated such a fire.

He adds:

"Strangely enough, a few days following this fire, the water mains in this same San Mateo region broke, and for hours streets and highways were flooded. The explanation was—just 'faulty valves'. . . . But much stranger is this: Two boys were riding bicycles in Milbrae, near San Mateo. They were not riding together, nor did they know each other; yet they suffered similar injuries at about the same time, 4 P.M. Neither could remember how the accidents occurred, or what happened just before the accidents. Both suffered head injuries and one was injured in other parts of his body. One of the two bicycles was smashed."

Just ordinary accidents, reader?
Mr. Worthley adds this:

"One of the boys said he had pedalled off to investigate *a mysterious sound like a shot*. And when he did not return his friends looked for him and found him injured. It sounds very suspicious to me, but proves nothing."

Or, as the old English monk, John Lydgate said, more than 550 years ago:

> "Straunge thynges ther be,
>   On lond, in sea."

What, or who made that mysterious sound like a shot?

THE NIHILISM OF THE OFFICIAL SCIENTISTS

Say it with guns, and bombs and bells.
    Shout round the world from pole to pole:
"Man is a beast without a soul."

Lines sent by the author of this book, to the late Senator Miles Pointdexter, of Virginia, from a hell corner in Kent, in war year 1943.

MOST PEOPLE ARE SURPRISED to hear that flying-saucer phenomena are as old as written history, and may ante-

date Egyptian hieroglyphs and cuneiform script. Certainly,
they go far back to the Roman annalists of the third and
fourth centuries, B.C. Livy, who died in A.D. 17, drew
from these lost records. Of his 140 encyclopaedic books
only thirty-five have survived. With those lost 115 books,
there must have been swept into oblivion a great corpus
of annals of strange, paranormal and phenomenal events,
records of strange things seen in the skies of Western
Europe, Africa and Asia.

In our sixteenth, seventeenth and eighteenth centuries,
academic skeptics, in those ages of dawning experimental
science, and prose and reason, censured Livy for "vulgar
notions and superstitious tales." Such tales also fill the
pages of the blackletter volumes of Conrad Wolffhart (or
Lycosthenes), professor of grammar and dialectics at
Basel, in 1559, and of his whimsical and tongue-in-cheek
successor, the late Charles Fort, of New York, who had
never even heard of Lycosthenes.

These were the stories about milk, flesh and blood
falling from the skies of old Rome. And they fell again,
1,000 years later, in Ireland; and many times in the nineteenth century of our own era.

Livy was also censured for speaking of changes of sex
in men and women. But this is now well recognized in the
psychopathology of modern medicine and surgery. In
1954, it was recognized by English High Court judges
as a valid ground for divorce. Livy said: "I record only
what have made indelible impressions on the minds of
my countrymen."

So time and history have their revenges. Science has
been forced to acknowledge the reality and existence of
derided phenomena. But, as some of us know, the lesser
breeds of scientists remain more obscurantist toward the
advance of scientific thought than are the priests of the
cloth.

Another enlightened old Roman who fared even worse
than Livy was the Roman consul, Varro, who took all the
knowledge of his day for his province. He put it into 500
volumes, *all* of which are lost, except some fragments.
These strongly suggest that Varro recorded great cataclysms in the remote past of the earth which annihilated
civilizations, but of which nothing save traditions and
strange monuments survive deep in central Brazilian jungles. He also recorded strange phenomena in the skies.

Cicero commended Varro for his erudition, and he was
no mean judge. St. Augustine, who preserved tantalizing
fragments, said of Varro: "I wonder how Varro, who read

so many books, found time to compile so many. Then, how he, who compiled so many volumes, found time to read such a vast variety of books and gain such great literary information."

"If these flying saucer phenomena are as old as·history, as you say," I am asked by a somewhat brash American gentleman (a by-no-means, altogether-to-be despised compiler of scissors and paste columns in a certain popular magazine), "how do you reconcile with this assertion your theory that these visitants of the remote past have come to this planet, since 1945, because they have been attracted here by our explosion of atomic and hydrogen bombs?" He further makes the exceedingly silly point— for which he has no shadow of proof—that, in the vast universe, including our solar system, the odds *against* anything human, or even humanoid, existing on any world but ours are astronomically great!

There is, today, a greater awareness of paranormal phenomena, and of extraordinary events of a cosmic nature, not to be explained away as something else, or as hallucinations, etc. Our whole world, having become one vast sounding-board and picture screen what is said or seen, one day, on sea, land, or in the sky, in China, Alaska or Kamchatka, or Patagonia will, an hour or so later, be known in faraway Cincinnati, Chester, Oslo, Iceland or Timbuktu. Among these events are those demonstrably proving that vast space ships, and the satellite discs called flying saucers, not only in units, but in fleets and squadrons, have quartered every land and sea, and surveyed our whole globe from pole to pole.

Why are these elusive and coldly indifferent aeroforms here in such increasing numbers? Why has the tempo of these strange and highly disturbing incidents so considerably increased?

The answer is that man, in 1945, started to use a force so devastating that it has the potential and cosmoplastic power to turn his earth into a flaming nova, and affect the whole solar system. By the appalling etheric upheaval he can set up, he can gravely affect fourth-dimensional worlds in space, whose existence he may accept in theory, and deride in fact. It is from these fourth-dimensional worlds, perhaps the doubles of visible planets, that some of these space ships come.

(But there are others which appear to be third-dimensional, and of our own order of matter.)

The fourth-dimensional beings really are there! It does not matter whether one calls them "Etherian beings," or as Blake might have done: "Mister Nobodaddies." To deny their existence is *not* to disprove them. "They" do not care who is right or wrong in this earth. They are indifferent and coldly disinterested in our -isms and our -ologies. They intend, in certain American opinion, to keep man from disrupting the solar system, and are prepared to do so, even if they have to take over and run our entire planet.

Since the late 1930's, our scientists have reduced matter to an unknowable and unpredictable noumenon about which your senses can tell you nothing certain. Bertrand Russell has concluded: All scientific theory is a matter of statistics. Some probability, but not certainty. "The wave which has nothing to wave in."

The most luminous of scientific intelligences has, at best, only a dim notion of the extent of the tremendous forces he has begun to unleash in the nucleus of the atom. Underlying the atom may be—probably *is!*—a *sub-atomic world*. So far, even the most powerful atomic bomb, detonated by militarist-physicists, blind servants of the anonymous forces of finance and power, including the most totalitarian of all so-called Christian churches (they are one and the same) have barely touched one-tenth per cent of the forces locked up in the atomic nuclei of the isotope of Uranum, U-235.

There is now said to be an even more Satanic weapon than the atom or even the hydrogen bomb—the L-bomb! It is at least a thousand times more effective than the H-bomb and, alas, it is much cheaper to make!

Since, in the United States, and probably in England, little or nothing is known about this L-bomb, I here give details which will be new to all except the "back room boys," and even unknown to some of them. The L in the L-bomb stands for Lithium.

Lithium is the lightest metal known, a soft, silvery element of the alkali group. It is usually obtained by electrolyzing fused chloride. It is believed that it was first found feasible for use as a bomb by the Austrian physicist, Hans Thirring, who later took refuge in Argentina. He created the first lithium hydride bomb.

This was exploded about January, 1953, by the Russians in the neck of the peninsula of Kamchatka. Its blast caused a major earthquake which actually "dented" the earth. The seismic wave it set up travelled several times round the globe.

When triggered off by an atomic explosion, both the elements in lithium hydride appear to pass fairly easily through a fusion process with the mass of lithium hydride in itself acting as a *tamper*. Like clay tamped into a blast-hole, it gets out the full force of the explosion.*

Lithium hydride is cheap and available in large quantities. Therefore, the number of L, or lithium-bombs is limited only by the number of atomic bombs available as detonators. Since the critical mass necessary to detonate the L-bomb has been reduced to about ten pounds, and the uranium isotope, 235, and plutonium are now produced by the ton, the L-bomb production is only too ample. It is calculated that Russia is now producing them at the rate of more than 1,000 a year.

Here are some words from an American engineer friend of mine:

> The Hiroshima bomb, equivalent to 20,000 tons of TNT which was the high explosive of World War I; Nagasaki, the first plutonium bomb, 40,000 tons TNT equivalent; Eniwetok type, 120,000 tons, TNT equivalent; weight of the Hiroshima and Nagasaki bombs was five tons; weight of the latest type of Eniwetok lightweight bombs is half a ton. Thus the weight has been cut to less than one-tenth. Hydrogen bomb, 500,000 tons, TNT equivalent; "L," or Lithium super-bomb, 13-14,000,000 tons, TNT equivalent. As of spring 1954, portable bombs, under ten tons weight, would create an explosion of 1,500,000,000 TNT equivalent!

One "L" bomb exploded over London would leave all that mighty metropolis a crater. Exploded between Liverpool and Manchester it would annihilate both cities. I will leave my mathematically inclined readers to figure out

---

* *Lithium:* Atomic number, 3; atomic weight, 6.940. Boiling point 1336° C., plus or minus 5° C. Melting point 178-186° C. Rather rare element often associated with petalite, lepidolite, (lithium mica) deposits in Montana, Manitoba, Sweden, France, Spain, Saxony, Bohemia, Namaqualand and the Karabib region of Southwest Africa. Also found in amblygonite form in California and South Dakota, Saxony, Bohemia, etc. It will be noted that some of these countries are "behind the Iron Curtain."

In metallic form, lithium is the lightest known solid substance. When heated in hydrogen gas, it forms lithium hydride which, when subjected to electrolysis, gives up hydrogen at the anode, the first known instance of that element functioning as a negatively charged ion.

how many of these Satanic contraptions it would take to destroy the British Isles. Since the Russians have a lead of two years in "L" bomb production, one may visualize the effect on certain American official scientists on learning this! Or the effect on the fire-eating politicians—those who are not as *dumb* as they are blustering poltroons? Will it enforce second thoughts on them when they contemplate, like Mark Twain's Yankee, at the court of King Arthur, on getting in a blow "fust." For the "fust" will also be their last, *and* ours!

It is believed that Russia has exploded at least thirty of these "L" bombs. That may be; for Russia, even in the days of the old Tsars, had some of the world's cleverest chemists, physicists and engineers. I well remember the engineer, P. P. Schilovsky (whom I met in 1924), inventor of the gyro-motor car, and the mono rail system with one-girder bridges.

It is likely that Russia has today some of the most powerful turbines in the world, and operational planes that in the U.S., have not even got beyond the stage of "thinking about them." However, not even Russia, to say nothing of the United States or Britain, will say another word about the "L" bomb.

No wonder, then, that these "mutant" aeroforms, and others *not* so mutant, from other worlds in space, are so plaguily busy in our skies! Some of us will be blowing the angels, wings, feathers and all, out of the skies, if *THEY* do not throw a cosmic monkey-wrench into our terrestrial wheels.

In the thermo-fusion-nuclear, or hydrogen bomb, the blast forces and radioactivity are many thousand times greater than those of the atomic nuclear bomb. And the end of the reactions—meteorological and other—set off by its tests is almost certainly not yet in sight. In late May, 1954, protests of appalled physicists induced President Eisenhower to call off a projected explosion.

Yet this is but the beginning. The next step will be for the atomic physicists to play about with the *sub-atomic* particles. The deeper one goes into the layers of this "onion," the denser, and the greater are the colossal forces that will be released.

It is said—who can *know?*—that, within these innermost layers, or more intense waves and radiation, of what we may crudely call energy-mind-stuff, the fourth-dimensional entities have their being. They are, it is said, also approached and disturbed by sonic barrier-passing, terrestrial aeroforms, which set up stresses in the ether of space.

Consequently, there have been reactions in the air, and on the land. "Manifest nonsense, or balderdash" or not, the British Government has thrice been forced to ground Comet jet liners. The causes of the recurring disasters to these are now, July, 1954, theorized by investigators to be "structural weaknesses, or metal fatigue, in the highly pressurized fuselages." Only that and nothing more, and "we shall see them back in the air by the end of 1954":

June 1, 1954: An official of the British Ministry of Civil Aviation tells the "London Daily Mail," that, *à propos* of a statement in a book by a former retired officer of the U.S. Marines, that an unidentified flying body hit and caused the crash of a British Comet jet airliner, at Dum Dum airport, Calcutta, on May 2, 1953: "Neither we nor the Air Ministry stated that the Comet crash at Calcutta might have been caused by an unidentified flying body coming into collision with it. It is utter balderdash."

Is that so? This is the official quibble which is more unmanly than *a downright lie.* Consider the following:

May 2, 1953: A British Comet jet airliner met disaster soon after taking off from Calcutta airdrome. Its speed was 500 miles an hour. Suddenly, it caught fire, disintegrated and crashed. The wreckage was strewn over a wide area. An investigator sent from London, Mr. J. H. Lett, of the British Ministry of Civil Aviation, said that he found that the airliner broke up in the air after striking some heavy and unknown body.

Subsequently, on November 17, 1953, an American paratroop plane, over Fort Bragg, North Carolina, hit an "invisible body" in the air, crashed and killed fifteen men. The survivors stated that the plane "hit something in the air, sounding like two automobiles in collision."

I leave my readers to make their own comments on this British official, and on the "public-spirited" newspaper which was (or its desk-men were) either too timid, or too lazy to look up the facts in its own files.

In this chapter, however, I am more particularly concerned with the highly dangerous reactions following upon the explosions of atomic and hydrogen bombs. If we do not approach the brink and topple into the abyss of cataclysm, it may be not because we lack destructive folly. It will be because of an enforced halt in our "progress" towards a red and sightless hell of another kind than was envisaged by Oscar Wilde in his "Ballad of Reading Gaol."

February, 1951: After five tremendous explosions of "super-atomic" bombs in one of the deserts in Nevada, it was reported, in both London and Paris, that a radioactive cloud was shortly afterwards detected 13,500 feet up over the Puy de Dôme laboratory, Central France. By the third and fourth atomic explosion, Geiger counters showed that the activity of this cloud had greatly intensified. Professor Garrigue said there "was no danger."

All I wish myself to say is that more than half England was waterlogged and the threat to food was serious. Right on the heels of these explosions, the barometer here in Kent and in Gloucester, at the opposite side of England, fell steeply and abnormally. It was exactly what happens in the China Sea before the coming of a typhoon!

Far away in Alaska, at the same time, the weather was, as a resident there air-mailed me: "Terrific. Never the like known!"

Garrigue may say "no danger," but the Alaskan people think very differently! Late in March, I took a train trip to Gloucester. At 2:30 in the afternoon, a black mist turned day into night. Near Didcot the track, waterlogged, sank under a landslide. Ten days later, revetments and walls of a tunnel were bulging with the weight of the waterlogegd soil overhead.

Let official scientists say there "is no danger." The ordinary man and woman *knows* better! Such insane playing with unknown forces and chain reactions must calamitously affect the weather!

If this happens after five explosions of American atomic bombs, what will be when these diabolical weapons are lobbed by tens and hundreds in a world war?

Numerous meteorological, tectonic, and geophysical phenomena in the years 1952 to 1954 might lead some to theorize that visitants from outer space, with a very advanced science, have been drawn here on investigations of their own. History has shown that often, in the last

3,000 years, these elusive visitants have come to spy on the earth. Fantastic beings to us, they may have a code of ethics and morality not ours. In a cosmic sense, they may be beyond good and evil, in the phrase of the almost forgotten Prussian philosopher and poet, Friedrich Nietzsche.

Let us summarize some of the more striking of these global incidents and phenomena:

October 8, 1952: More than a hundred tons of rock crash off the 4,995 feet high Monte Leone, in south Switzerland. The entire side of the mountain is crumbling.

1953: A subtropical weather line is creeping northwards. One American meteorologist predicts that North America may presently know only two seasons: summer and winter.

Mysterious double explosions and a shock-wave sweep the Medway, Kent, killing one man and injuring another. No sonic barrier-passing plane was up, but at Shorne, near Gravesend, fifteen miles away, a "paroxysm of light" was seen in the noon sky, and was followed by two violent blasts. A trench caved in, killing a man in it, and shaking villages for miles around.

Three weeks later, at Islington, strange reverberations and noises, like those of an earthquake, scared people who rushed into streets in night attire. Six days later, December 23, at 3:38 P.M., a mysterious and violent explosion shook south and west London. The police remain baffled.

1954: A sea of mud rolls down the hills of Sierra Madre, South California, causing 8,000 people to fly in terror. The hip-high slime could not be dammed. Fire had denuded the mountains of their forest cover and abnormal rains followed. These coincided with hydrogen bomb explosions in the Pacific, lasting three days.

An east-west air current, moving at 300 miles an hour, altitude 40,000 feet, and 400 miles wide, sweeps across the United States.

British atomic experts plan new device to trigger off hydrogen bomb at Woomera, Australian desert range.

Four inches of rain fall in five hours in Santa Monica, California.

About forty miles from London, a very hush-hush

underground citadel, invisible from the air, has been built for "safety" in future H- and A-bomb explosions. Scientists said to have been taken there "in blinkers." (If *official*, surely the scientists did not need them?)

Strontium, made radioactive, is expected to produce a cheaper and better bomb than even the Satanic cobalt bomb. Since vegetable and animal life react strongly to strontium, in two weeks, it is claimed, strontium dust dropped from planes would annihilate all life in the area. (Present use for strontium is in fireworks, flares and paints).

The National Trust of Scotland has lost £26,000 by the devastation of woods and forests attributable to hydrogen bombs, detonated either in Russia or the Pacific. These are believed to have caused a tornado in North and Highland Scotland, and great floods and breaches of sea-walls and dykes in eastern England.

Ash from the Bikini explosion was so strongly radioactive, it registered on a Geiger counter three yards away. (*Tokyo University*) Twenty-eight Americans and 236 Marshall Islanders were contaminated by this ash. Standing for one hour near a trawler carrying radioactive fish, proved fatal. Fishing crews burned by it infected others.

Stated that hydrogen bomb, exploded at Bikini, in April or May, 1954, is equivalent to fifty megatons (fifty million tons) of TNT. Effects would force evacuation of cities hundreds of miles from blast center.

Shock-waves of the Bikini explosions were felt 176 miles away.

Abnormally high radioactivity found in surface snow in Winnipeg, four times greater than any previously measured.

Professor Hermann Oberth, inventor of the Nazi V-2 rocket, says that by 1955, a hydrogen-rocket-bomb can reach any part of the world in forty-five minutes. He is corroborated by W. S. Cole of the U.S. Atomic Energy Committee.

Nevertheless, a heavenly British professor, Otto Frisch, says the air, sea, or earth cannot catch fire when an H-bomb is exploded, nor will any radioactivity come down. Frisch must be interested in a new soothing syrup factory. His optimism is *not* shared by British "working stiffs," who in the Forest of Dean, threaten to strike if atomic waste is dumped into disused coal pits in that national park area.

I give special mention to the item following:

March 23, 1954: Dr. Eugen Sänger, well known rocket expert who formerly worked for the German government, has developed "the Sänger Project," whereby a piloted and manned rocket-bomber plane can reach any part of the globe within seventy-five minutes, and return to its point of departure in the same time. According to the "Interavia Journal," Sänger estimated the cost at about ten billion (*sic*) dollars. This colossal sum, says "Interavia," could be raised without great difficulty by either Russia or the United States.

It is said that Russia is developing a giant rocket with a thrust of 118 tons, at sea level. Some of the work has been carried out at the Khimki rocket station, near Moscow. This rocket, it is said, could carry an atomic warhead over a distance of 900 to 1,000 miles in thirty minutes.

Switzerland is also said to have built a manned rocket plane.

I continue my summary of our new and *far* better age:

1954: The sixth Earl Nelson, in England, warns that winds distributing radioactive dust could infect cattle thousands of miles away. When "we learn to split the atoms of oxygen and hydrogen and lighter metals, we can destroy all the people of the earth in 1 millionth of a second."

No one, so far, has attempted to estimate the probably serious effect on health of the future use of atomic power and radiation in industry, apart from war uses.

British, New Zealand and Australian governments warn that H- and A-bombs exploded over the sea, will induce very dangerous radioactivity in the sodium and chloride contents of salt water for over thousands of miles.

Sound waves, travelling the 8,000 miles from the Pacific to Britain through solid rock, in less than one hour, are recorded on delicate barographs.

Mysterious black ash rains down on New York state. Comes from the west in large black curls, quite unlike soot or smoke.

Nehru, Premier of India, warns that even *before any world war*, the hydrogen bomb can cause uncontrollable and devastating effects.

Bigger yet, H-bombs are promised by America's Atomic Energy Commission. (One may be sure that their effects will *not* be shut in behind the closed doors so favored by martinet Admiral Strauss and his Congressional friends.)

"Red Star," Moscow, described the explosion of a Russian H-bomb as comparable to the impact of the million-ton aerolite that devastated the Stony Tunguska region of North Siberia in 1908, whose flash was seen 750 miles away.

The United States admits that the H-bomb at Eniwetok *got out of control*.

The three items following may be singled out:

April, 1954: In New York, Civil Defense chiefs are dismayed by disclosures of the effects of hydrogen-bomb explosions at Eniwetok, Marshall Islands. All within a three-mile radius would be annihilated; destruction within seven miles would be severe, and would extend, though with diminishing force, as far as ten miles. If detonated near Washington, D.C., the White House, the Capitol and all main government buildings would have been destroyed.

A fire ball 3½ miles in diameter was created. The coral island on which the explosion took place disappeared. Big blocks were bitten off two adjacent islands. A crater a mile wide and 175 feet deep was blasted out. In ten minutes, the radioactive cloud climbed ten miles high, and spread out a hundred miles. Yet this bomb was called "not really *the* bomb, but only a 'device'!"

"Going down into shelters is obsolete. Evacuation of populations is all we can do." (Mr. Herbert O'Brien, New York Civil Defense chief). Well, a large part of *any* population will "evacuate" any way, if it knows that "peace-making" gentlemen are about to unloose, or already have sent this super-civilizing device their way!

April 2, 1954: Mr. Herbert Morrison, deputy leader of the British Labor Party, informs the House of Commons that he has been told the Russians are developing *nitrogen* bombs even bigger and far "better" than the others.

(*Author's Comment:* Hasn't anyone told Mr. Morrison about the L-bomb—better than either—which Russia, but not the United States, already has.)

The Japanese Maritime Safety Board alleges that twenty-three fishermen injured by a radioactive ash fallout from an American hydrogen bomb, were in a ship nineteen miles outside the danger zone. Their blood-count has fallen sharply. The Diet in Tokyo demands international control of A-bomb and H-bomb production and use. All the tuna fish of another ship were found radioactive and were destroyed after the blast of a bomb which Admiral Strauss of the U.S. Navy says was twice as devastating as scientists expected.

When the leucocytes (white corpuscles in the blood) drop in number, after exposure to radioactivity, medicine ceases to have any effect.

Tokyo twice alleges that radioactive dust falls fortnightly on Japan from the *direction of Siberia*.

Prof. Tzusuku (medical faculty of Tokyo University), found that the Japanese fishermen had lesions of a form of dermatitis never seen before. He urged, at a Geneva Red Cross conference, that the H- and A-bombs be banned to prevent wholesale destruction of peoples. Nehru, of India, demanded at New Delhi, the immediate cessation of all H-bomb explosions.

I continue my summary of our brave new world, whose population of scientific "lunatics" must be very large or whose official toadies appear to count the whole world well lost, if such destruction gains them titles and offices. Perhaps, if the spook of Huxley is glancing back from the world of shades, he may now think that, after all, it was just as well that the Unnameable and Unknowable did not grant him the longer years he so ardently desired:

1954 (April and onwards): Sweden builds tunnels under deep lakes and high mountains and in vast caverns to shelter civilians and defense and radar staffs. These subterraneans are fitted with dockyards and airdromes, one under a huge cliff, and 120 feet high. Ships may enter it from the Baltic. It is hydrogen-bombproof. Her nationals have done very well, indeed, out of two world wars, so she has plenty of kroner to spend on jeeps to tow planes into the works, via long tunnels.

(*Comment:* History repeats itself, as in the legends of the Patagonians and Alaskans, that far, far away and long ago, after a great catastrophe, people had to live for years in great tunnels.)

President Eisenhower assures TV listeners that the United States will never use the H-bomb in war. He meant that it is a deterrent against the other rascal's use of it.

Storm in the British House of Commons when Sir Winston Churchill points out that ex-Premier, Socialist Attlee, sold out British right to be consulted by the United States before the A- or H-bombs be used against third parties. Attlee, like a prudent politician, left the world mystified about what actually did happen. He demanded that no documents be divulged. So, if someone *was* sold down or up the river, we shall never now know.

Eisenhower says that no bigger H-bomb will be made by the United States.

Man and wife injured on highway near Mt. Shasta, California, by blue-green phosphorescent snow—after Nevada A-bomb blast. No physician can find a cure for the blister and skin-disease so caused.

I again single out two items:

April 8, 1954: The "N. Y. Times" (Mr. W. L. Lawrence, science editor), says that the cobalt-hydrogen bomb was detonated at Eniwetok, Marshall Islands, on March 1 and 26. The cobalt shell, unlike the steel shell which becomes only "mildly radioactive" on vaporizing, is transformed into a deadly radioactive cloud, 220 times more powerful than radium. It travels with the wind over thousands of miles, annihilating all life in its path. If exploded from a ship in mid-Pacific, the cloud would travel towards and over all North America.

Radioactive poisoning of the atmosphere and annihilation of all life on the earth are now technically possible. Lawrence added what may be a pious opinion that nowhere in the world could such a Satanic weapon be tested.

April 9, 1954: Professor Leo Szilard, of Chicago University, estimates that 400 deuterium-cobalt bombs, each weighing one ton, would discharge enough radioactivity to annihilate all life on earth.

I proceed—still in April, 1954:

Coventry Town Council, England, decides that hydrogen bombs make civil defense waste of time and money. So Home Secretary Maxwell-Fyfe steps in and runs the city's C.D. himself, at the taxpayers' expense.

Sir Edward Appleton, quite forgetting the experience of two world wars, declares cheerily that H- and A-bombs will forever stop war.

Snow and ice block roads in the Apennines. Italians blame H-bombs for the worst spring in living memory.

British Air Marshal, "Bomber Harris," poses the question: "Who dropped the first bomb in air war?" *Answer:* In 1848, the Austrian Imperial Army dropped bombs from hot-air balloons over Venice. In 1911, the Italians dropped them from airplanes upon Arabs at Benghazi, North Africa. In 1914, the Germans threw out bombs from early planes over the Vosges mountains, nine days after the First World War began. A week later, the British Royal Flying Corps dropped a bomb on grounded German planes, in the British retreat from Mons. So we "progress."

The United States tells Japan that no more American H-bombs will be let off after the end of June, 1954. Another Japanese fishing boat comes back from the Carolines and Marshall Islands with signs of radioactivity. India says that dust collected on the wings of Indian airliners proves radioactive. She ascribes it to American H-bomb explosions on April 6.

Radioactive snow in Italy, bitter gales of 110 miles an hour, landslides in mountains, collapse of building. Italian meteorological office denies that H- and A-bombs are to blame.

Abnormally cold and dry weather in England. Even in wet Westmoreland, streams run only in a trickle.

Craig Hosmer, formerly of the U.S. Atomic Energy Commission, says Russia stole a march on the United States with the first H-bomb.

In Britain, so much damage to houses has been caused by blast effects from sonic barrier-passing planes, that R.A.F. pilots are ordered to fly them over sea or moors.

April 13, 1954: Archbishop Dr. Garbett, of York, England, says: "The early Christians believed the end of the world was imminent . . . but the end they expected would have been owing to acts of God, not to man's sin and folly."

Professor Joseph Rotblat, physicist of St. Bartholomew's Hospital, London, shows TV audiences a map outlining destructive path of a heat-wave from a hydrogen bomb, dropped in Whitehall, London. It would blast Tilbury, Sevenoaks, Dorking and Windsor.

Probabaly interplanetary aerofoil enthusiasts will have noted that, in April, 1954, what is possibly a new source of energy for *terrestrial* space ships was discovered in the laboratory of the Bell Telephone Company of U.S. This is implied in the item following:

April 25, 1954: Thin strips of silicon, found in sand, have generated electricity when sunshine strikes them. A battery has been made, the size of a man's hand, that when held up to the sky, generates enough electricity to operate a pocket radio. A voice transmitted over this radio has been picked up many yards away. (*Bell Telephone Laboratories, U.S.*)

Yet another step in progress seems implicit in what is below:

April 29, 1954: The Russians are said to have constructed a "two-stage, eighty-ton, super V-2," with a range of about 1,900 miles. A 97-ton "multistage rocket, with a range of 2,500 miles," is said to be under development, with German technicians' aid. It is also said that a Russian launching ramp can fire rocket-missiles at the rate of 800 an hour. If each one of these carried an H-bomb and was aimed at targets ten miles apart, England "could be destroyed in thirty-five to forty minutes"(!).

Soviet experimental aircraft, thirty-eight feet long and about 15,000 pounds in weight, are said "to have a maximum speed of 1,700 miles an hour at a height of about twenty miles. Test flying of experimental planes "of 2,500 miles an hour at about forty miles up, are said to be about to be carried out at Tomsk, Siberia."

Mr. Scott-Crossfield, American test pilot, has flown a Douglas sky-rocket plane—jet and rocket motor—at 1,320 miles an hour, at a height of about twelve miles over a Southern California desert. But it had to be carried halfway up by a big mother-plane before being released under its own power.

April, 1954, ended with the information that under a mountain, seventy miles from San Francisco, an abandoned railroad tunnel had been turned into an air-conditioned vault for valuables, against the Last Days when the H-bomb climaxes Progress. None seem to have reflected that, in that dire event, there will be transvaluation of *all* values *and* valuables.

Came May, 1954, and our old earth began again to quake with an intuition of wrath to come:

A crack, 600 feet deep, opens on the slopes of the Culebra Cut of the Panama Canal, and threatens to end in landslide of the entire hill.

In the Brenner Pass, in the Austrian Tyrol, fallen boulders cut the main railroad line from Italy.

At Nelson, England, a sudden wind-stream of hurricane force hurls a half-ton screen over the wall of a cricket-field. (The British Meteorological Office shuddered when impious people spoke of convection currents set up by H-bomb blast forces on the other side of the world.)

Lightning hurled laborer, Sam Armstrong, ten yards across a tile works at Prudhoe-on-Tyne, England. Man who rushed to his aid got a "hell of a shock," as he touched Sam's shoulder.

Phenomenal frosts ruin plum and cherry harvests in England. Prof. Powell, physicist of Bristol University, proclaimed that the tolling of the great deathbell of history was heard all over the world, and no birds sang when in the Pacific, a bomb 2,000 times more powerful than the Hiroshima world-ender, blasted out to the empyrean its Valkyrie music.

Cracks appear in the walls of the 1,800-year-old Colosseum in Rome, threatening its dissolution.

The worst weather known in a century, with floods and landslides, cuts off Cape Town from the rest of South Africa. Ships are caught up by Titan winds and hurled onto stony beaches off Table Bay; and even the 27,000 ton British liner "Capetown Castle" cannot dock.

All Italy swept by hurricanes; international express trains are held up by thunder and lightning; two locomotives struck by thunderbolts. Rich folk, fearing the end of all things, pack the churches to the doors, and the keepers of Italian casinos and purveyors for dope orgies of high society in Rome have a thin time. Temperature in Italy falls ten degrees below zero.

At this juncture on May Day, 1954, Uncle Sam cheers them all up by announcing that he has a new atomic gun firing explosives at least as powerful as those dropped in Japan, in 1945. Alas, again the fanatic world-enders raise their heads! The pastor of an Adventist sect proclaims over the radio and on billboards in California and Melbourne:

"The End of the World is near at hand, and whatever hath to be done hath better be done quickly."

I do not know exactly what this reverend gentleman deemed it expedient to do in this desperate case; but a cable I sent him, to which no reply came, caused me to enter in my diary what followeth:

My sporting offer to certain American newspaper prophets who have written me forecasting the end of the world, any time between 1954 and 1960, to relieve them of all unwanted bank balances and dangerous securities and valuables, without any demand for free fire and life insurance, has I regret to note, found no takers. I fear, therefore, that my pristine faith in their panic has been sadly shaken.

I wrote to one American gentleman: "Come, come, buddy, you appear to be backing the Horse of the Apocalypse both ways! Delay no longer. If it be fire you fear, then the filthy root of all evil 'must infallibly engulf you in the flames of Tophet. If it be water, then load not yourself below the Plimsoll line with what must certainly consign you to Davy Jones's Locker.' "

June, 1954, opens ominously all around the world:

More than twenty-two inches of rain revived second thoughts of another Great Deluge in Cape Town, South Africa. Farms and orchards became quagmires.

President Eisenhower says his scientists advise him of two new H- or A-bombs which are really *too* dangerous to explode.

Berlin newspapers allege that Russia has tested improved V-2 rockets in the Arctic breaking up vast ice-floes, which have drifted into the Atlantic and cooled the Gulf Stream.

British government admits that it blew off an H-bomb in the Montebello Islands, off the coast of

Australia. For years those islands will be dangerously radioactive, and anyone found there—vain hope?—will be given seven years in jail.

Five weeks after an H-bomb test in the Pacific, radioactive rain falls in Birmingham, England. Similar effects noted at British atomic factory of Windscale.

Worst snowfall in twenty years covers Griqualand and the Drakensberg range in South Africa.

Singular, light-grey rain, silky in texture, falls in Leicester, England.

The Marshall Islanders, in the Pacific, many of whom have suffered burns from drifting radioactive ash, petition the United Nations to stop H-bomb tests.

Worst storm ever known washes away roads and bridges in Iceland.

Raging flood-waters from the roaring Danube menace Austria; the Tyrolian mountains all aquake with landslides.

Another step in Progress has been recorded; except that the physicists are too modest to assess its possible use in accelerating a global *bouleversement:*

July 9, 1954: An atomic particle has been detected coming, it is believed, from outer space that speeds with an energy of 10,000 billion volts. The discovery was made by Dr. Marcel Schein of Chicago University. Dr. Robert Oppenheimer, atomic scientist, says: "The particle is trying to tell us something, if we could only understand it. No one knows what it really is, but it may throw new light on the nature of physics."

The particle was trapped in an aluminum pack of special photo-plates in a high altitude balloon over Texas last winter. It burst like a bullet penetrating a pack of cards and left behind a track of dots.

Some theorize that the particle may be an anti-proton, sought for years; and the contra, or negative force, in relation to the core of the hydrogen atom. In forcing a way through the photo-plates, it may be that this anti-proton came into collision with a proton and they annihilated each other.

At any rate, its velocity was far beyond anything so far known in nature, some 1,200,000 times faster than any particle accelerated by an atom-smashing device in a laboratory. It may indicate that, somewhere in the vast universe, matter is annihilated and transformed into energy.

July, 1954, opens with this cheer:

Floods rage all over western Austria. American soldiers stand by sirens, waiting to blast out warnings of collapsing dams, dykes and Danubian banks. In the Tyrol Alps roar the thunderous voices of landslides, amid the muted music of falling rain and snow. Thousands are homeless in Central Europe. Main railroad lines under water. Damage estimates run to over $30,000,000. Mass evacuation starts, aided by American and Russian troops. Balkan countries quake to see ruin and deluge coming down on them. Far away in Kansas and California, folk wilt under 110 degree temperatures. Stalingrad, Russia, has an intense heat wave.

(*Author's Comment:* As already stated in this chapter, we do not even yet know the price the world will have to pay for these thermonuclear experiments. Ever the toll mounts, while fools prate that "science only saves." No doubt it could; but we have the official Martian scientists to reckon with, and it is not *saving* they have in mind. As Shakespeare did *not* say: "A plague on your ideologies and freedoms!")

On rolls the Juggernaut of Progress:

Ten nations in five continents have been devastated by the "worst floods in history."

A veritable cataclysm and deluge falls on the North German plain as the Elbe bursts her banks. At Budapest, the Danube is twenty feet above normal.

In China, 1,500,000 volunteers fight the "worst flood China has ever known." In Tibet, the town of Gyantse is destroyed when Lake Balung bursts her banks.

In the United States, deluges sweep Richmond, Virginia, and ruin $20,000,000 worth of property. South Africa quails under appalling floods, while every steamer in tornado-swept Table Bay sends S.O.S. One British steamer loses twenty-three mooring ropes, worth £2,340, snapped by tidal waves in the docks. Landsliding mountain falls upon naval base at Simonstown.

In Hungary, large industrial town of Gyor hemmed

in by swirling flood-waters. Russian troops and Hungarian Army engineers blow up Hungarian dykes to draw off the water, but thereby flooding three other Balkan countries.

Author's Comment: Like a Valkyrie dirge sounds the warning: "The end of the hydrogen bomb explosion devastations may not even yet be in sight over the world!"

July 22, 1954: United States Defense chiefs say they believe that, by 1960, or even 1958, Russia will be able to send H-bomb rockets from Moscow to New York. These V-2 type rockets may have war-heads of the H-type, accurate over a range of 5,000 miles. The Pentagon, at Washington, D.C., says these Russian weapons will be the ultimate in striking power.

August 5, 1954: Ex-Major-General Walter Dornberg, head of the Nazis' V-2 rocket project, clearly not a man to care a damn about the devastating effects of any project on which he may be engaged—tells the "London Daily Telegraph," that in the establishment of the Bell Aircraft Corporation in the United States, he has blue-printed a new bomber plane with a speed of fourteen times that of sound (say, 10,000 miles an hour, near sea level). It will be launched from a carrier plane at an altitude of about sixteen miles. After detachment, the pilot will accelerate to maximum speed, using a rocket-motor, and climb to an altitude of thirty miles. As this bomber cannot turn, its residual velocity, or momentum, will take it on a straight line to a base even 10,000 miles away. On its way, it will scatter twelve-ton bombs, demonstrating what some American politicians and British militarists mean by the *higher* civilization.

Be it noted that, by July 17, 1954, repeated Austrian and German broadcasts roundly asserted that the excessive rains and catastrophic floods were the direct result of American H-bomb explosions in the Pacific. But who *knows* what "beneficial" experiments of this type have synchronously been conducted by Russia? It is also asserted, and not only by Communist organs and radios, that the Adenauer Government has spent so much money on armaments, that it has none for dams and other flood controls:

August 2, 1954: The East and West Lyn Rivers in England suddenly rose four feet after ten hours of rain. Two years before, thirty-one people had lost their lives in floods. A tornado ripped roofs off houses and killed people in Dakar, West Africa. In East Pakistan, India, vast areas are under floods from the river Brahmaputra and affluents. Dacca's fruit market has been swept away in a deluge, and in Northern Bihar, cholera and malaria are rife. Tens of thousands homeless.

August 2, 1954: Floods in Persia have killed 450 people, ruined twelve villages, and cut off all roads between Teheran and the Caspian Sea.

August 3, 1954: The East Pakistan city of Narayangang is completely submerged by floodwaters. Scores of people who sought safety in trees were fatally bitten by snakes. In the flooded city of Muzaffapur, Bihar, snakes entered houses and caused fifty deaths.

It is hardly matter for astonishment that old Mother Earth suffers vulcanism and earthquakes. People in both England and the United States, and by no means the least intelligent, theorize that the A- and H-bomb explosions, which approach a cosmoplastic catastrophe, are disturbing the equilibrium in the deep-lying strata of the earth. In April, 1954, came reports that previously inactive volcanoes in Alaska were beginning to jet out plumes of smoke, and fears were expressed that sacred Fujiyama, in Japan, might be about to blow its top.

Geophysical changes appear to be under way that may be dependent on causes lying far out in space beyond our earth. These might produce internal pressures, disequilibrium, earthquakes, volcanic eruption, sudden elevations of volcanoes where none existed before, alterations in etheric pressures and gravity-thrusts, and phenomena triggered off by A- and H-bomb explosions.

There may be reason to suppose that the tempo of cosmic radiation from outer space, pouring in upon our earth, has accelerated the distintegration of its crust. It should also be noted that, when hydrogen bombs are exploded, dreadful vibrations descend vertically more than 1,000 feet into the earth, fan out, and travel thousands of miles far more rapidly than the waters of the ocean would transmit them. (Sir Winston Churchill told the House of Commons in March, 1934, how barographs and other delicate instruments in London, had detected the tremendous explosions in the Marshall Islands.) Among his other follies, man does not seem to realize that other inhabitants of the universe may be indifferent or even hostile to him and his earth for good cosmic reasons.

The general theory of relativity is that space is expanding. It is highly probable that some three billion years ago, the stars were much nearer each other than they now are. On the other hand, the celebrated mathematician, Professor de Sitter, of Leiden, Holland, has pointed out in *Cosmos*, that, on the existing data, an oscillatory condition of the universe is equally probable. There are, as yet, no adequate grounds for decision.

But whether the universe is expanding, or oscillating, there is a *real* motion of recession of the nebulae. It does not greatly matter, in relation to tectonic effects on our earth, how one interprets the "Doppler effects." (This is the principle that the light emitted from a receding stellar body appears redder in color than that of an approaching star, which is bluer. This can be partly attributed to the gravity-pull of the stars and nebulae on light passing near them). It may be that less solid bodies in the stellar universe are attracted towards central bodies within the orbits of suns, or return to the suns.

Some of this matter is extremely heavy or dense, like sub-plutonium. An excess of it, falling into our own sun, causes the discharge of longer waves of electrical or radiant energy. It may be that these increased discharges of radiant energy, from our sun, break up magnetic or etheric pressures, and produce disequilibrium in the crust of the earth; and so, earthquakes and vulcanism.

Below are recent reports that are certainly significant:

1953: Submarine volcano, 200 miles south of Tokyo, suddenly erupts and blows up 270-ton research and oceanographical ship, "Maiyo Maru." Crew of forty-one, including eight scientists lost. American military planes see below them in the Pacific, a hundred miles southeast of Tokyo, a new volcano, not on any chart. Its smoke-plume resembles an atomic bomb blast. Ten quakes felt in California.

Just as *some* scientists are not so sure that the continual release of blast-forces of H- and A-bombs may not have a cumulative effect on the world's weather similar to violent solar disturbances, so others have similar skepticism about other official dicta:

November 20, 1953: "Scientists are dissatisfied with

the official dictum that there is 'no connection' between A- and H-bomb blasts, and tornadoes. The dictum is based on the irrelevant contention that 'weather
forces' are more powerful than atom-bomb explosions.
The question now is: 'Can an atom-bomb explosion
trigger an explosion in the atmosphere?' "

Author's Comment: The "Philadelphia Bulletin,"
from which the above is taken, can do as I did: motor
from John o'Groats, extreme north of Scotland down
to the central highlands, and see the vast area of
devastation caused by a tornado of 120 miles an hour,
and accompanying inundations from the sea. These
followed hydrogen-bomb explosions at the end of
December, 1952. Scotland has now ceased to import
timber. She is using trees blown down by the tornado.
1954: Four townships in Chiapas, Mexico, wrecked
by violent earthquakes, *everything in an area of fifty
miles being pulverized.* Tila township (pop. 1,165)
wiped off map. Power lines, cables, telephones cut
off; death toll heavy.

Violent earthquake at 5:13 A.M. rocked Calcutta,
causing pandemonium among Hindus who blew on
conches to scare off demons. Simultaneously, severe
quakes felt all over northeast India, with epicenter at
South Manipur.

Death toll in successive Greek earthquakes in Thes-
saly would have been much greater, but for warning
given by agitated storks, thirty minutes before shocks
began. Violent earthquakes rock Dodecanese Islands
off Greece.

People in Huancayu, Peru, rush into streets in night
attire when violent tremors shake the ground.

A violent earth-tremor shakes Geneva, Switzerland.

At San Francisco, the Seventh Day Adventist
Church leader, Branson, announced that the "closing
hours of man's existence on the earth were at hand.
We must do what we have to do quickly. Christ will
come without tarrying. We have a million members,
the greatest gain being in the south Pacific."

Earthquakes shake Cyprus, at Paphos, where about
a year earlier forty people were killed by tremors.

In Alaska, long inactive volcanoes are smoking.

Mt. Ngaurhoe, New Zealand, warms up for the
biggest eruption since 1839. It shoots 500 feet into
the air, a fountain of incandescent lava, seen 100
miles away.

Mt. Cameroon, 13,350 foot volcano in west Africa,

smokes and glows, and tremors foreshadow eruption. In Europe, three tremors rock Mons, Belgium; and the most powerful earth tremors felt since 1924 rock Bergen, Norway.

A new volcano jets smoke and lava and suddenly shoots 200 feet above the floor of the south Pacific, between Sae (Lae) and Manus Island, Bismarck Archipelago, in Australian New Guinea area.

Mountain of Simonstown, South Africa, about to collapse.

Part of Prospect Point, Niagara Falls, collapses with a roar, and hurls 265,000 tons of rock into the gorge, carrying away 170 feet of the rim of the Falls. More cracks appear and a new rock-fall threatens.

In northeast India, great quakes and vast floods.

September 9, 1954, violent earthquakes and night of terror at Orleansville, central Algeria. Thousands flee in terror, after 1,000 people die and 2,000 are injured. Town turned into vast heap of rubble, and 600 people dead under ruins. Big buildings crumple like cards. "Hell let loose," amid shakings like terrestrial hiccoughs, and subterranean booms like powerful artillery. On September 26, another violent earthquake shakes Algeria, a country normally without such tremors.

Tremendous hurricane sweeps across the United States into Quebec, Canada. Death toll forty in the United States; in Canada, road between Montreal and Quebec cut for hours.

Observers in the United States point out that cosmic radiation is pouring in on the earth at an accelerating tempo. These are breaking down the underlying strata of the earth, already shaken by H-bomb blast forces transmitted through the rocks and the oceans. These vibrations penetrate about 1,200 feet vertically, then fan out and travel thousands of miles.

As stated elsewhere, previously inactive volcanoes in Alaska are beginning to smoke up. It is said that the cosmic rays tend to heat up the earth's lower strata, and that the increasing radiation from space causes a mutation in the rocks and strata, and a sort of chemical crystallization of the surface. It is pointed out that flying-saucer entities are suspected to have taken samples of the earth's water and soil, in order to test the effects of radiation.

Cosmic radiation will prove a very serious problem in

terrestrial voyaging to our moon which, as Professor Hans Thirling pointed out at the Innsbruck Astronautical Congress, August 2, 1954, is *not* for the near future. Apart from the cost, which must run into billions, he does not think the moon could be reached in one hop. Intermediate bases would have to be established first. Our possession of some of the atomic energies still leaves us short of the powers needed.

I am unable to say if schools of what is called "space medicine" have seriously estimated the risks to personnel from lethal cosmic radiation. Even in the crude prophylactic of lead shields, it is likely that, five or ten years later, those exposed to this radiation would show cancerous growths. It may be only by using electrical impulses to "jolt" and align the molecules and atoms in shield structures that an impassable barrier could be opposed to these penetrating cosmic rays. Clearly, that is something still beyond us. Such a revolutionary discovery —which must, long ago, have been achieved by nonterrestrial space-voyagers—would also render the aeroform applying it, weightless and therefore of immense velocity.

So-called "death rays," which some of these elusive space ships seem to possess and, at least on one known occasion were used on an American plane (over Fort Godman, January, 1949), have long been the subject of terrestrial experiment. On October 26, 1944, Brussels newspapers reported that, in 1937, German experimenters used them with lethal effects on animals. It was said the blood corpuscles were shattered. Earlier, in the closing years of World War I, it was alleged that airplane motors had been stopped by such a ray.

The first 1937 test was made in the Templehof Airdrome, Berlin, when an electrically produced ray stopped an internal combustion engine 500 yards away. It killed guinea pigs at 200 yards range in ten minutes. At the secret establishment at Peenemunde, apparatus generating what was called "The X-Y ray," killed a pig in ten minutes. As in atomic radiation, and also in suprasonic experiments, the white corpuscles were shattered.

Few people know that radium burns, following on the A-bomb explosion at Hiroshima, had uncanny after-effects. When the first trial atomic bomb was exploded in the New Mexico desert, it was reported that a *blind* girl, many miles away, said when the first flash occurred: "What was that?"

Gamma rays of radium can make the blind see, "paroptically."

Professor Frederick Soddy had observed these strange effects as far back as 1903:

"When radium, put in an inch-thick lead box, is brought near the forehead of a person in a dark room, he experiences a flash of light on the retina of the eye, even when the eyelids are tightly closed. The blind, apparently, also experience this sensation; hence, the rumors that radium can make the blind see. I think it was the late Sir James MacKenzie Davidson, one of the first pioneers in the medical use of the Röntgen and radium rays, who told me this."

In November, 1945, Russian physicists in a mountain laboratory in Armenia, used a three-ton magnet in investigating cosmic rays. They found a group of particles which they named "component cosmic rays." They separated the heavy from the light particles and measured their energy. Among them were *un*charged particles which penetrated more than five inches of lead.

The items following are interesting:

July 7, 1954: Mason Sears, United States delegate to the United Nations Trusteeship Council, says that American H- and A-bomb tests will continue in the Pacific Islands trust territories. The Marshall islanders had petitioned that the tests should stop.

In western states of the United States, in 1952, mysterious green "fire" balls hit water tanks, giving rise to a theory that there may be "reverse" or "contra-terrene" matter, in devices used against the earth by hostile flying saucers. At Tucumari, New Mexico, on a night in January, 1952, mysterious red balls hit a big tank and released 750,000 gallons of water which destroyed twenty buildings and scattered sheet steel around.

July 5, 1954: In the British House of Commons, Sir David Maxwell Fyfe, Home Secretary, reported on the effects of atomic bomb radiation: "Protective clothing and washing of the body avail nothing. Those who absorbed the gamma rays would experience no immediate sensory effect. That came later, in the form of radiation sickness. Some little protection was afforded by screening with various materials, or by walls of houses.

"The heat flash lasted at least thirty seconds. Its intensity was enormous, varying with atmospheric conditions, being greatest on a clear day. Outside the area of devastation, as far as the fringe of damage, fires might be started and people in the open badly burned." Civilization as we know it, would require decades for restoration.

Fyfe is a political optimist, for no one seems to have informed him of the period of 2,000 years thereafter, during which lethal radiation set up by these Satanic weapons would persist.

IS THERE A COSMIC GENERAL STAFF?

JUDGING FROM THE INNUMERABLE and world-wide reports of flying-saucer sightings between 1944 and 1954, the earth has been surveyed from pole to pole by these mysterious and elusive entities from outer space. For what purpose?

Proof in the forensic or juridical sense, of course, is at the moment unobtainable. Statistics alone may induce the belief that some of these visitants, coming from nobody knows where, may be acting in the fulfilment of some strategic plan of a general staff.

But whether or not *all* these entities hailing from unknown worlds, some of them fourth-dimensional, and others from unknown worlds akin to our own three-dimensional planet, are in any sort of alliance or confederation in relation to the earth, no one knows.

For reasons equally unknown all over the world, from February to the end of May, 1954, sightings of saucers heavily decreased. But it is not easy to say how far this had anything to do with a semi-secret, official censorship exercised in the British and American press, and more overtly, by War and Air departments. Their commanding officers and directors have vetoed, under penalties, any public communication of saucer sightings by airforce pilots or ground staff men.

One country alone did not enter this official conspiracy of silence. That was the great Commonwealth of Australia. There, as this book shows, reports of saucer incidents continue numerous and startling.

In June-July, 1954, the red planet Mars, in her fifteen-year orbital periodicity, came within forty million miles of the earth. Johannesburg (South Africa) astronomers said the planet appeared to have undergone changes. Not unnaturally, there have been people who have suggested that saucer entities are Martians; but of that there is not now a shadow of proof. If the saucer entities have any connection with Mars, it may not be more than using it, like the Moon, as a stopover or way-station on their cosmic voyages through space. I say *may*, for obviously no one can yet know.

A citation of the world-wide sightings of flying saucers up to July, 1954, makes plain the remarkable exploratory ways of these elusive and utterly indifferent entities. Another singular aspect to which I shall recur later in this chapter should be noted. The apparent fact that while many of these mysterious aeroforms seem to be *mutants,* changing their shapes, and alternately disappearing and reappearing as from nowhere, there are other aeroforms, described by observers as having what look like conning towers, observation windows, louvers, mechanical appendages, etc., which may import that, from whencesoever they come, they may be of an order of matter akin to our own. *If* this be so, it would be inferred that between them and the fourth-dimensional, non-terrestrial aeroforms there may be little or no relation, or anything like an alliance:

August 8, 1953: Two ground watchers reported to the airforce base, at Moses Lake, Washington, that they saw a flat, bright object, about 250 feet wide, rushing overhead. Sabrejets were sent out to quarter the region, but finding nothing, concluded that the mysterious object may have been merely lights reflected from a small township onto a cloud layer.

October 13, 1953: The sensitivity of birds and animals such as sheep to strange phenomena in the skies has been frequently noted in the United States and in England. Over Pleasant Hill, California, when four round objects flew at a great height, and glistened in the sun. Mrs. E. Cortsen, feeding her turkeys, noticed that the birds were greatly excited. As she looked up, she saw the objects throw off a mysterious white substance. (*N.B.* Ejection of unknown substances by flying saucers was noted at Brisbane, Queensland, Australia, on September 3, 1950; at East Grinstead, Sussex, on December 1, 1953; at Oloron and Gaillac, France, on October 17 and 29, 1953; in Victoria, Australia, on January 3 and 6, 1954.

Mrs. J. L. Gee, a saucer enthusiast of Hampstead, England, tells me that an American wrote her that in February, 1954, a saucer ejected a lacy substance over the San Fernando Valley, California, which "fell onto bushes and jumped out to passersby as hair does to a magnetized comb." As in France, this mysterious substance appeared to vanish, or dematerialize, when held in the hand. Mrs. Cortsen, above, says that a strip of white stuff settled in a tree. The strip was twelve feet long. American Air Force authorities were trying to analyze this strange substance.

Four continents have been narrowly surveyed by these most elusive visitants from outer space. However, none but blatant hoaxes and imaginative liars, or impostors and psychopaths claim to have had personal contact with them:

1953: Elliptical object, rounded and with an appendage like a "flag," shines like silver, spins fast and flies low near London, Ontario. Two boys were given their fares by their schoolmistress, Mrs. Grace Williams, to go into town and tell the local newspaper.

A radar team at Cape Point, South Africa, tracks a mysterious object flying at 1,278 miles an hour. It did six turns at under 5,000 yards range, at from 5,000-10,000 feet, until mountains masked it. Its size, as registered on the radar screen was vast, yet it was not visible in the sky.

More saucers reported seen inside than outside the Arctic circle. Alaska has sighted 128; Greenland, 103; and 187 have been seen elsewhere in the Arctic.

Six gleaming spherical objects, coruscating in the sunshine, dived vertically, rose, moved horizontally, criss-crossed, then hovered over Kimberley, South Africa. At Bloemfontein, South Africa, two circular objects, dark in color, circled over each other at immense speed for three minutes.

Over Hengistbury Head, Dorset, England, at 10:20 P.M., an unknown silver object revolved for thirty-five minutes, then shot towards Bournemouth, appearing larger than a star.

At 2 P.M., December 11, a gleaming cigar-shaped object glided over Wensleydale, England, moving slowly. It did not seem of large size, and was silent. Visible for six minutes under a clear sky.

Queer object, like two globes on top of each other, the uppermost smaller and with apertures like ports, travelled across the sky leaving smoke trails, over Berks, England.

On the last day of the year came the following report:

December 31, 1953: Marines at Quantico Marine Base, Virginia, say that a flying saucer landed for a few minutes near the base, and took off. It was round, throbbed and pulsated, and emitted red lights. On four previous nights, near the same base, saucers have been maneuvering in the air. One was at tree-top height. They seemed under control.

A mysterious object of large size hovered over an Army base in Bermuda. It was around 250 feet in diameter, low in altitude, metallic with golden round rims and it streaked off at fantastic speed.

Rumors that a saucer, forced down by radar, is locked up at the secret base of Muroc, in the Mojave Desert, Southern California.

February 15, 1954: In England, a boy, fifteen, Stephen Darbishire, saw on Coniston Old Moor a strange object rise from a valley, circle and make off. He took a photograph of it which shows a thing like a large white hat, with wide brim and a conico-cylindrical crown. About a fortnight later, the boy was invited to Buckingham Palace, London, to tell his story to the secretariat of the Duke of Edinburgh. There subsequently appeared in a London Sunday newspaper a reproduction of a sketch with this caption: "Stephen Darbishire's drawing of what he saw."

It is nothing of the sort. It is really a sketch by someone of an alleged saucer from Venus, whose occupants were communicated with "by telepathy and gesture for one hour," by a man who says he met them on a ridge in Arizona. This man hails from Palomar, California, but *not* from the well known observatory there!

Two people in Sydney, Australia, saw very high in the sky, at 3 A.M., a strange object like two shades of white tapering at one end, and surrounded by a halo. Object much bigger than a plane, hummed strangely.

A thing like a ball, forty feet in diameter, came rumbling like a heavy truck towards a native fellow, Johnnie, riding a horse over a low ridge near Todd River Downs station, in central Australia. "It nearly skittled me off my horse," he says, "and lifted sharply as it passed, causing a heavy wind. It rumbled and there were four columns of smoke on each side of it. I was terrified and galloped to a mission station fifty miles south."

Other natives here say they had seen this strange object and it made a similar noise. "We all know airplanes, but it was nothing like them." In January, 1954, a photographer took a picture of a saucer in the same area.

Johnnie says he had never heard about flying saucers before his adventure.

May 8, 1954: An American correspondent tells me that on the night of January 9, 1954, an orange light was seen about thirty feet above the tree tops near Warrenton, Virginia, moving in undulating fashion. The impression of observers was that the strange object may have been searching for something, or sending back visual or television reports.

My correspondent also reports that at midnight on November 9, 1953, several people near Omaha, Nebraska, saw high in the sky, an object like a cylinder, bright red in color, and flashing lights on and off. In a few seconds a number of other lights, flashing like stars, clustered around the cylinder, which was visible for six minutes. The cylinder seemed to be in a line with Venus, clearly visible at the time, and the earth, and slightly to the apparent right or eastern limb of Venus.

In June, 1954, singular objects were seen in the skies over England and Australia:

Mysterious light seen over Canvey Island, Thames estuary, after dark. It was like a small globe ascending and vanishing towards London.

For six minutes, until 8:30 P.M., a thing like a green ball with long, tapering yellow tail, first flew very high, then came down to roof-tops in Victoria, Australia. There it split in two and "blacked out."

Three "weird objects," flying at tremendous speed, passed over Melbourne, Australia, at 10:30, 10:32, and 10:45 P.M. They were silent. One left a wake of yellow lights.

Mr. P. F. Sharp, of Knutsford, England, sends me some interesting diary extracts. I would stress the similarity, and in some cases, even the identity of the phenomena he records, with unidentified objects seen in the skies over Victoria and New South Wales, Australia, from May to June, 1954:

November 10, 1953: "At 7:10 P.M., Miss M. Brockle-hurst, head girl of Knutsford Secondary School, was on Shaw Heath when she heard overhead a whine like that of a plane. She looked up and saw a strange object in the sky with five or six lighted windows or ports. A yellow glow came from behind it, and the ports emitted a golden illumination. At first it hovered, then moved north. The object was fairly low in altitude, its apparent size that of the full moon. It moved off at very high speed. Night: clear and starry. Her brother also saw it; and a pilot reported the object to the Ringway Airport. A man and a boy at the nearby village of Toft also saw it. It was also seen over Warrington. R.A.F. officials at Ringway assured Miss Brocklehurst that it was just a helicopter or weather balloon."

(*Author's Note:* A year later, the same officials would have told her: "We can tell the public nothing—by orders of the British Air Ministry.")

December 7, 1953: "At 5:30 P.M., Mr. D. Haigh and three others were outside the railroad station of Moston, when they saw in the sky a globe emitting a white glow. Visible for three seconds. It was silent. It went off at a high speed towards Manchester."

December 9, 1953: Mrs. J. L. writes to the "Manchester Evening News" that she saw the object seen over Moston the evening before. It was spinning like a top and shedding a bright white light. She watched it for twenty seconds. She observed it over Chorlton, near Manchester.

April 12, 1954: "Mr. C. Evans, a former member of the R.A.F., was having tea in his house at Macclesfield, at 6:15 P.M., when chancing to look out of the window, he saw to the north, a flying saucer. In a slow turn it passed a cloud at a speed faster than a jet plane, then vanished in the east. The object was silent. He said the thing resembled a balloon with a flat top—but was *not* a balloon. Its course was about forty-five degrees from the horizon, wind about ten miles an hour, west to east. *Apparent* size about six inches. He assures me there was no window distortion that would have created an optical illusion."

"I wrote to the R.A.F. air base at Ringway," says Mr. Sharp, "but the commandant there said: "'I can make no comment on this phenomenon. I have forwarded a report to higher authority.'"

Author's Comment: Three months before this incident, the British Air Ministry and the British War Office ordered that soldiers and airmen should tell the public *nothing* of saucer sightings. Further comment is needless.

The incidents below were reported to me by correspondents in South Africa, Germany, and Nova Scotia:

July 9, 1954:

Airport officials at Dusseldorf, Western Germany, see a saucer travelling at immense speed, at a height of 18,000 feet, June 9.

Fifty people telephone the police at Zurich, Switzerland (June 11), that they saw a saucer circle the city for twenty minutes.

Two warships called their crews from shore at Halifax, Nova Scotia, and prepared to speed to a point off the coast where an unidentified object crashed into the sea. Some say it was a flying saucer.

A curious type of flying saucer was sighted July 2, over Kimberley, Transvaal, South Africa. It bore what looked like a numeral "I," followed by "3," or as some say, the capital letter "B."

About 300 independent observers report having seen "glowing discs," at a great height, and flying at great speed over Berlin, Germany, on July 3. These objects have been sighted since May 11, and always between 10 and 11 P.M. (*Sunday Times, London.*)

On May 9, 1954, I received a batch of saucer reports from correspondents in the United States, Canada and Europe, covering the period between June and December, 1953. In some of these sightings there appears to be a synchronism with a nearer approach to the earth of the planet, Mars. It is, however, *not* at present possible to say whether or no such apparent proximity of Mars and the earth is related to the periodicity of saucer sightings: ·

June 13, 1953: For about fifty minutes, at 5 A.M., Mr. J. Weger, his wife and daughter, watched a strange round object, as big as a street light, emitting a noise so loud as to produce vibrations of the air. It had neither wings nor fuselage, and moved up into the sky at an angle of fifty degrees with the horizon.

June 15, 1953: Two men, R. Lambert and F. Toupance, were driving a motor truck to a reservoir near Pittsfield, Massachusetts, when at 8:45 A.M., they were startled to see a gleaming object like a cylinder with round nose and "open tail," from which jetted puffs of blackish gas. It drifted over trees which were ahead of the truck, was travelling at about fifteen miles an hour, and was about seventy feet long. The day was sunny. The object had no wings, made no sound, and had neither louvers nor ports, nor windows, except that the nose had an aperture like a shutter. As it was only some five feet in diameter, the men concluded that no human or humanoid entities were inside it.

We now come to sightings in all parts of the world of a type of saucer described as being equipped with "conning towers," or windows, or appendages. These may be of the order of matter from a three-dimensional world like our own planet. In some cases, these mysterious objects have been seen to divide and separate, or to send out satellites which have been seen to divide.

Mr. H. K. Hotham, an old friend of mine, airmailed to me on June 10, 1954, sightings of saucers in Victoria, Australia, on June 5, 6, 9 and 10, 1954:

June 6, 1954: Seven people at East Malvern, Victoria, Australia, see an oval-shaped saucer with objects inside it fly at fantastic speed just over the tops of trees. One man was standing at his gate, talking to a friend at 12:25 A.M., when the saucer flew over. It climbed upwards at very great speed. The first sighting of it was May 30, 1954; but it was seen again May 31, at the same place at 8 P.M., when it swooped across the sky, backed, vanished, flattened out, then reappeared. One account said it was like a white football, and left a wake of sparks. Another says it was as big as a railroad car, and there were dark shapes inside it like people. Speed varied from a floating grace to a vertiginous velocity, when it shot straight up and vanished. As it dived, it jetted out a "yellow gaseous matter from its stern." It later appeared that three saucers were seen that evening in various parts of Victoria; one fading away suddenly, as if someone had switched off a light; the second, appearing as a dull glowing object in the sky; the third, like a star, hovered then dashed sideways for two miles, and was visible for twenty-five minutes.

Author's Comment: The Australian government, unlike the authorities in the United States and Great Britain, has not adopted the ostrich policy of imposing a censorship on saucer reports.

June 6, 1954: A weird object, described as like a white balloon, flying at tremendous speed, with a long tail tapering, and with an umbrella or mushroom-shaped object inside it, seemed to travel towards the ground at Melbourne, Australia, at 5:45 P.M., on June 1, 1954. Another object seen the same evening, carried a revolving red light. The light did not come from a plane, nor was the object a weather balloon of any type. One observer, a Mrs. Wiley, said it was silent, floated in the air, and then shuttled back and forth. Suddenly, it spun three times as if it had been a plate, and then vanished. The Australian Air Force asked for written reports, and an official spokesman stated: "We do not pooh-pooh these things. We take a lot of them quite seriously."

June 9, 1954: Janette Brown, a sixteen-year-old schoolgirl, of East Dandenong, near Melbourne, Australia, stood "frozen with fright," at 6:20 P.M., when about a hundred yards away in the air, she and a girl friend, Jeanette Johnston, aged thirteen, saw a flying saucer hovering for three minutes.

She told the "Melbourne Argus": "I was so scared that I begged my parents to move to another suburb, in case the saucer tried to destroy our home and us. I was standing on a highway, waiting for my girl friend, when I heard a loud drumming; but there were no cars or motor-cycles around. Then a large, dark shape appeared over a factory, and whirled towards me when I shone my torch. It got above the house of the factory caretaker, and when I shone my torch, whirled towards me. Then it burst into light: a gleaming, bluish, silver-grey light. It hovered twenty yards away on the top of the factory gate as if it wanted me to look for it, or as if it wanted to look at me. It was cylindrical, about thirty feet long and fifteen feet high, with a canopy and window on top, and a window on each end. Then my friend arrived, and I told her to watch the house. She did. She said: "A silvery cylinder rose above the house, and swept away in a wide circle to the International Harvester factory, a few hundred yards away. It stayed on top of the factory for about a minute, and then vanished behind some trees."

Miss Brown made a sketch of the saucer—I have a copy of it. Parents of both girls say that the girls have had no sleep since the night they saw the saucer and are nervous and frightened.

For some reason unknown, the month of June, 1954 was remarkable for saucer incidents in Australia. The "Melbourne Argus" offered £1,000 for the first authentic photograph of a saucer.

I summarize the incidents:

Three saucers seen near Shepperton, Victoria, the apparent length of a telegraph pole. They were vertical in the sky, then swung into a horizontal position and flew southeast at about the speed of a plane. The third object, says Mr. Dave Heritage, "wriggled like a snake."

A weird saucer of discoidal shape was reported by J. Machen, a policeman. It was clipped through the center of the minor ellipse of its axis with a thick metal-like band passing and girdling the shorter axis, with three things like fins, or clamps on the major axis, from end to end. Machen said it emitted a bright yellow light, was stationary for one minute, and swished off towards a park lake. It seemed about eight feet in diameter, with "three rows of funny (queer)-looking things around it." He adds: "When I saw it, it was very low in altitude—hardly seventy feet above the horizon—and I estimate only 300 yards from me, in the darkness." (*N.B.* In Australia, the season was winter.)

June 20, 1954: Summary of reports from three people in Somerset and Hampshire, England—counties separated by about eighty miles, on an east-west line as the crow flies. On the night of June 9, 1954, they saw a "huge thing like a globe surrounded by a brilliant flame." It was only forty yards from the observers, an eighteen-year-old boy, Nigel Frapple, and a sixteen-year-old girl, Doreen Heffer. The object was seen by both, but hours apart. They say it seemed to have something like a central conning-tower from which a flame came. It was fifty or sixty feet across, and silent as the grave, except for a slight "swish." For about two minutes it hovered, then sped off at high speed. The youth Frapple was returning home from a village dance, time 2 A.M. He was so startled he got off his cycle and hid behind a hedge. He tells me the body of it was metallic. Later on he got on his bike and tried to follow it, "but it was far too swift for me." The girl who saw it from a window of a house, thought it was a forest fire.

(*N.B.* On 11 June, 1954, a bright unknown object was seen circling over Zurich, in northern Switzerland.)

Author's Comment: The British Air Ministry is said to be puzzling over "this extraordinary phenomenon." If this cosmic drama mounts to a climax —as it may—not only the British Air Ministry, but every service and defense department in the world will be more than "puzzled." They will be *stupefied* by what may happen.

The predicament of the serious student of these phenomena is grave: he *dare* not inform authorities of what he may theorize may be happening, and is forced into the position of the "dumb cluck," which is exactly their own. We may wake up too late, for these entities from some world in outer space behave as if they were carrying out the plans of a cosmic general staff!

June 22, 1954: A correspondent in Miami, Florida, tells me that on May 6, 1954, a queer disc with something flashing at its rear, moved slowly across the night sky near Miami.

July 10, 1954: A dazzling object bigger than a plane passed at great speed over Pascoe Vale State School, Victoria, Australia, at 8 P.M. Two youths saw it, Tom Blake, nineteen, and Allan Jackson, twenty. Blake said the object moved too fast for him to distinguish its shape, and it made a soft buzzing sound as it flashed across the roof of the school, only thirty yards from them. No plane would have disappeared in a few seconds as did this mysterious object, nor have made so low a sound.

I am told, but cannot vouch for the story following: Late in the summer of 1954, an American physicist was driving home in his car from his job in an atomic-pile plant in the Middle West, when he saw ahead a brilliant object like a large, hot sphere, which forced him to stop the car. There stepped from the sphere a giant entity, very well-proportioned, and radiating great heat, who appeared to know the scientist, and conversed with him. "I am Moroni," said the entity. "We fear that your scientists will cause great disasters."

The long drama of the flying saucers pays no heed to any Aristotelian dramatic unities of time or place. In the war year, 1944, an American pilot, flying over the Burma road, said his plane was held motionless and the engine propellers stopped, while far aloft a mysterious disc appeared to be putting some sort of immobilizing ray onto his plane. After this seeming "inspection," his power came on again, the propellers resumed turning, and the mysterious object vanished into the far blue.

By the kindness of my friend, Eric Biddle, editor of the London journal, "Uranus: Space Travel and Flying Saucers," I have been shown an extract from the German monthly, "Neu Europa," dated September 1, 1954. This records not merely an alleged projection of a flying saucer's immobilizing ray, but an abduction. I summarize the account, but for reasons that will appear, I am able neither to vouch for, nor dismiss outright, what is alleged:

On June 11, 1954, the airport staff at Buenos Aires, in Argentina, stared at a large plane apparently floating, with propellers slowing down. It was the twin-engined Portflighter, from Bogotá, Colombia. As it approached the runway it yawed and zigzagged, and as the undercarriage touched the ground, the propellers stopped automatically. The airdrome staff rushed to the plane, opened the cabin-door and found no one inside. It had landed unmanned. On the telephone, the Buenos Aires staff were told that the plane had left the Andean region of Bogotá with both pilots aboard. There was no landing-place on the 2,300-mile route over the "green hell" of Amazonas, the Matto Grosso, Bolivia, and the edge of the Gran Chaco to the Argentina. On the seat of the second pilot, Juan y

Genza (*sic*) a scrap of paper bore the words: "Stunned! Hands trembling. Impossible steer plane. Controls out of action, won't function. Something astounding is happening. A huge flying saucer seems to guide our plane. . . . Controlled by something unknown." The first pilot attached his signature to the message. Both seats of the pilots showed bloodstains. The manometer (*sic*) showed a position 4,050 meters (approximately two and a half miles) above Santa Cruz, Eastern Bolivia. Then it had stopped.

Certain questions arise about this story:

A *manometer* does not indicate altitude, but gastension. Is *altimeter* meant? Would any air transport company fly a plane for more than 2,300 miles, merely in ballast, with no freight, mails, or passengers? If not, what had become of the passengers? The name "Juan y Genza" is "phony." It is not in Spanish or Spanish-American style. If—who can say? —the two pilots were abducted, why should a space ship (non-terrestrial) take the alleged trouble to steer an unmanned plane for at least 1,300 miles across the Gran Chaco wilderness to Buenos Aires?

Until these and other questions are answered, the story remains dubious.

In July, 1954, the Australian Flying-Saucer Investigation Committee issued an interesting report on fifty-five sightings. The Committee interviewed twenty-five observers of saucers. I congratulate the perspicacity and rare insight of this Committee for excluding from its board those most hopeless of all men: the conventional astronomers and the crassly conceited science-chairsitters who consider themselves Sir Oracles, have the whole truth under their mortar-boards, and forbid any dog to open his mouth after they have deigned to enlighten our earthly darkness. Such do not deserve the name of scientist. Real scientists in every age recognize that they are *not* omniscient, and are duly humble towards the vast extent of what they do *not* know. Humility is the characteristic of the *great;* arrogance the mark of the petty, overwise in their own conceit. On those it is vanity and folly to waste time.

I summarize the Committee findings on some of the forty-seven cases which they could not explain:

"*Cigar-shaped objects:* Regular symmetrical shapes, at night emitting a phosphorescent glow. The covers of their bodies seem to glow, and it is not a translucent effect. Their motion is smooth and regular, and they glide in the sky—not zig-zag. There are six of them in our fifty-five reports."

As I have said, I believe these cigar-shaped objects are space ships, and have shown themselves to be hostile.

"*Rotating discoidal flying saucers:* Appear often in pairs. By day, they look like discs. When seen low in the sky, their upper portion seems to revolve. They have windows and ball-like wheels underneath. They number fifteen of our cases."

"*Shooting Moons:* At night, they appear luminous, like a full moon, and travel at great speed, shooting across the sky, then hovering in one place, mostly for about a minute. They appear suddenly and just as suddenly vanish. Six have been seen."

"*Small hovering lights:* They hang suspended in the sky, then dart off at high speed; often racing off at right angles. Sometimes, they look like small balloons with an apparent diameter of two feet. In daylight, their surfaces flash in the sunlight like highly polished metal. About twenty have been reported."

The Committee sums up, as follows:

"We are still far from deciding what these things are. It would be only guesswork to say they are actual space ships from another planet. But we are fully agreed that these things are material objects—and *not* optical illusions or hallucinations."

They add *this*—and the reader will note I have ventured to make a similar suggestion:

"*They are getting lower, seemingly to land.*"

Here follow two of the more remarkable incidents mentioned in the Committee report:

No. 2: "At Templestowe, nine months ago, a woman heard a loud humming noise outside her house. It was early in the morning. Hovering over a paddock, at a height of only about thirty feet, *was an enormous*

THE EARTH'S GRAVEST HOUR

saucer-shaped object. It hovered for about fifteen seconds, then shot off at great speed. It had a strange superstructure, but no port-hole or windows.

No. 3: "On January 7, at Bonbeach, a woman going to bed at about 10 P.M., heard a loud humming that seemed to come from a fuse-box in her hallway, or from wires outside. She woke her husband and they went outside to investigate. They saw nothing and went back to bed. But the humming continued. Twice the woman went outside again, each time returning to bed to forget the noise. Finally, outside the window, she saw a shining, round gold object circling in the sky. It had hazy edges, was of the apparent size of the moon. She hurried outside and saw it travel for five seconds and vanish over the horizon. It had been brightly illuminated by the light of the moon. For three more minutes she watched. *Then a cigar-shaped object shot up into the sky from the same place where the round body had disappeared*. It did three or four loops, with a slight pause between the jumps. It left behind it, each time, a puff of white smoke. This happened each time it looped. Then it, too, vanished and the noise, which had continued during the two sightings, stopped abruptly.

THE EARTH'S GRAVEST HOUR

THERE ARE REASONS for people naïvely supposing that the flying-saucer phenomena have ceased to exist. In 1953-1955, Great Britain's Air and War Office authorities imposed a rigid ban on the communication of such information, not only on officers and all ranks of air and army departments and branches, but even through civilian air-transport ministries on the personnel of *civilian airports*. Similar bans have been imposed in the United States. In 1954, President Eisenhower was publicly assured by his military and airforce advisers that no non-terrestrial or cosmic aeroforms are traversing the skies of America.

Nevertheless, reports of strange sightings and incidents between summer, 1954 and late spring, 1955—the time this is written, continue to come in.

But before I set down these sightings, I should like to summarize a few remarkable earlier incidents. They are of phenomena either unknown to the public, or which have belatedly come to my knowledge, and which have not been reported in widely-read media.

"Foo fighters," seen by American air pilots of the Second World War over the Rhine, and in Far Eastern operations in 1944, were actually seen *twenty-six years earlier!* But then their nature was not recognized.

In January, 1919, my brother, Mr. Gordon Wilkins was stationed at an army post on Salisbury Plain, England. He told me in January, 1955, of a curious incident of which he was then an eye-witness:

"Early in January, 1919, about 8 P.M., I and another man of my corps were returning to our camp. We had been on a ramble to Figeldean to look at an old church. On a sudden, I was startled to see in the night sky on the western edge toward Netheravon, three weird colored globes—red and orange—at a height of about 3,000 feet. They looked like lanterns illuminated with a very strong glow. As I watched, they floated downwards, and then suddenly and inexplicably vanished. The famous prehistoric monument of Stonehenge was some miles south. There were airdromes and British Royal Artillery camps and ranges some miles away. But, at this time, there was no firing at night. The man who was with me had evidently seen these globes before.

"Said he to me, noticing my astonishment: 'They must come from the Royal Air Force drome at Boscombe Down,' (about eight miles away).

"I think that *very* unlikely! At that date, thirty-six years ago, airplanes had no apparatus capable of firing off such globes. Nor would there have been any object in doing so. Moreover, the cockpits were then open, not closed in as now. At that time—it was three months after the Armistice—most of the camps and dromes and firing-ranges had demobilized their airmen and artillerists. Certainly, when I saw these globes, no plane was to be heard or seen, and on that eerie plain of prehistoric monuments and Neolithic barrows and other memorials of the long unknown dead, the air was as still as death. In the silence and darkness, the effect of these apparitions in the starry sky was most startling and unnerving!

"I wish to draw attention to the fact that my companion had seen these phenomena at least four times, in 1917 and 1918. Hence his lack of surprise; for he evidently—and I think wrongly—assumed they were devices of the R.A.F., or perhaps the Army."

Two years after, about 4,500 miles away on the Texan shores of the Gulf of Mexico, some men shooting ducks saw at dawn, in June, 1920, four discs. They were travelling very fast, one behind the other and emitting a soft orange glow, but alternating with sea-green and blue. They were like two large silver plates canted on edge, apparently about thirty feet in diameter, and slicing through the air as if they had been naval monitors with rams. With amazing speed they ascended sharply into the sky and disappeared inland, in the direction of Austin, Texas. Since few people look up at the sky, it may be imagined that nobody who had then been comfortably abed believed the report. And how many patrol cops, with the watchdog air, look upwards to the skies—unless they happen to have been around, say, in southeastern England in 1944-45, when German flying-bombs or rockets seemed to be converging on them from the skies.

I now summarize a curious report made by Mr. H. B. Williams to the Borderland Sciences Research Associates, of San Diego, California:

"In 1936, Major Green, U.S. Army Engineer Corps (he died that year), told me of a strange experiment some years before, at Wright Field, Dayton, Ohio (I think it was). Those who participated were ordered to deposit all metal objects on their persons in a room. They then went out to the center of the airfield. Men placed a section of railroad rail upon cross-sticks, and held it suspended between them. A plane then took off from another part of the field, circled and then flew over the group. Whereupon the rail disintegrated and disappeared. Major Green said they were given no details by those in charge of the experiment."

In a previous chapter of this book, I have referred to mysterious disappearances of men and women, which may or may not involve the "psi" phenomenon of teleportation. Among unsolved missing-person mysteries on the books of the police of Winnipeg is that of Mr. and Mrs. Earl Kirk, of North Bay, Ontario. On October 4, 1940, Kirk, a wholesale merchant and importer, and his wife, left by car on a vacation trip. Their route took them from Sudbury, along a lonely highway running along the northern shore of Lake Huron, to Sault Ste. Marie. The last man to see him and Mrs. Kirk was a gas-station operator at Sudbury, who directed him onto Highway 17.

I summarize the report in the "Winnipeg Tribune":

"Not until the end of October, 1940, was it known that the Kirks had disappeared. Kirk's affairs were all in order. He had a good balance at his bank. The immigration officials at Sault Ste. Marie had not passed the Kirks into Michigan, nor had anyone at Sault Ste. Marie seen them. So the mystery was narrowed down to the 195 miles of highway between Sudbury and Sault Ste. Marie. Lakes and rivers and creeks were dragged, bush and woods combed by 150 men for six weeks, until the snows fell and ice froze over the lakes and put an end to the search. Kirk's friend at Sudbury, Mr. John Newstead, said it was extremely unlikely that Kirk would have given a lift to any paranoiac wanderer. To this day, in 1954, no one knows what became of Mr. and Mrs. Kirk. No motorist on the highway had seen him, nor was there any sign of an accident anywhere on that 195-mile-long stretch of road."

In the summer of 1942 a fantastic incident occurred in the waters off Tasmania, a large island off the South Australian coast. My informant is a major in the Australian R.A.F., whom I will call Brennan. He is now stationed at the secret weapons and long-range missiles experimental desert station of Woomera:

"The whole yarn is so odd that I must ask you *not* to give my name if you write of it. We had orders not long after the Japanese attack on Darwin, to patrol the Bass Strait where fishermen had reported seeing mysterious lights on the sea at night.

"At 5:50 P.M., of a lovely sunny evening, we were flying some miles east of the Tasman Peninsula when, on a sudden, there came out of a cloud bank, a singular airfoil of glistening bronze color. I'd say it was around 150 feet long, and about fifty feet in diameter. It had a sort of beak at its prow, and the surface seemed burled, or rippled, or fluted. On its upper surface was a dome, or cupola, from which I seemed to see reflected flashes as the sun struck something, which might or might not have been a helmet, worn by something inside. The other end of the airfoil fined out into a sort of fin. Every now and again there came from its keel greenish-blue flashes. It turned at a small angle towards us and I was amazed to see, framed in a white circle on the front of the dome, an image of a large, grinning Cheshire cat!

"The damn thing flew parallel to us for some minutes, and then it abruptly turned away and, as it did so, it showed four things like fins on its belly-side. It went off at a hell of a pace, turned and dived straight down into the Pacific, and went under, throwing up a regular whirlpool of waves! Just as if it had been a submarine. No, the Japs had nothing in the amphibian line like that mysterious bird!

"I've read your 'Flying Saucers on the Attack,' and saw what you said of the 'Foo Fighters.' We were in the same predicament as those American airmen. If we reported to intelligence what we'd seen, we should likely have been grounded as suffering from nerve-strain. So we did *not* report it! What do *you* think the damned thing was?"

Your guess is as good as mine, Major Brennan. All I can say is that queer objects like that have been seen both on the North and South Atlantic, in 1872 and in 1882—but on the surface of the ocean, and not in the air. It may be that the shipmasters who saw them arrived after the things had risen from the depths or come down from the skies.

Here follow American reports of either a squadron, or a unit of singular, unidentified objects, seen in 1949, 1950, 1951, 1952 and 1953:

June 20, 1950: The Rev. Ross Vermilion, a wartime flier, was driving a car at midnight on U.S. highway No. 54, nine miles west of Kingman, Kansas, when he and his wife saw a strange red object, as large as a B-29, whirling like a huge red light in the moonlit sky. He turned his car to drive under it when, as if aware of his intention, it went off at a height of about

500 feet, at a vertiginous speed, far beyond that of any jet.

April 14, 1949: Charles Moore, testing balloons eighteen miles south of Hot Springs, New Mexico, and fifty-seven miles from the White Sands provingground, picked up on his theodolite a strange elliptical object, a hundred feet wide, and crossing the path of a balloon at an altitude of over fifty miles. Its speed was five miles a second, a force equivalent to twenty times the pull of terrestrial gravity. He and five other units saw the object alter course and flash upwards.

April 11, 1951: J. C. Kaliszewski, and another balloon expert, flying a plane high over Minneapolis, see two strange and extremely fast objects emitting a queer glow. They were neither balloons nor conventional aircraft. Ground men at General Mills sighted them with a theodolite.

September 11, 1951: Huge, white silvery thing, at 11:25 A.M., moved inland, as pilot Lieut. Wilbert Ballard flew passenger plane over New Jersey, U.S. The thing moved in an arc from Sandy Hook to Red Bank, thence out to sea at Asbury Park. Speed: over 900 miles an hour.

August 4, 1952: Off-duty, jet pilot Lieut. D. Swimley, in his garden near Hamilton Airforce base, California, watched with neighbor for fifteen minutes a formation of eight shining discs. The things maneuvered, broke off into trailing formations, and one dived, its size enlarging as it came lower. Registered on radar. Emitted flames from rear, as jets do not.

June, 1953: Strange object seen over Kansas City, in bright daylight rising from horizon to zenith. Appeared to be of burnished metal, with keel gleaming like aluminum. Altitude about 3,500 feet. Apparently thrice the size of a large freight plane. Hovered for five minutes, visible for ten minutes. Appeared symmetrically round, but had no wings, fins, or exhaustports. Some people said they heard a vibrant hum coming from it.

November 4, 1953: Mr. Edward Lake, of Torrington, Connecticut, got out of his car to stretch his legs on Route Seven, near the Vermont-Canada border. The night was clear and stars could be identified. Towards the big dipper, he saw a round, flat, fiery object shoot across sky towards Lake Champlain. The object was very large, with a narrow blue streak. Soundless and very fast. "Left me with a vibrating feeling." (*Communicated to author by Mr. Lake.*)

At the end of August, 1954, there came in out of the cosmic cobalt an extraordinary object which appeared like a mechanical-minded boy's dream of Vulcan's underworld. It entirely "demogalized" a hard-boiled Canadian R.A.F. "sarge," and other tough groundsmen who saw it. Its startling annunciation was very close to the region where saucers have been seen to alight: namely, North Bay, on Lake Nipissing, western Ontario. It was preceded by a curtain-raiser, which I here summarize from a Toronto evening newspaper:

At 8:30 P.M., on August 27, something suddenly appeared in the starry sky that shook up tough Bill Supa, handyman of the Caswell Construction Corporation, which has a factory at Boston Creek, Ontario. As it neared, he saw that it was a wingless airfoil. He watched it land, about a mile and a half away. Supa made tracks for the spot. The thing looked like no airplane he had ever seen or read about. He was 300 yards away when he saw it shoot up into the air and flash off so darned quick he could not make out what propelled it. His impression is that its shape was circular. Where the queer thing had rested, the grass was flattened down.

Three days later, August 30, 1954, came the *real* mystery:

At North Bay, western Ontario, is a station of the Canadian R.A.F. There, at 5:25 A.M., Sarge Durdle stood at the door of his Nissen hut, rubbing his "peepers" to get out of them the last dews of night. He let out a cavernous yawn, which got somehow badly fixed, when he saw in the sky, something coming straight at him across the waters of Lake Nipissing, and so tarnation fast you would not have been able to say, "This is it!" before it became "What in hell was it?" It made no sound and Sarge Durdle braced himself against possible accidents from aloft. As he did so, the sky-borne juggernaut pulled up abruptly, and Durdle gasped!

Said he: "On top of the mystery was a circle—all the time, a brilliant glow came from the center—and this top part had hanging down an oblong sort of canister. From the center of the circle stuck up a long cone, with, on its top, a globe rotating like hell and shooting out rays, like that rotating trademark which opens up on the films of a Hollywood concern. It illuminated something like a lattice-work of gleaming metal. As I watched, I was startled to see the whole darned thing turn through an angle of ninety degrees from the vertical to the horizontal. It now looked entirely different!

"I could not now peek into the inside of the circle. That had canted right over and looked hollow, with knife- or saw-edges. The cone with the rotating light was now not horizontal, *but vertical*, and was revolving on its base, like the globe at the top. And the glow emitted was enough to burn one's eyeballs out! On part of the canister-side, there was a vertical slit of light, like the loopholes you see in old castles, where they used to fire arrows! But I guess *this* thing was not for bows and arrows. Old Robin Hood would sure have made tracks pronto, deep into Sherwood Forest, had he seen it. This slit was in the side that was turned towards the circle that was attached to the canister.

"It was like an open door, and inside it, I could see gadgets like throttles or regulators in a locomotive cabin. But there was something even more startling. As the thing swung to the horizontal, six of the weirdest contraptions you might see in a nightmare hung down and shimmered. They were like huge dazzling necklaces. Six of 'em, and they seemed to shine independently of the light from the cone and the globe. And the whole darned nightmare was hovering only at the height of a tall telegraph pole. I reckon that the canister might be around twenty feet in diameter; the circle might be, say, seven feet across; and the cone stood up about eight feet from the center of the circle. The rays shot out of the globe over twenty feet.

"As soon as I could recover what the Froggies call me *sang frowd*, I dashed into the hut and woke up the fellers who, by rights, ought to have been up. Only four of 'em ventured to look. By that time, the weird thing was moving on and up, in a sort of corkscrew or spiral fashion. About two miles away, it stopped and hovered over some woods, where it seemed to pulsate like a throbbing heart, with the lights expanding and contracting from its center and top. Then it corkscrewed higher into the sky and its shape was lost in one blaze of light. Over the skyline it hovered for twenty minutes."

This beats anything yet seen by the author, who has witnessed some mighty queer things in many parts of the world. And this was seen by five air force men. From what bourne in heaven or hell, or the vast cosmos this thing came; what was in it; and what their business might be on our planet—for it has doubtless been seen before—is something that every Government and Security and Defense Department on earth ought to be trying to discover.

In the same Ontario region two other strange incidents occurred shortly after Bill Supa saw something land from the skies:

At 12:25 A.M., August 31, 1954, a policeman, Grabovski, on patrol in a car, near Kirkland, Ontario, saw about 1,500 feet up in the sky, a shining elliptical object going slowly north, parallel with the railroad tracks. From it an intense light shone. He could hear no sound, and was startled when the object disintegrated in a shower of sparks. He drove the car to the tracks, but found nothing. An air pilot reported having seen this object a few hours earlier.

Later the same night, at 3:15 A.M., William Martin of Kirkland, Ontario, rang up a local newspaper and said big drops of blue rain were running like ink down his window-panes. A reporter sent to Martin's house saw the blue drops change to ordinary water. The drops were of very large size.

On December 30, 1954, I received a bizarre story from a young woman, a cashier in a store in a Kentucky township. Apparently in the late summer of 1954, this girl, who had read my "Flying Saucers on the Attack," and remembered my account of mysterious giant footprints on the Isle of Wight, had the following encounter:

"Several months ago a young man, boarding at my house, took me to lunch in a basement restaurant. When we had finished eating our lunch, we each went to the Rest Rooms. When I came out of the Ladies Room, my escort was standing by the revolving doors that lead upstairs. He said: 'Meg, did you see that man sitting on that seat back there, with shoes that had a place for every toe?' I said: 'No, Jack.' He suggested: 'You go back into the Rest Room, look at him, and come back out.'

"I did. This man was sitting there with his hands on his knees. He was a tall man. His head and shoulders were higher than any other person's there. He did not say a word. He just watched everyone. When he saw me look at him and at his feet, he got up and walked out. He was wearing a dark brown suit, and *his five-toed shoes* were dark brown. His toes were *long* and big, and his foot looked narrow at the heel."

My correspondent added irrelevant details about a nearby coastguard station on the Ohio River. She gave her name and full address, and I airmailed her, asking some questions. Would she give me the name of the young man, and his address, who, she said had been an eye-witness; and, especially, could she give me a sworn statement that she had not read a story like this in some sci-fantasy magazine?

She had enclosed with her letter, a clipping from a local newspaper about a brilliant and unknown object seen on a bright afternoon, on November 12, 1954, for at least forty-five minutes, over her township. Its color had changed from amber to white. It had been tracked by radar and theodolite, from Godman and Standiford airfields. It remained motionless for two hours. At one time it rose more rapidly than any up-current could have lifted it. Officials who refused to give their names said it was a "Moby Dick" balloon. Others swore it was something else far more exciting. It also appeared that at 7:40 P.M., the same day, at Oolitic, seventy miles away, quarry-workers had seen a white ball emit an explosion high in the sky, and then rapidly move south where it hovered for over an hour. All these sightings, however, had happened months before the man in the toe-gloves had been seen around her burg.

Alas, from that day to this, three months later, not a word has come from that young lady!

Mind you, ladies and gentlemen, I do *not* assert that with all these many hundreds of unidentified objects flying and quizzing in our skies, over all our lands and seas, from China to Peru, and from Alaska to the Antarctic, not one of them might have dropped some entity to canvass our cities and countryside. *But,* that he would draw marked attention to himself by wearing his long toes in gloves . . . that calls for witnesses and affidavits, does it not!

Here follow more incidents:

January 15, 1954: Two women and a man, travelling by car, at 2 A.M., over a stretch of desert road in Nevada, were startled by the sudden apparition in the eastern sky, of an eerie blue light that stretched near- ly half the distance to the zenith, and ranged all along the eastern skyline. It seemed to rise from the ground. No one could offer any explanation. It may, or may *not* have been an aurora, but auroras do *not rise from the ground.*

January 30, 1954: In a house at Gadsden, Alabama, Mrs. Robert Arledge, wife of a policeman, was stand- ing in the dining-room when there came a terrific ex- plosion. Folks outside said they had seen a flash like lightning. Rushing in, they found that Mrs. Arledge had been hurled to the floor. She was bruised and had slight burns. Firemen found the floor tiled up and one wall-foundation pushed out, but no light fixtures broken, nor any glass fissured, save one front-door panel. The investigators found no other signs of fire or explosion. The blast remains a complete mystery.

Author's Comment: In a parallel case in South Carolina, where an explosion shook a house, a noise like a plane had been heard passing over the house; but no plane had been up!

February 2, 1954: Strange and unexplained mirages have been seen on No. 4 runway, at a London airport —the airport whence the Pan-American airliners fly for New York or Idlewild. Sir Jack Albiac, the air- port commandant, says it is the first he has ever heard of it; but one man says he has seen a mirage or a sheet of water at the end of the runway. Members of the British Royal Meteorological Society swear that mirages are not infrequent on this runway. (*N.B.* At this airport, in February, 1955, an outward-bound airliner smashed up by taking off from a runway blocked by a concrete wall, and not supposed to be in use; and a mysterious caller got hold of a private air- port line and said he was from the moon.)

February 15, 1954: The city of Auckland, New Zea- land, is struck all of a dither by nine flying saucers that flew over in the daytime. Some say there were twelve of them.

February 27, 1954: Two women at Hillsboro, Oregon, see six strange objects very high in the sky, shaped like large white birds, soundless and moving their wings. They went in and out of the clouds, and then moved west. In the Middle Ages, and as late as the seventeenth century in Switzerland, they would have been called "Dracones volantes" (flying dragons).

What follows is concerned with phenomena of mysterious tracks in lonely places, referred to elsewhere in this book:

February 5, 1954: Mrs. Weiss and Mrs. Sanders of Las Cruces, New Mexico, saw in the desert, queer round marks one and a half to three feet wide, imprinted about half an inch in the sand, the edges sharp as if made by a metal object. The impressions were a series of concentric circles. Some of the tracks had an impression of an "arm" above the rim of the circle, with three talons, or hooks, dug into the sand at the end. Several miles away they saw mysterious lights, one yellow, one red, winking at irregular intervals. What these lights were no one knows. (*Extracts from local newspapers*).

Another case of unexplained fissuring of glass in France, called "cancer de verres":

February 6, 1954: A terrific explosion startled Mrs. H. Dressler of Houston, Texas. She rushed into her drawing-room and found a fish bowl on the coffee table, perforated and the fishes lying on the carpet. She had had the bowl for a long time, and the room had always been kept at a constant temperature. She placed the bowl in the kitchen but, next morning found that it had shattered itself to fragments. Mystery unexplained.

Curious incidents in March and May, 1954, reemphasize the fact that our planet is a more mysterious place than the laboratory scientist imagines:

March 10, 1954: Aboard the U.S. destroyer "Marshall," escorting an aircraft carrier steaming across the North Pacific towards Hong Kong, an alarm bell rang. Commander Noel Bird, of Oakland, California, who was reading a book, rushed to the bridge and found that a plane had fallen into the sea. The destroyer circled the spot for three hours, but the pilot did not come to the surface. Half an hour later, another plane crashed into the ocean. Again, the pilot did not come up. Bird was suddenly startled to realize that the book he was reading was titled, "Go Down Death!"

March 13, 1954: Enough red snow, at 129 tons per square mile, to cover 1,600 square miles, fell over Minneapolis and neighborhood. Röntgen ray devices showed that the red snow had adhered to dust containing felspar, quartz and hydroxide of iron. But where on earth did this dust—75,000 tons of it—come from? We know no more than did the Romans in B.C. 230, who also recorded red snow; or the monkish chroniclers in Western Europe's middle ages, who chronicled similar falls.

March 14, 1954: Small jellyfish suddenly appeared in Crystal Lake, Ohio. Very seldom are they found in fresh water. The mystery is as insoluble as the provenance of two jellyfish, the size of big baseballs, found after torrential rain in a garden in Austin, Texas.

The very mysterious incident below has an extremely disquieting aspect for those who are forced to believe that, among the many hundreds of flying saucers in the world's skies, there may be some whose entities are hostile and malevolent towards our own planet. Was it they, or their like, who brought "wyld fire" on England 920 years ago?

I summarize reports from various middle western newspapers:

May 1, 1954: Driving on a highway near Logan, Utah, Mr. J. Fuller was startled almost out of his wits when, on a sudden, he saw a dazzling red half-globe come out of the ground, ahead of his auto, and to the left. Eight seconds later, as his auto drew opposite the glaring semi-globe, there came a violent blast and concussion that nearly overturned the vehicle. At the same time, over an area of 250 square miles, doors of houses and factories, some bolted, were violently thrown open, and there was an earth-tremor.

Investigations started next day. A game warden found a sixteen-foot crater from which earth had been hurled over an area of 290 feet. Dr. Lincoln LaPaz, director of the Institute of Meteoritics of New Mexico, arrived along with J. S. Williams and C. T. Hardy, Utah state geologists. They found some strange things: the crater was too small to have created the shock wave that had been recorded. Drilling to a twenty-five foot depth brought up no meteoric debris. An artesian well suddenly appeared in the crater. In the scattered earth no nickel, iron, or meteoric stone was found.

Professor Hardy, using a Geiger counter, found no unusual radiation. Eye-witnesses in the region say they saw a flash, or paroxysm of light at ground-level which is not the characteristic of meteorites, which never flash on impact, as did this phenomenon. Drag electro-magnets sieved the soil, but found no metal particles.

May 6, 1954: "Curious celestial object seen in Arizona today. It was low on the southern horizon, and looked like a nebula, perfectly circular with bright center. Just like a nova after it begins to cool. Got only an evasive answer from La Paz." (*Letter to the author from Mr. Frederick G. Hehr, engineer of Santa Monica, California*).

May 16, 1954: A strange thing like a white "flying sausage" hung for three minutes in the sky over Currumbin, Queensland, Australia. It then vanished.

May 21, 1954: The Miller family of Pasadena, California, report seeing in the sky at 9 P.M., a strange thing like a "house on fire." The apparition was noiseless and moved fast to the south; stopped, hovered and showed a dome and something like a band on its keel. Apparently some American military base put a searchlight on it. It passed through the beams and vanished in the west. The strange object emitted blue, amber, red and yellow flashes. Next night the same, or a similar object was seen, at 9:30 P.M., moving fast and illuminated. It was seen again in mid-June.

(*Author's Comment:* I have several accounts from the Middle Ages to the 18th century of phenomena in the sky, like this "house on fire.")

May 24, 1954: "Light from an atomic explosion can turn fluid in the eye into steam and 'explode.' At night, in exceptionally clear air, rabbits inured to night vision, forty-nine miles distant, showed eye injuries after an explosion." (*U.S. School of Aviation Doctors.*)

June and July, 1954, did not fail to enhance that sense
of mystery in the skies, and on the earth that Einstein
says "is one of the most beautiful things in life." The
discovery below is of contra-terrene matter in space. It
may be recalled that impact with a presumed contra-terrene matter, appearing like a fire-ball, on a January night
in 1952, shattered a 750,000 gallon tank of water and
wrecked twenty buildings at Tucumari, New Mexico:

June, 1954: Cosmic ray expert, Dr. Marcel Schein of
Chicago University, reports detection of a new particle which, when striking a proton in the aluminium
covering of photo-plates, converts matter into pho-
tons or light-units of energy, and then re-converts the
energy into pairs of electrons, the free-flowing waves,
or negative particles of electricity. He calls the annihilating ray an anti-proton, or reversed matter. He
estimates its energy at ten million billion volts. These
particles enter the earth's dense atmosphere from outer
space, but usually vanish before reaching the soil.

Another Chicago University professor, James Arnold, has developed a scintillation-counter, 10,000
times more sensitive than the Geiger counter. It de-
tects radioactive carbon-14 by the light of its radiation in samples dissolved in a fluorescent solution.
Photo-multiplier tubes are used. This discovery is of
use in estimating the approximate dates of prehistoric
monuments, and has reduced to a thirty-seven year
margin the probability of error in carbon-14 dating
of archaeological material up to 25,000 years old.

June 10, 1954: A woman driving a car at 4:10 P.M.,
along a highway at Woodside, California, heard an
explosion, and saw the bituminous road surface
aflame. She warned the fire station, which found a
spray of hot metal fragments, ranging from a dime to
half-a-dollar in size. A local sheriff found some of
the metal to have come from a cylinder. But the
Stanford Research Institute said the metal was cast
iron. No clue to origins.

June 18, 1954: Unknown object shaped "like a railway car," and jetting blue flames flew in from Botany
Bay, Australia, at 5:55 A.M. The night before, people in nearby Sydney saw peculiar multi-colored lights
hovering in the sky at 7 P.M.

July 17, 1954: Astronomer Rolf Brahde, of Norway,
examining films of two flying saucers photographed
by John Bjornulf, from a plane over the North Sea,

commented on the curious "dragon-shaped tails" of the objects. He surmised that they received solar energy, but can give no explanation of the objects, or of their connected shock-waves.

On the road to Istres, South France, a woven-fabrics merchant and his wife, driving a motor truck, saw a short distance from their windshield a queer, bluish light, which then shattered the glass. At the same time, a singular, impalpable, whitish mist pervaded the inside of the truck's cab. The woman felt an inexplicable heat envelop her; and her nylon vest stuck to her skin. Nylon under-garments turned from white to pale yellow.

In the U.S.A., and other parts of the world, the month of August, 1954, unreeled mysteries calculated to bemuse any scientist. Elsewhere in this book, I refer to the mysterious noises heard in the Chalfont and Westcliff regions of England. A similar but not identical phenomenon, was reported at East Haddam, Connecticut, as far back as 1788.

August 1, 1954: Scientists have been investigating mysterious, apparently subterranean noises, around Moodus Village, Connecticut. No smoke, explosion, or steam is ever seen, and no buildings are rocked by earth-tremors. It is impossible to determine the epicenter, or exact direction. Observers stationed at varying distances report only that the noises were heard near them. Harvard seismologists theorize that they may be of earthquake type, but Moodus citizens point out that no quake-effects have ever been felt. One man says he heard an explosive sound around and above him.

August 3, 1954: At Gainesville, Texas, orange light moved in the sky from apparent direction of Mars. Visible three minutes, then vanished. Size larger than plane. Similar phenomena seen next night.

August 4, 1954: At 4:45 P.M., while driving, Mr. R. C. H. Townsend of Penroy, Southern Rhodesia, saw a flash of green light in the sky. He drove his car forward, and pointed out to his wife a queer object in the sky, shaped like an English army helmet. The domed surface was uppermost. The throbbing movements of the object gave shimmering reflections of the sunlight, but they were soundless. Altitude probably about 10,000 feet. (*Summarized from letter to author, by Mr. H. Neal of Southern Rhodesia.*)

August 5, 1954: An unnamed California woman who dozed on her porch found, on waking, some drawings in her lap. She called in the boy next door, who was a ham radio fan, and asked him if he had put the paper in her lap. The boy got "all het up." He is said to have devised a box which gave off light signals, in series of three, from which he made out the letters "O B S E R V A M U S," (We are on the watch). The boy's father, perhaps concluding that the watchers were the well-known gentlemen with horns and tails, put an axe into the gadget. Apparently, one is to assume that the paper left in the lady's lap came from the same mysterious source, and was the boy's blueprint for the "box."

August 6, 1954: Sportsmen at Santa Fé, New Mexico, startled by a brilliant white ball in sky, which left a luminous trail, and was visible for fifteen minutes. It shot up, and not down. Dr. Lincoln La Paz says it was not a meteorite. It left a white cloud, seen in San Francisco for half an hour. Later story says the phenomenon put TV and radio on aircraft, out of action; but oddly (see above) not ham radio sets! Is this not what is said of the cosmic phenomena called "the whistlers"?

August 7, 1954: According to the Dutch newspapers, Capt. Jan P. Bos of the "S.S. Groote Beer," reported that enroute from Amsterdam to New York, a queer moonlike thing rose out of the ocean, ninety miles east of Cape Cod light. Bright on keel and had what appeared to be illuminated ports on its rim. Speed fantastic.

August 8, 1954: Long Beach, United States Coast Guard Radio intercepts radio from Honduras steamship, "Aliki": "Saw fire ball move in and out of sea without being doused. Left wake of white smoke; course erratic; vanished from sight."

August 9, 1954: Artist, sketching in eastern Utah, saw porcelain-like disc in sky, undulating about an axis parallel to its course. One moment it looked fusiform in shape; next moment it was circular. It was soundless. Estimated speed around 1,000 miles an hour.

August 10, 1954: Close to Hemmingford, Quebec, children named Coupal were in field, at 9:30 P.M., when they said a bright light followed them home to the farm. Father and older son went to the field, and

saw orange-hued object rise and speed off into the
Western sky. Left grass flattened for forty feet, and
with two tracks about fifteen feet long. (*From the
Gleaner, Huntington, Quebec.*)

August 11, 1954: "Flying tadpoles," seen in skies of
Austria—by police, priests and fifty other people. Also
in Yugoslavia. One was reported seen flying at immense speed, at about 4,000 feet, shooting off green
flashes. Others say it emitted a humming noise and
showed signs of being steered.

(*Author's Comment:* There is a story that a Scan-
dinavian skipper of a small trading schooner found
a strange disc—apparently pilotless—that had crashed
and burnt out, near a Kamchatka coastal village. He
says it had Soviet markings. Whether or not these
Austrian reports relate to a Russian airfoil, or to
real or cosmic saucers, who can say?)

August 17, 1954: At 10 P.M., a woman saw a luminous, white, globular object approaching Long Island,
N. Y. Soundlessly it *slid* across the sky. As it ascended it turned pink, and vanished into cloud. Next
day, a Long Island newspaper said a red object in the
sky had been chased by Air Force planes. The Air
Force at once denied any knowledge of the incident.

August 18, 1954: A stratocruiser plane's windshield
suddenly cracked, fifty minutes after it left London
Airport for New York. The plane had to return, and
was grounded.

August 26, 1954: Mrs. Jeanne Macdonald Gregory, of
Southsea, England, writes me: "I am an ex-airwoman.
I saw today, about 7 P.M., in a clear sky, a strange
object with a long trail resembling a jet bomber's
wake at 40,000 feet. But it was *not* a jet plane. Visible nine minutes. I estimate its altitude as not less
than twenty miles."

(*Author's Comment:* The lady, who is an experienced airwoman, sends a sketch from which it may
be deduced that the mysterious object was of very
large size, and may have been a space ship.)

About 8 P.M., Mr. and Mrs. Faris of St. Louis,
Missouri, saw what looked like a star move to and
fro, in the region of the sky where could be seen the
handle of the Big Dipper. It finally faded away.

End of August and early September, 1954: A whole
crop of reports from Europe about alleged contacts
with saucer entities. In Portugal Senhor Ferreira, a
landowner, said he met "two eight-foot giants in

metal suits, who emerged from a thing like a flying cup."

Signora Rosa Danielle of Bucine, Italy, came out of some woods barefoot, carrying her silk stockings when, she said: "Two laughing little men snatched them from me and made off in a thing shaped like a spool. They wore helmets with a bulge in the center of the forehead."

A man in the south of France says he was scared almost to death by a small, bearded entity with an eye in the middle of his forehead!

John Swaim, a twelve-year-old boy on a farm at Coldwater, Kansas, says a little man approached him while he was on a tractor. The entity jumped while he was on a tractor. The entity ran towards a saucer hovering five feet in the air. The entity jumped in and took off. "He was dark, wore shiny clothing, and had two cylinders on his back. The saucer was fifty feet wide, and lights shone from portholes as it ascended." The "Wichita Evening Eagle" says "the small man had pricked ears." Local sheriff and the boy's father found footprints four and a half inches long, and two inches across the toes, with the "narrowest heels you ever saw." There were about 100 footprints in a ring.

In Rome, Italy, there was an epidemic of pitted windshields and shop windows. Theories range all the way from radioactive bomb fallout to impact with an order of matter, contra-terrene, not our own, or to "panspermist" germs brought from outer space by flying saucers.

The month of September, 1954, was remarkable for more than "nuts ripe brown all tumbling down":

September 2, 1954: Mr. W. K. Kitchener of Rye, England, saw from his garden "two objects like giant feathers floating towards the ground. I next heard the drone of accelerating engines and the two feathers shot away towards London, at about 2,000 miles an hour. Air Ministry, London, said: "We've heard nothing."

September 4, 1954: Planes are searching for a Dakota with four people, which vanished somewhere between Platinum and King Salmon, in west Alaska. In this region, since July 20, eleven planes have crashed, and ninety people are dead or missing. (*New York newspapers.*)

September 5, 1954: Three amateur astronomers at Rockford, Ill., claim to have seen through a six-inch telescope, a spherical object ascending from Mare Humboldt area of the moon, of a size estimated at one quarter of the diameter of the lunar crater Vlaco. Velocity very great—over a 29 feet 30 inch arc in 40 minutes. They think it travelled under power, and was ascending in space. They estimate its length as close to two and a half miles!

September 10, 1954: An Algerian road-sweeper said: "I saw a *sun in the sky at midnight*, and the moon turned red, one hour before the great earthquake struck Orleansville, Algeria." (*N.B.* The appalling earthquake at Orleansville, which began at 1 A.M., killed more than 1,000 people.)

(*Author's Comment:* I was a boy of four, at Gloucester, England, in 1895, when an epidemic of smallpox, of the virulent North African type, hit the city. One night at 1 A.M., a violent earthquake hit the house in which I slept, and the town rocked. At midnight, strange and mysterious lights had been seen in the sky. This phenomenon has been seen before and since, but remains a mystery. It may be aligned with what was seen at the village of Aston Clinton, England, on May 21, 1950, when just before a tornado hit the place, a mysterious, vast red fireball was seen in the sky. It turned green and disappeared.)

September 12, 1954: Red flares seen near St. Tudwall's Island, in Wales, caused lifeboats to search for seven hours without finding anything. Off Beaumaris, Anglesey, thirty-five miles northeast, on the other side of the Lleyn Peninsula, a lifeboat searched for three hours, in vain, to find a rowboat with three people in it, reported drifting off Anglesey.

September 19, 1954: Thousands of people in Rome, Italy, see a flying cigar about two-thirds of a mile up in the sky. It was picked up on radar, and the Italian station followed its course for half an hour. Intelligence of the Italian Air Force say the object was "bisected and had a big antenna amidships. From its pointed stem, a smoke trail projected."

September 30, 1954: At Valence, France, a woman with a dog on a leash, came face to face, she says, with a form swathed in "cellophane." Seeing the dog, it climbed into a saucer, and shot up with a deafening hiss. Police examined the parking-place of this saucer and found that cornstalks, in a radius of about ten feet, were pressed to the ground.

At Nantes, a driver and fireman of a train watched for ten seconds a saucer ascending perpendicularly into sky. The fireman had to be treated for shock.

In the Pyrenees, France, director of a Parisian cabaret saw a saucer 2,297 feet up. With presence of mind, he photographed it.

In the Savoie, Franco-Swiss frontier, fifteen persons watched for five minutes a saucer maneuvering in the sky.

While all this was, or was *not* happening in France, certain saucer entities of a different type, if we may believe a story told by a laundryman of a township in Michigan, were trying their prentice feet on the soil of that state:

September 30, 1954: Driving to his work at a laundry at Dearborn, Lawrence Cardenas, aged forty-five, slowed down his car at a traffic light at 4:45 A.M. To the right was a field through which a road was being driven. Close to the derricks, Cardenas was dumbfounded to see about fifteen little men who were speaking an unknown tongue. They were around 5 feet 4 inches tall, in dark-green uniforms, had on their heads tightly fitting skull-caps, with pointed peaks in front. A larger entity, in a brown uniform, about six inches taller than the rest, seemed to be addressing them. All wore heavy goggles over their eyes, and what looked like oxygen cylinders on their shoulders. Dawn was breaking, no other car was in sight, and Cardenas had just started up the car, when he was even more dumbfounded, he says, to see some 250 feet away, a big oval thing resting on the grass, with colored lights on its upper surface, flickering on and off. It seemed about twelve feet high, and had smoothly finned sides suggestive of a seashell. He was not, he says, scared, but did not wish to be late for work. The entities seemed quite friendly, and curious about their surroundings.

Mr. Cardenas is a reliable man and not given to tall stories. (*Various Michigan newspapers.*)

October, 1954, in no way came short of the previous month in the way of mysteries and sensations from the skies:

October 2, 1954: Jean Narcy, a road-mender, cycling to his job, near Haute-Marne, France, saw in a wheat field a strange whiskered being, four feet tall, clad in a fur coat and an "orange corset and plush cap." Narcy said: "Bon jour, Monsieur," but the little man turned and jumped into a *soucoupe volante* (flying saucer) and buzzed up into the clouds.

October 2, 1954: The U.S. Navy Hydrographic Office reports a mystery: The American tanker, "Dynafuel," bound for New Orleans, saw in the Gulf of Mexico, smoke coming from underwater. It was seen for twelve minutes. No explanation offered. No planes known to have dropped bombs onto targets there.

October 3, 1954: Roger Barrault was halted near Lavaux, in southern France, by a singular being with "brilliant eyes, and an enormous moustache, who spoke Latin." (Whether Barrault knows Latin, cannot be said.)

While ten young Italians at Tradate, Italy, were being fined for impersonating "Martians," with trunks like elephants, and turkey-cock wattles, hoaxing a Milan newspaper man, crowds in Rome and Florence saw fleets of saucers passing in their skies.

October 4, 1954: For the seventh time in nine days, an unknown being has set cars and things in them afire in Birmingham, England. The police are baffled.

On a hundred-foot stretch of road in Sussex, England, cars "just slide off the surface." There have been thirty serious accidents here. The police are mystified.

October 7, 1954: At 6 A.M., Claude Lasselin, ten, and his sister, Francoise, nine, of Henzies, France, were on their way home. They were passing a lonely field, newly plowed, when they saw in a hollow about 600 feet away, an object shaped like an egg, red in color, with its top pointing upwards. They silently approached it. At about 300 feet away, they saw that it had a sort of black lid, or cover. Said the boy: "At this moment, I saw, and so did my sister, two men of normal height come out of the 'egg.' They were all in black, and their faces seemed black. We were seized with fear and flew home, and did not turn our heads." The father came back to the field, but the object had gone. Questioned by local authorities, the boy stuck to his story. "Everybody laughs at us, but we saw what we saw." (*Courtesy of M. Marc Thirouin, Flying Saucer Journal, "Ouranos"*).

October 5, 1954: Some unknown force pulls cars off the road near Barrie, Ontario. Recently a girl aged seventeen, Marlene Holmes, was killed in the third fatal crash in a month. Motor truck drivers say the road at this spot seems to slope the wrong way. Police say that although the road should be safe for autos at 50 miles an hour, some unknown force seems to pull them off the surface.

(*Author's Comment:* It may be that a mysterious vortex, or warp, in the gravity-field, acts here. What *is* gravity?)

October 5, 1954: A French Army "projector" at an exposition at Metz, sighted a mysterious metallic globe, motionless in the sky for more than three hours at altitude of 6.2 miles.

October 5, 1954: For twenty minutes, in the skies over Mehalla-el Kobra, Egypt, a thing like a spindle was seen by hundreds of people. At Behnay, cylinders in the sky emitted a thick smoke. One exploded, and hurled to the ground a fellah (peasant), and killed two cows on whose hides showed burns. Lieut. Tewrik took a photo of a rotating saucer that emitted smoke above East Kantara (Suez Canal). He sent the photo to Egyptian Army Public Relations, and to Helouan Observatory. Admiral Youssef Hammad, director of Ports and Lighthouses, alerted airpilots and astronomers to keep watch on a saucer seen over Cairo.

October 6, 1954: The Vienna (Austria), meteorological station sees a queer object terminated by a panache of flame, very rapid and high in the sky, and silent. *Not a balloon-sonde* (weather balloon), it says.

Five sightings of saucers in Holland, in September, and one in October.

Prague, Czechoslovakia, reports violent detonations during passage of unseen objects in sky. Watch kept on Tatra Mountains.

Yugoslavia reports many saucers, very high in sky, extremely rapid, luminous, and seen flying in formation.

October 7, 1954: Prof. G. Umani sees a cigar-shaped, rotating saucer flying over Rimini, Italian Adriatic. Says its course was absolutely parallel to the horizon; rotated at a very sharp angle. Italian Air Ministry orders day and night vigilance at detection posts by saucer spotters. Astronomers at Lucques set up office for flying-saucer observations.

Kenya Colony, Central Africa, reports numbers of saucers.

Object like a star moves quickly, cork-screwing across the sky, and then stopping over Mildura, Australia. (Not star, comet, or plane.)

October 8, 1954: Man near Mertrud, France, says he saw being, four feet tall, take off from a field in a thing like a "flying red knob." It was spherical, orange-colored, thirty-feet across, and had a sort of spindle sticking out underneath.

October 9, 1954: E. D. Farthing, Texas Airlines meteorologist, believes that red and green rays in sun's corona may turn on and off our rain. Heaviest rain appear synchronized with emission of intense green light from sun, when directly facing the earth.

October 10, 1954: Milkman at Le Mans, France, alleges that shining red and blue cigar-shaped saucer, about three feet long, sped over his truck and stopped his engine. As soon as force-field was removed, his engine re-started, and his lights went on. Other parts of France report flying, illuminated "mushroom," bright orange disc, and a gray object emitting a whistling sound.

In Alexandria, Egypt, observatories see cylindrical flying saucer, red and green. Royal Belgian observatory, at Liege, opens a dossier on saucers and asks for public reports of sightings.

October 11, 1954: At 4 P.M., "I saw soundless object of grey metallic color, about 300 feet up, moving horizontally, disc-shaped, speed not fast, about thirty feet in diameter with no tail or wings. I was wondering at the air-resistance it must meet, when it suddenly made a very sharp turn, and rolled upwards vertically, at angle of thirty degrees to the horizontal. It rolled like a wheel, until it entered thick clouds. Visible for thirty seconds. Seen over Cherry Valley, N. Y. State. I am an engineer, used to working with finely graduated instruments. Am member of the American Society of Mechanical Engineers." (*Letter to the author, from Major Abraham B. Cox, Cherry Valley, N. Y.*)

October 12, 1954: Near Münster, Germany, film-director Herr Hoge says he saw a landed flying saucer. Location: Rinkerode, near Münster. From it came a dazzling blue light. It hovered about sixteen feet above the ground; a peculiar cigar-shaped object surrounded by blue light. Under it there walked four entities about four feet tall. They had enormous heads and slender legs. They wore rubber-like (gummy) clothes. Hoge says he stood off about sixty-five yards and watched for forty minutes. He had not the courage to venture nearer. The entities were noiseless. Suddenly they vanished into the saucer up a kind of ladder. The craft tilted, then like a flash of lightning, took off into the sky. In a few seconds, it looked like a shining disc.

October 13, 1954: Report that two men at Castelibranco, Portugal, saw two entities in shining metal dress, emerge from grounded saucer, and pick flowers, twigs and shrubs, as if gathering data.

Mail-carrier in Belgian village of Huy, saw saucer hovering near ground, with silhouetted roughly human shapes inside it.

Two men in France, at Châtellerault, and another at Bugeat, 120 miles away, allege independently that normal-looking beings approached them, kissed them, jabbered unintelligibly, then got into cigar-shaped saucers ten feet long, and took off.

A saucer grounded at Drôme, Dauphiny, S.E. France, emitted sound like a musical top as it took off vertically after a "plastic-garbed being" had approached Madame Leboeuf, at Drôme. (Lady *did not* say that he tried to snatch a kiss!) At Bressuire, France, Angelo Dinardeau, at dawn, saw a saucer in a field, all aureoled with light. A being in a sort of "diving suit," fled into the saucer and took off in a flash.

October 14, 1954: Jules Martin, schoolmaster, swears that in the lone, rock-begirt island d'Oléron, in the Bay of Biscay, he encountered two pretty ladies from "Mars," in leather helmets, gloves and bootees. They had borrowed his fountain-pen, jotted down some hieroglyphs, then took off without making a date with him.

Farmer and wife, in Kenya, East Africa, saw a circular object in the sky, half the apparent size of a full moon, streak south with an undulatory notion. Light green in color, and with a distinct "aura." Speed might have been about 3,000 miles an hour. (*Letter to the author, from Lieut.-Colonel N. W. B. B. Thomas of the British Army in Kenya Colony.*)

October 15, 1954: Man sitting in his car at grade-crossing, near Modena, Italy, reports seeing a flaming, white hot, cigar-shaped thing whiz past at immense speed.

Twenty other saucer sightings reported in Italy, including a landing in a field.

In Norway, farmer saw triangular objects of mauve color over his farm.

Customs officer at Perpignan, France, attests on oath that a strange reddish object landed near him, that out of it came a man in a sort "of space suit," who, apparently scared by barking dogs, climbed back and took off at fantastic speed.

October 17, 1954: Is an alleged "Martian" saucer masquerading as Frenchman? A café owner, Alphonse Rapellini, told the police of Toulon, that he saw a being come out of a saucer, with domed top and discoidal shape. With Alphonse was Philippe Ottovani, an engineer. The being said: "I am not a Martian. *Je suis Français* (I'm French)." He asked where he was, then took off vertically at high speed.

October 18, 1954: A London evening newspaper asserts that monkeys in oxygen masks and helmets, used in cosmic ray test balloons, account for stories of queer beings in landed saucers. (Another scientific brushoff!)

October 21, 1954: Was it a meteor that was seen at 7:40 P.M., over Youngstown, Ohio? A husband and wife in a car saw a huge white star come out of the sunset. No explosion heard. Nearly twice the size of the full moon.

October 22, 1954: Denied by Sir Lionel Heald, M.P., British Crown lawyer, that Martians downed the British Comet airliner that sunk in the Mediterranean, with a loss of fifty-six people, on January 10, 1954. He said: "We found no signs of explosives in the wreckage, unless the Martians use ammunition very different from others."

(*Author's Comment:* Why necessarily "Martians"? Also, why should cosmic entities use terrestrial type rockets, cannon, or what-hev-yer in the arsenals at the Tower of London, or Woolwich?)

October 23, 1954: Residents of Berri, Australia, saw a most mysterious thing, six feet long with scaly back and tapering tail, odd-shaped head and eyes like round plates, curled round a branch. "Like an animal from another world!"

(*Author's Comment:* See chapters in this book on teleportation.)

October 25, 1954: People in Austria and Italy see gleaming, whirling disc with tail of flame shoot through sky at dawn. Police and newspaper overwhelmed with phone calls. At Pesaro, Italian Adriatic, red ball with blue-green tail shoots towards Austria.

Dr. E. C. Slipher, of Lowell Observatory, took 20,000 photos of Mars, in South Africa, through a twenty-seven inch telescope. Saw gleaming white Martian polar ice-caps, clouds, dust-storms, and two new hazy canals. 1954 seemed fertile year on Mars for vegetation, since color markings were intense.

Belgrade (Yugoslavia) Meteorological Bureau reports seeing V-formation of three shiny metallic discs, with luminous blue tails. Estimated altitude: 9,000 feet; speed: 2,000 miles an hour.

October 27, 1954: Any "Martian" landing at or near French vineyards of Chateauneur du Pape, is to be offered a bottle of the local wine. But his machine will be confiscated by the Maire. It is *not* stated whether he will be called on to pay in good U.S. dollars for the wine.

October 28, 1954: Dr. Sutton, of British Meteorological Office, pontificates that atomic explosions have no lasting effect on the weather.

(*Author's Comment:* Has he never heard of the Wilson Cloud Chamber showing that, when a *radioactive* particle passes through suspended droplets of water, they lose their natural electrostatic charges, coalesce, and fall as heavy rain?)

October 30, 1954: From Harika, Algeria, M. Yves Vernet writes: "With prismatic telescope, twenty magnification, I watched the sky at high altitude. I was *stupefied* to see a brilliant object fly high above cloud-layer at great speed. Five minutes later, I saw another object pass. Since October 26, when the first sighting occurred, every day between 1 and 2 P.M., I have not ceased to see flying saucers passing *every 5-10 minutes.* More are visible at midday than at morning or evening. Their frequency *in a field so reduced is of grave import.* Such a number of discs is great enough to *alarm!* Their performance is far above that of our best terrestrial aircraft; and their number seems higher than the greatest aerial concentration we could effect.

(*Author's Comment:* The above is *extremely grave.* It was in Algeria that a terrible earthquake occurred, late in October, 1954. When will the Governments of our planet wake up to what this portends?)

November was marked by episodes involving dogs, and in the American Middle West by the reception of singular radio messages from outer space, which probably ought *not* to be dismissed summarily:

November 1 (and later), 1954: French encounters with saucer entities in early November were reported by Gilbert Lefay, thirteen, of Chateaubriant. He was told in French that he could look at but not touch the saucer, a large ball that radiated purple light. Henry Lebrisse, of Aude, reported a small saucer, about three feet in width, containing midget-like entities, in his barnyard. Took off on sight. Saucer entities patted a little dog belonging to Charles Garreau, of Chalais, but others buzzed off from barking dogs, at Perpignan.

At Diges, a tall, dark entity in a "khaki space suit," standing by a cigar-saucer, pointed at both ends, looked hard at Madame Simone Geoffrey, who took to her lightsome heels. She did *not* wish to be kissed. At Montluçon, it is alleged that a railroad porter actually caught an entity, landed from a twelve-foot torpedo saucer, in the act of helping himself to the railroad company's gasoline. The entity, who was described as exceptionally hairy, uttered some *galimatias* (gibberish), then whizzed up into the skies.

November 2, 1954: An "oblong saucer" startled Arab bedawin when it whizzed, with lights all around, through the skies over Nablus, Jordan.

November 2, 1954: All glowing in the western night sky, a cigar-saucer was seen over St. Austell, England, where it hovered for five minutes. Had vertical tail. Lost in clouds.

At 6:35 A.M., what looked like three "hot steel bars" were seen in sky over New York State. Apparent size: seven feet.

Alexandria, Egypt, saw a "vermicular" saucer running the gamut of colors from red to green and gray, and whizzing at fantastic speed.

Inquest at Calne, England, failed entirely to discover—nor could British R.A.F. authorities help—why the wings fell off a four-engined plane, which crashed from a cloud, killing all aboard. Plane did not catch fire, but disintegrated.

A new Gloster Javelin, all-weather jet vanished mysteriously over England.

Over Torquay, England, mysterious orange and

fiery red-balls seen moving at dusk, high over the English Channel.

At Dhubri, India, a thing like an illuminated dinner-plate flashed towards Assam, leaving a fiery wake.

November 3, 1954: For fourth time, car windshields fissure near Chalfont St. Giles, England.

November 5, 1954: While investigating a mysterious affair on a former "pagan hill," near historic Winchester, England—I, the author of this book found that, on night of November 5, 1954, two hundred yards of turf had been removed, to a depth of about six inches, forming a symbol somewhat like a mark of interrogation. Up to date, the mystery remains unsolved.

In the course of my investigations I met an ex-airwoman who told me that, on that very night, about twenty miles from this hill, her radio set suddenly went dead, about 9 P.M. Her thoroughbred bull-terrier rose and growled. This has happened before. Also, in 1931, on one occasion she heard, outside the window at night, a queer swish, which, as an airwoman, she recognized must have been made by some type of aircraft. But when she and her daughter went outside, they saw nothing in the sky.

From another part of England—Bradford, Yorks —some hundreds of miles north, another woman, who does not know of the existence of the first, also found her radio unaccountably go dead, and her cat showed signs of uneasiness, and had its eyes fixed on the window, against which there suddenly sounded a queer swish. This woman too at once went outside, saw nothing in the sky, and found no evidence of wind-disturbance, or pranks of boys.

November 6, 1954: Belgian professional men form "Committee to Welcome Martians." A company director, Marcel Rubens, wants to "get in first with interplanetary trade."

Reports appear that Uncle Sam plans to set up, next year, an artificial planet 500 miles out in space.

Primitive rock-painting of *very* ancient date, found in South Africa, shows strange red circular objects landing, and men running away in panic.

South Africa Air Force plans research on flying saucers. "Extremely important," says Air Chief.

November 7, 1954: A motor-cyclist and a taxi-driver separately gave the police at Nucro, Sardinia, detailed corroboratory descriptions of a saucer they said had landed in a field, on the slopes of Mt. Orto-wene. Gianni Camabosu, the motor-cyclist, said the saucer gave him such a turn he fell off his bike. To prove it, he showed a grazed forearm. The taxi-man, Francesco Tanda, got out of his taxi and walked towards the discoidal saucer. As he approached it, it took off at high speed, emitting a low whistle. Peas-ants, and three girls on the other side of Mt. Orto-wene, later reported seeing the disc in flight on that afternoon. The saucer was around fifteen feet in diameter, silver in hue, and of metal scaled like a fish. On top was a kind of turret, with a port of ap-parently thick glass.

Six times in late October and November, a queer pattern of blobs was seen on radar sets in England. Their course: east to west. The War Office and Air Ministry do not know what the blobs are. As in a recent case over Berlin, the objects suddenly appear about 1 P.M., at 11,500 feet altitude heading west, always in similar formation. Since they are invisible to the eye, they appear to be fourth-dimensional. Their trajectory passes from a loop into parallel lines, and finally into a curious Z formation, when they vanish off the radarscopes.

November 8, 1954: Almost all Italy again "het" up. Saucers appear and discharge the filmy woolly stuff, called "Virgin Mary's hair," and also seen in France, the United States, and Canada. Formations of un-known sky-objects have panicked the fishermen of Leghorn. Newspapermen have seen them, and spec-tators at a football match at Florence watched a flight of saucers pass overhead. Mrs. Clare Luce, American ambassador, believes they are extra-terres-trial. In Monza, at 10:30 P.M., man going home from a cinema, got off his bicycle when he saw an intense light on a sports field. He peered through some boards and saw a luminous body and two small shadowy ob-jects. Crowds gathered and spectators say they saw "figures in white pants, grey jerkins, and transparent helmets." Under the intense glare from a saucer, there was silhouetted a "queer luminous body and two little entities who emitted guttural sounds. One had a black face with a sort of trunk," perhaps a breathing-apparatus. Bricks were thrown but when they struck the saucer, there was no clang. They seemed to have impacted on soft stuff!

The disc was in two sections and seemed to rest on

the ground as if on a tripod. On top, from a half-circle conning-tower or cabin, so strong a light came that it was blindingly silver. Over it was a thing like an antenna. Breaking down the gates the crowd rushed the saucer-entities, who retreated to the disc. One sicced a boxer dog onto the entities, but the intelligent beast turned on *him*, and bit *him!* The entities got aboard the disc, and with a whuff, and a shrill siren hoot, it rose vertically from the field and vanished at high speed. (Reported that 150 Italians saw the saucer and entities.)

November 9, 1954: A sheep station hand at Wilcannia, Australia, took three photos of an object moving in the sky 500 feet up, and making a "terrible noise." It looked like an inverted saucer, with an inverted teacup on top.

Two villagers at Bois de Villers, Belgium, say they saw a "flying egg," six feet tall, land in a cow pasture. "Screams came from it," they say.

November 11, 1954: Small, dull red cigar flies at 600 miles an hour, at 5 P.M., over Whitstable, England. Skeptic said it was just neon-lit plane advertising varnish for "young bitches' nails." (Did he lose in a breach-of-promise action?)

Professor Hermann Oberth, famous rocket expert, theorizes that the saucers may bring us "Uranides" from a distant world.

Police and coast guards at Lowestoft, England, off North Sea, unable to find origin or explanation of mysterious explosion heard by hundreds, after dark.

November 12, 1954: Vatican, Rome, offers gold medal and twenty dollars for a story on a trip to the Moon. *Snag:* Must be done in Latin.

November 14, 1954: Three hundred Swiss soldiers, on maneuvers at Grandvillard, southern Switzerland, see a disc with red glow on silvery side hover motionless, 10,000 feet above.

British Interplanetary Society complains that British War Ministries are strangling all rocket and interplanetary research, and even the most harmless technical information is suppressed.

Police at Helsinki, Finland, find that a shoemaker at Alavieska, hitched a small flashlight to a tame crow, and passed him off as a saucer! We suggest that he—not the crow—be sentenced to live on bird-seed, two days a week.

November 15, 1954: Strange gleaming white object

hangs motionless (about fifteen miles) over Louisville, Kentucky, from 3 to 6 P.M. Jet pilot failed to sight it after climbing to over seven miles up.

November 16, 1954: Glowing object, emitting bluish-yellow light, flies very high and very fast over suburbs of Melbourne, Australia. *Not* a meteor or plane.

Many shapes of saucers seen over Palestine (Israel and Jordan), Sea of Galilee, and Jerusalem, and along Levantine coast. One, like a rocket, zig-zags in flight, very fast and brilliant. Saucer like "flying house" has smoke billowing from its windows; globe, emitting dazzling light, seen at 300-foot height. Cigar-shaped saucer speeds with two fire-tails behind; egg-shaped saucer, at great speed, is aureoled with clear and powerful light. Daylight flight of saucers seen over Safad, Galilee.

November 18, 1954: "Flying grape-fruit" saucer seen over Camberwell, England, at 11 P.M. "Grape-fruit" saucer has ball of orange fire and jets out smoke. Vanished southwards.

November 18, 1954: National Geographic Society, Washington, D.C., reports an expanding shell of dust and gas in the Crab nebula, remnant of a gigantic explosion seen by Chinese astronomers in A.D. 1054. This holds one strong cosmic radio source. Others are in Cassiopeia, Sagittarius, and Cygnus constellations, and two turbulent gas-clouds in the Milky Way.

November 19, 1954: Hermann Klein, former German Nazi scientist, now in Zürich, Switzerland, says he was present, in 1945, in Prague, Czechoslovakia, when Germans started work on a terrestrial saucer. In 1942, they sent up a pilotless, tele-guided disc that flew from Stettin, on the Baltic, to Spitzbergen, in the Arctic. It was made at the V-1 and V-2 Nazi base at Peenemunde, now under Soviet control. These Nazi airfoils, he said, were very maneuverable. They left trail of vari-colored flames. They had a central stabilizer to prevent overturning. Of the three men who built them, Schriever died at Bremen in 1953; an Italian, Belonzo, died in 1952; and Miethe is now in the United States. Klein says he is now constructing a small saucer driven by electricity. Klein says American air force is instructed not to shoot down foreign terrestrial saucers but to force them down.

November 20, 1954: "I was recently in Austin, Texas, when I heard of a mystery in the neighborhood. A woman had 'seen and heard' blasts. The American

Air Force denied that any jets were the cause. The blasts occurred mostly in the night hours. About the same time, there fell, in an inaccessible forested area of Minnesota, a flaming, cone-shaped object. Seen as far north as Canada." (*Letter to the author from Mr. Ed. Worthley, San Francisco.*)

November 21, 1954: A fleet of nineteen saucers caused a panic when they flew at "tremendous speed," fewer than 350 yards from an airliner, bound for Rio de Janeiro, Brazil.

November 25, 1954: Meteorite crashes through roof of house in Alabama, and injures hip of woman, sleeping on couch. Husband threatens suit if the United States Air Force does not return the fragment, for which they have been offered $5,000.

November 25, 1954: Two discoidal saucers, with a sort of conning-tower, flew over Taormina, Sicily, in broad daylight. Were watched by many people on the beach.

November 27, 1954: Why did the South Goodwins lightship, in the Straits of Dover, send out no radio signals, when a violent storm drove her from her moorings? Why did she not send up flares or rockets? She was in a busy steam lane, yet all men in her vanished off the lightship, fate unknown. Why, in the North Sea, have similar radio failures occurred in airliners, some of which met disaster? *Who,* or *what* is busy on these occasions? Echo in a sea-shell merely answers: "WHO? WHAT?"

November 28, 1954: A light green, pear-shaped meteor, big as a moon, was seen flying over Austria and Czechoslovakia, about twenty miles a second. Whether or not it *was* a meteor, a Yugoslav scientist asserts that seven flying saucers, about this time must be secret weapons of the United States or Russia! (*Author's Comment:* No doubt, from the old planet called Baloney.)

November 29, 1954: At an official inquiry into the loss of the Dutch K.L.M., Super Constellation, Triton airliner, which mysteriously crashed almost immediately after taking off from Shannon Airport, Eire, the Captain (Viruly) says he had noticed a peculiar noise from a port engine, when the liner took off.

Viruly made a strange remark whose significance he may, or may not realize: "Just before we crashed down from the air, I had the feeling—instinctive and not derived from instrument-indications—that the aircraft I was *in was not meant to fly.*"

(Suppose *something unseen* in the sky had deliberately intended that the airliner should not fly? *Author.*)

Edward Whitney of the Shannon Airport's fire and police force, said he had seen a light flashing in the estuary after the airliner took off in the darkness. The control tower signalled: "Who are you?" but got no reply, although the light kept flashing.

November 30, 1954: Using light beams—not radio or teletype waves—in a test to find if they could get any reply from saucers in space, three Illinois engineers and other observers heard sounds like the ringing of bells, and unintelligible vocables. These messages, whether or not from outer space, seemed machine-keyed, as well as very rapid.

November 30, 1954: The Great Mystery of the alleged two lunar satellites of the earth: U.S. press reports say that the earth has captured two large chunks of meteoric origin, orbiting the earth at 650 to 1,000 kilometers' distance, respectively. But Copenhagen astronomers report nothing even remotely like such satellites. *Very* unusual circumstances are required for the capture of a new "moon" by the earth; and satellites rotating 621 miles from the earth, would reflect so much light, that even the smallest telescopes would see them.

November 30, 1954: Why the unknown stuff—referred to as "Angels' Hair," or as the Belgian and French call it, "Cheveux de la Sainte Vierge" (Virgin Mary's hair—albeit, why the Lady should be so prodigal of it as to fling it about this planet's *airways,* I know not!) Is it jettisoned from cigar-shaped, or other saucers to sterilize the air, or render radioactive fall-outs innocuous? Has it any connection with their propulsion in our atmosphere? Who *knows?*

It is called "spun glass," in Italy, and theorized to be of silicon. Mrs. Dittmar, of Marysville, Ohio, saw a silver cigar-form saucer, emitting an eye-blinding light, discharge it. It drifted to the ground, in long fibers. "It is soft and fine to the touch, but not sticky, and stretches without tearing, although it stains the hands green." It seems to vanish without trace or residue.

November 30, 1954: At 7:55 P.M., Mr. Albert, Mayor of Abbey Wood, on the southeast edge of

London, saw a long, flaming tube with rounded ends, in the sky, hovering, and glowing red. Its trailing edges swelled with white flame, which rose and fell.

(*Author's Comment:* An object like this was seen by me, at Bexleyhealth, five miles away from Abbey Wood, at 6:25 A.M., on July 23, 1954. It is likely to be seen again and again.)

Old Father Time, in the closing month of 1954, must have wrinkled his brows and scratched his gray head over still more mysteries, not all of them in the air:

December 1, 1954: The Canadian Minister of Trade, Mr. C. D. Howe, says in London, that the loudly trumpeted hush-hush project of the flying saucer of the Avro airplane firm, Canada, is to be dropped. "Had no useful purpose," says he.

(*Author's Comment:* Then what in heaven, or the other interesting place, *was* its purpose? For the Canadian tax-payer lost $155,000,000 on it—not that that will deprive any politician masquerading as a statesman of sleep.

December 2, 1954: Strange thunderstorm over London flooded West End and Trafalgar Square, and southern England. As Mrs. Jeanne Macdonald-Gregory, ex-airwoman who watched it, wrote me: "The sky did not contain the normal heavy electric thunderclouds, but moving layers black in parts. Two falls of hail large as marbles. The one thing that will certainly interest you is that during the *whole* of this gale-period, the R.A.F. had jet fighters up! *Why?* I ran into a blank wall of silence.

"I watched no fewer than five jets climbing like mad to their maximum height, the cloudbase, at that period being around 50,000 feet. I saw two of the fighter jets break away and dart off at right angles, as if they had suddenly seen something else in a different quarter.

"No Air Force would send up planes in that sort of weather, if they had not been at *panic stations.* Was the phenomenon induced by the sixty-three atomic explosions, or by those watching us from outer space? That electric storm made me wonder. Am I crazy to think it was not quite 'natural'?"

(*Author's Comment:* No! Nor is the author of this book crazy. She adds that she is logging all mysterious interruptions to her radio. It is to be noted that animals and birds are sensitive to queer things in the sky. Mrs. J. McG. adds: "My dog's antics are peculiar. These past two nights he wakes me up at from 2-2:30 A.M. He is very intelligent. Next time he does it, I'll get up and look at the sky.")

December 6, 1954: The phenomenon of "whistlers," theorized to be musical-quality signals from outer space, picked up on radio sets and supposed to be electric discharges, going back and forth, pendulum-like, twelve times and lasting a minute and a half, are being studied by Stanford University, California, and the Bureau of Standards.

The first one was recorded by a German field operator in World War I. A U.S. Navy icebreaker is to use instruments for listening in to "whistlers" in the Antarctic. The British are cooperating at Bermuda and the Falkland Isles. Dr. Helliwell, Stanford University professor, does not believe they are signals from other planets. Believed that masses in outer space play some part in the phenomena.

December 7, 1954: Trawler in Loch Ness used echo sounder and found its "monster" on bed of this very deep lake. It measured fifty feet long, with an eighteen-foot tail, and a small head. It had eight legs and the silhouette of a mammoth scorpion! It was detected at depth of 540 feet, the lake being at least 750 feet deep. Trawler, turned round, startled monster. I have, myself, toured this loch, but did not see the famous monster—which, however, is very far indeed, from being a product of Scottish whisky distilleries. Mystery is: where does it go in the intervals of its disappearances?

December 8, 1954: Why did the ebb tide in Leonardville harbor, Bay of Fundy, suddenly flow back, quite out of the order of nature, and rise perpendicularly one foot, three or four times, at half-ebb, before it resumed its normal fall? Was there a submarine upheaval? No one knows the solution of the mystery.

December 9, 1954: Woman at Melbourne, Australia, in early morning, hears a buzzing, and sees saucer of "enormous size," hovering over a field. Another woman at Bonbeach, Port Phillip Bay, sees golden object circling in sky. It whizzed over the skyline and, a few minutes later, a cigar-shaped saucer came up from where the other had vanished. *It* looped, leaving puffs of black gases, and shot off.

In Australia, investigators find four main types of

saucers: (1) cigar-shaped, glowing, seen mostly at night; (2) rotating discs, often in pairs, rotary motion being in upper sections, with ports, and small, ball-like wheels underneath; (3) bright lights like "moons," which flash, hover and suddenly vanish; (4) largest class of all—small, hovering lights, hanging in sky, and dashing off at high speed. In daylight, their surfaces gleam like burnished metal.

December 12, 1954: Monster saurian seen in deep subterranean canyon off shore at La Jolla, California. Was also seen in 1944. Scared fishermen fled from "horrible sight." Manning Edmundson also saw it from U.S. cruiser's deck, whose officers thought it was a big stump and changed course. (Volcanic and submarine convulsions, probably along with rising temperatures on sea-beds, force these unknown monsters up from great depths.)

December 13, 1954: Birmingham, England, police are baffled by a mystery of fire. Eleven times in eleven weeks, cars, vans, cycles and trucks have been found on fire. Fingerprinting and police cordons cannot trap arsonist. No signs of what caused the fires.

December 15, 1954: Australian Navy pilot, chased by two saucers as he flew back to base in the dark. Radar at Nowra, showed the saucers flying together. "Unknown objects," says Australian Navy Minister. (*N.B.* On radar, the objects were seen to draw away from the plane, and gradually vanish. Incident kept dark for three months.)

December 16, 1954: Mr. and Mrs. Chapman, driving in car to Oklahoma City, saw bright blue light, a hundred yards east, moving parallel to car. It carried small red and white light, in front, and larger blue light at rear. Silent, vanished in flash. Seen from location, mile south of U.S. Highway 66.

December 17, 1954: D.C. airliner (British pilot), between Malmo and Stockholm, Sweden, startled when metal sphere flashed at amazing speed under his plane. Object was completely symmetrical.

U.S. Air Force has "no evidence that we are being observed by machines from outer space, or by a foreign power." (Long John Silver had no evidence that ole Ben Gunn was around in the night, until he found all the gold had gone from the cache, in the day!)

December 18, 1954: Thing like large electric globe, pear-shaped, and tapering to a point, whizzed across the sky, in daylight, at Black Rock, Victoria, Australia. Seen by seven people.

December 19, 1954: A strange "boiling" of the water, half a mile off Kentish coast, at Dungeness, England, tore to pieces a net worth $1,500. When they unravelled what was left of the net, they found in it an unknown monster, fourteen feet long and a ton in weight. It had slate-blue, smooth skin, huge mouth with teeth, eyes like those of a horse, and rows of gills like those of a shark. London zoo expert wonders if it is an extinct species.

Mr. Fox Holden tells editor of the American magazine, "Imagination," that some months before, he was gazing through a telescope at the moon, when he saw a small dark speck move in a straight line and then make an abrupt ninety degree turn and vanish.

December 19, 1954: A milkman and four security guards at Daudenougar, Australia, saw at 2:55 A.M., a blue light flash up the ground. In the sky a strange object with a tail jetting flames like red-hot lava, rushed out of a cloud, 1,000 feet overhead, and streaked across the sky. It had a silver-yellow tail. At 3:25 A.M., in the same region, a thing with blue-green tail of light coming from underside, appears and suddenly disappears.

December 25, 1954: "Marvellously warm night. I and my son were out on our gold-reef in Victoria, Australia. Stars magnificent in cloudless sky, light northerly airs. Dead overhead, suddenly, a thing meandered in a curious undulatory flight, quite unlike that of a plane. Vanished over trees in darkness. Flew lower than east-west passenger planes which cross this region. Bill saw it first and let out a yell. I rushed around and saw orange flying saucer, in undulating flight, going southeast. My first saucer! As if to confirm it was no plane, later saw a red light top a ridge half a mile north. Low across our camp came a four-engine passenger plane all lights on, flying beautifully, for Essendon airport. Quite different *its* flight from that of the saucer, which was noiseless."

(*Letter to author from his friend, H. K. Hotham, of Melbourne, Victoria, Australia.*)

December 20, 1954: Three Uruguayan towns report round, brilliant objects going south at great speed. Towns are miles apart.

December 24, 1954: At Sao Paulo, Brazil, eye-witnesses allege that fragments of metal came from a flying saucer. Brazilian Air Ministry says analysis showed eighty-nine per cent of it was tin—but have not analyzed the eleven per cent residue.

December 27, 1954: Brilliant "triangle" hovered low in sky over Cobalt, Ontario, for five hours. It rose and descended, sometimes slowly, sometimes at fantastic speed. Moved north and vanished.

December 28, 1954: Three people in a car near Chippewa Falls, Wisconsin, were terrified to see a red thing the size of a baseball, strike their radio antenna, and hit the chrome trim over the driver's window with a clang like metal impacting on metal. It then whizzed off into the night.

December 28, 1954: At 3:45 A.M., in Paris, M. Paulin saw in the sky, between the Eiffel Tower and the Parc des Expositions, at a height not easy to estimate, a disc emitting a bluish phosphorescence. It was motionless. Having a camera, he took a picture of the object, giving the film an exposure of two minutes. In this time, the disc slowly shifted to the right. It appeared to be studying the center of Paris. The Observatory had no comment to make. The disc vanished at very high speed.

December 29, 1954: R.A.F. expedition announces that the North Magnetic Pole is not on Prince of Wales Island or Boothia Peninsula, but in the Sverdrup archipelago, 500 miles north of these locations. The Sverdrups are about 770 miles from the geographic North Pole. In certain quarters this set off a panic yarn that the North Magnetic Pole is moving and that, coupled with a toppling of the axis of the earth, a catastrophe is at hand.

Author's Comment: For many years past, the North Magnetic Pole has been periodically moving from east to west of north and back again. The phenomenon is *not* new. It has long been known as variation or declination. In 1652, and again in 1669 and 1670, the Magnetic North coincided with the *geographic north.*

Whether or not these secular changes are owing to geological changes in the earth's crust, we do not don has diminished from 24½ degrees West of North to 17 degrees West.

The phenomenon was brought to my personal attention, in 1937, relative to a strange chart of Captain Kidd's Island, in Oak Bay, Nova Scotia, of which chart I shall some day tell the singularly romantic story. This vellum chart showed *true north.* It was found in old French records in Ottawa that, in 1669 and 1670, when this treasure island chart was made, the magnetic and geographic North coincided.

There is a curious sort of pendulum swing from west to east, and back from east to west. It is *not* new, nor an indication of coming cataclysm. I do *not* say that ominous climatic changes in the Arctic and Antarctic may not prelude or portend trouble; but this secular shifting of the North Magnetic Pole is *not,* necessarily, such a portent.

I am aware that Mr. H. Auchinloss Brown of New York, has compiled data, according to which the five and a half million square miles of ice, two miles thick in the Antarctic, may eventually aggravate the oscillation, or mutation of the earth's spinning axes and cause the earth to topple over and rotate about a new axis.

(This has happened ages ago, the gamut of strata in Spitzbergen indicates.) I also know that another authority, Dr. Laurence Gould, of California, points out, that if the ice of Greenland and Antarctica melt, the sea-levels may be raised a hundred and fifty feet and bring about another deluge.

I have also myself pointed out, that not only is the Arctic Sea slowly warming up, but ice-floes from the Antarctic have, for some years past been found nearer and nearer Australia. But this may be trouble that is not imminent; and the secular shifting of the North Magnetic Pole is probably not connected with the other phenomena.

1955 opens with a fresh spate of mysteries, portents, "signs of the times," and riddles:

January 1, 1955: One of my readers in Australia, Mr. Griffith P. Taylor, of Miranda, writes: "Between 9:35 and 9:45 P.M., January 1, I and my wife were on the Manby Ferry, in Sydney. The sky was cloudless and the moon in the first quarter, low in the western sky. Suddenly a luminous cloud, abnormally persistent in shape and position, appeared moving slowly right and downwards. After it had disappeared, another luminous cloud appeared. This was bell-shaped, and brighter in its upper and outer parts. For sixty seconds, it moved down to right, and split up into four ovoids reminding me of the four luminous clouds seen over Salem Air Station, in your book, 'Flying Saucers on the Attack.' These ovoids, too, vanished gradually. Now a smaller cloud appeared to the right, and condensed into two more ovoids waned, formed another luminous cloud, and vanished. I fancy it is only when these phenomena come between the moon and the observer that they are seen." (Mr. Taylor sends a sketch of what he saw. *Author*.)

January 1, 1955: Fifty people in Lima, Peru, see about 9:30 P.M., five saucers, brilliantly silver and emitting intense light, hover over the city for eight minutes.

A letter from another of my readers, Mr. Robt. C. Walker of Barker St., S.E., Washington, D.C.: "I'd like to ask you if there is anything in the Bible about flying saucers?" (*N.B.* Mr. Walker was referred to *Ezekiel*, chap. I, possibly showing that the ancient Hebrews, like Pharaoh Thutmosis, his army and his priests of Amon-Ra, saw a fleet of them). Mr. Walker adds: "My stepfather and others in his crew of the U.S. Air Force, flying on a mission from Panama to Bolling Airfield, had a saucer visitor for a few minutes, on their flight in June, 1953. It made a forty-five degree angle and vanished."

January 2, 1955: Metallic, mushroom-shaped object seen by air pilot Capt. D. Barker, flying low above the Yarra Valley, Eastern Australia, at 10:25 A.M. The object was four times the size of a DC-4 Convair airliner. Speed around 700 miles an hour; in sight for ten seconds. Under it hung a glittering thing like a gondola. Shafts of light occasionally shot through as if it were of plastic or celluloid. Pilot was sure the object was of solid metal. (*N.B.* A similar sighting reported by a pilot over Queensland, Australia, in the summer of 1954. It seemed to have a "glass dome.")

January 3, 1955: Six silver saucers, with red wakes, watched by panicking Viennese.

January 4, 1955: "Vegetable life, possibly, but no warm-blooded creatures on Mars," asserts astro-physicist Strughold. (*Author's Comment:* But what about the *underground* of Mars?)

January 10, 1955: Mr. Derek Laweden, mathematical lecturer at Birmingham University, England, complains of stifling by British scientific and official bureaucrats of free discussion on space-rockets. British have to turn to Switzerland or America.

(*Author's Comment:* Alas, there is a pronounced recent dry-up of such technical data from the United States, where also the ineffable bureaucrat is in the saddle and is riding the free American to death!)

January 11, 1955: Dr. V. Hajek, scientist, was motorcycling across a bridge near Victoria, Australia, when he heard a "sudden dreadful noise." Looked back expecting to see the bridge collapsing, but saw an object in sky like "a large metal propeller rotating at high speed." The mystery thing was travelling at around 800 miles an hour, about 300 feet up. It was highly burnished and elliptical, and slightly blurred. Diameter: about forty feet; visible twelve seconds.

January 16, 1955: I myself was startled, when at 1:30 P.M., a sudden black pall turned day into night over my house in Kent, and all over the county of London. Some folk said they saw a strange yellow star in the sky. Other folk thought the end of the world was at hand! Ships in the Thames dropped anchor; birds flew into windows; people ran out into the street. Phenomenon lasted ten minutes. Meteorological Office said: "Just smog—smoke trapped between two winds." Well, that may or may *not* be the explanation; in sixty-three years I have never seen the like. *Author.*

(*N.B.* Accounts of this sort are recorded in Byzantine chronicles. In the eighth century there were "months" of total darkness over Constantinople. The ancient Roman annalists had recorded this phenomenon a thousand years earlier.)

January 19, 1955: Amazing so-called "zephyr" *roared* (not the usual way of a *zephyr!*) several miles up over Philadelphia. Speed: 322 miles an hour. At San Francisco, surface winds of 100 to 225 miles an hour. Inland: two feet of snow in desert. (*Author:* Could it be caused by radioactive spores in stratosphere? Denials from official scientists come rather louder than natural.)

January 21, 1955: A weird black object, about thirty feet in diameter, came down rapidly in sky and halted for four minutes at the height of Carew Tower, Cincinnati, at 5:25 A.M. It was watched by Mr. David Owen, who as the British say, "had the wind put up him." It was, he says, like ebony. "I'd like to know what it was." (U.S. Weather Bureau Chief, A. W. Walstrom, is candid. "It's anybody's guess. I don't know what it was.")

January 21, 1955: French Air Ministry, which does "not believe in flying saucers," nevertheless orders pilots to chase them if they appear in the sky.

Port Elizabeth, South Africa, sees ten large egg-shaped, glowing objects travelling in the night sky in formation. In the van was a "purple, sausage-shaped object, which went out over the sea, glowing in its flight."

January 22, 1955: Near the Bonin Islands, in the Pacific, is a mystery spot called the "Devil's Deep," where nine ships have vanished without trace, between 1949 and 1955, with a loss of 215 men.

On January 5, 1955, a 144-ton survey ship, "Shihyo Maru," vanished in it, with all aboard. As in previous mysterious sinkings there, the sea was calm and the skies fair. The "Shihyo Maru" was blown up by some mysterious underwater explosion, while charting a reef, which had risen, smoking like a volcano, in September, 1950. Wreckage has been washed up, but not a single body. Air-sea searches find no clew. Japanese Maritime and Coast Guard now list it as a danger zone, but can offer no solution of the riddle. No fishermen will venture near it.

(*Author's Comment:* Gold Hill, Oregon, and Santa Cruz, California, have strange areas where gravity-pull and magnetism are distorted with optical and visual inversions. My friend, Dr. Meade Layne, of San Diego, California, wonders if fragments of very high-density matter embedded in the earth at these spots exert "contra-terrene" effects. Is there in this "Devil's Deep" an analagous submarine phenomenon?)

Reports from area of great earthquake (Nevada, December, 1954). Found to have ripped a fissure sixty miles long and twelve miles wide. Area looks as if angry Titans had been demonstrating against radioactive fallouts and explosions, waking them up from immemorial sleep. Mountains gashed for miles, with twelve foot horizontal slips forming, says geologist Gianella, the "most spectacular faulting ever seen in U.S."

January 23, 1955: Mysterious object crashed through bedroom window of William Cunningham of Darby, Pa., started a fire in the house, and wrecked upper floor. Fireman tested the metallic fragments, in a temperature of 2,700 degrees. They did not melt, merely glowed cherry-red, and rapidly cooled off, *with retention of shape!* No magnetic reaction; resistance to electricity almost zero. Mr. Cunningham, aged 50, was burned to the bone when he caught up fragment and tried to hurl it outside.

(*Author's Comment:* Did this fireball come from one of the *hostile flying saucers?* It is certainly no terrestrial bomb. Note too: steel melts at about 2,800 degrees Fahr., aluminium, tin, nickel, cobalt, silver, copper, zinc, cast iron, gold at temperatures, respectively of, 1,215, 449, 2,781, 2,786, 1,764, 1,949, 2,780, and 788 degrees Fahr. This metal is hardly meteoric.)

Five days earlier, two meteorites, larger than golf-balls, punched holes through the aluminium dome of the private astronomical observatory of Mr. L. Hawthorne, at Kirkland, Wash., at 11:45 A.M.

Uncle Sam now has guided missiles with transoceanic range, and speeds up to 9,000 miles an hour. Said to be ten times more accurate than the Nazi wartime V-2 rockets; will land within any given area of ten square miles.

January 28, 1955: A strange blue light has repeatedly been seen, by the Oregon State Highway Department snow-plow team, bobbing in the air over the Blue Mountains. Manuel Erikson dimmed his lights, and stopped. The blue light also stopped. Then it began to oscillate; it vanished with a hum, over some trees. When Erikson re-started his plow, the blue light re-appeared in the air, to his right, gave occasional azure flashes, and then vanished. Later, another man stopped his plow to adjust it, when he was surprised to find that he was casting a shadow. Looking up, he saw a blue light emitting a humming sound, and bobing up and down. His hair rose on his scalp, when it followed him and the plow, and leisurely moved into a canyon.

January 29, 1955: An engineer in Cracow, Upper Silesia, Soviet-controlled zone, read a story about saucers in a Western periodical. He translated it for Polish, Czechoslovakian and Hungarian engineers, who said *they* had seen them in in their countries, but thought they were British or American inventions.

February, 1955, rolled out its panorama of mysteries:

February 5, 1955: Chinese, at Singapore, start club for saucer enthusiasts and space-rocket fans.

February 6, 1955: Cigar-shaped silvery object in sky flashed at tremendous speed, throwing a blinding light over west coast of South Island, New Zealand. Seemed to split in two, lost altitude and vanished with an appalling explosion. Earth-tremor and smoke followed. Hundreds of square miles in isolated region were shaken.

February 9, 1955: Tram-driver Ryan, and bus conductor Dalvine, see at 9:40 P.M., over Malvern, Australia, strange object with a yellow center hovering high in the sky. Estimated five times the size of a plane.

February 11, 1955: Three girls, lunching in their office at Chichester, Sussex, saw six gleaming "tadpole" saucers frisking above clouds. Very high and fast, and seemed to reflect light like metal. Not long after, at West Wittering, a few miles away, a boy (14), saw a cigar-shaped saucer moving slowly. It was presently joined by small discs, and vanished into clouds. (Looks like a mother, or cosmic space ship, with satellite discs. Some say, or theorize that these discs televise scenes back to the mother space ship. Old England, like France, Italy, and the United States, seems to attract this cigar airfoil.)

February 14, 1955: As thousands in the district around Grisi, Sicily, abandon town after a week of terrifying and weird "hiccuping" earth tremors; as Stromboli belches out flame, white-hot lava and gases, flowing into sea and air, and raining rocks and red-hot ash; as old Etna goes into action, as he did in the days of Plinius Secundus, a new volcano rises from the ocean, at East Tuluman, off Manus Island, in the South Pacific.

February 23, 1955: Mysterious explosions shake eastern shores of Japan. Tokyo meteorological experts say: "Cause is sudden changes in atmospheric pressure." (*Author's Comment:* If so, *what caused them?* Aftermath of hydrogen-bomb blasts?)

Electronic brain machine, UNIVAC, of Mt. Wilson Observatory, re-discovers Jupiter's 8th moon, about 15,000,000 miles from the planet.

February 24, 1955: Dr. Walther Dronberger, one-time Nazi rocket man, predicts in New York that, fifteen years hence, rocket plane will transport people from San Francisco to Sydney, Australia, in an hour and a half. Altitude will be thirty miles, speed 13,000 miles an hour.

February 25, 1955: U.S. icebreaker, "Atka," returning from forty-one days of exploration of Antarctica,
finds like the Australians—that pack-ice is farther
south than in former years. Indicates that earth may
be entering on a cycle of warmth. Some observers
even suppose that, within the time of some now alive,
Arctic and Antarctic pack-ice will thaw in summer.
The Atka sighted a berg fifty miles long, and took
four hours to steam round it. Even its peaks were
shrouded in mists. It had a "calf" more than a mile
long.

February 26, 1955: Reported on this day, a sighting
on January 5, at 7:29 P.M., by S.S. "Bendigo,"
freighter in the Red Sea, west of the Arabian Hedjaz.
Greenish-white object in the sky, astern, maintained a
steady height, course and speed, and left a vaporous
wake.

The month of March, 1955, all around the world, certainly did not suggest that our mysterious visitants had
left off snooping, prying and peering around every corner
of our old planet. In more than one case, guys and ladies
who did *not* stay up all night, were fetched out of bed
on the run, in pyjamas or mid-Victorian night-shirts.

March 1, 1955: Silvery object, very high in sky, seen
to reverse course from N.W. to S.E. over Moola
Boola station, 240 miles from Perth, Australia.

March 1, 1955: Curious details continue to reach the
author of this book about mysterious messages in
code, reaching ham or amateur radio operators, one
at least of whom appears to have a connection with
a certain big short-wave station. It is possible that
these incidents have not gone unmarked by national
security authorities at Washington, D.C., but *their*
interest is not necessarily identical with that of the
"interplanetary enthusiasts."

I am informed that coded messages have come in
for one hour; the next message having a time interval of two seconds fewer; the third, four seconds
fewer; the fourth, six seconds fewer; and so on, in a
kind of geometrical progression. It is also alleged
that, in the background, is the hum of very powerful
motors. Five amateurs are concerned, and one of
them is said to have worked for the United States
government. There is said to be a call sign, "S.R.,"
and the messages are said to come in on a forty-

meter waveband. In one case, the message faded out nine minutes before the end, or zero. The receivers —the operators—assert that these messages are from entities unknown, in outer space. Miss Mildred M. Maier, of Ashland Avenue, Chicago, whose remarkable photo of cosmic phenomena and weird saucers, or space ships, seen over and near Chicago, appears in this book, was called on by a security officer who asked for a copy of a coded message, apparently from outer space, which message she tells me she received over WGN station, and that it was preceded by a silence of fifteen seconds, asking for "space to come in."

Author's Comment: No one can tell, as yet, if these coded messages emanate from outer space from entities attempting to contact the earth. If so, why do they not use some terrestrial code in some terrestrial language? Or why do they send to hams, or for that matter, official radio operators, messages impossible to decipher? It is *not* my business to suggest what Washington security officers, or do not think, about these strange messages; although I might have no great difficulty in forming a theory.

A certain Mr. John Otto, patent engineer in Chicago, and a group of associates are using a receiver composed of a photo-electric cell, and an audio-amplifier varying infra-red or "black light beams"— for transmitting and receiving. They assert that, not only have they picked up from outer space an unknown code, somewhat like the Morse code, but "voice-messages in a syllabic language, and voices in chorus saying the same thing, one sounding high-pitched and feminine, another masculine and guttural. *March 3, 1955:* Taking a closer peer-in at the unfashionable Moon, Dr. Gerard Kuiper, University of Chicago, saw through the eighty-two inch McDonald telescope, at Fort Davis, Texas, glittering white spots on the lunar surface. Adjusting the lens, he made out largish boulders, and he theorizes that the Moon was not torn off our own Pacific, but was earth's binary, and passed through a host of cosmic satellites to where it now rotates.

ALL THROUGH THE MONTHS of May and June, 1955, the British, as now the Australian press, was singularly silent on the subject of saucers and I am of opinion that, in the case of Britain, the silence is *not* to be attributed to the wave of strikes: shipping, railroads and newspaper. In Britain, as in Australia, there is good reason to suppose that the press and the governments are engaged in a conspiracy of silence on this very serious theme. A woman correspondent of mine writes me, from a British naval dockyard town, where strange phenomena, concerned with continued and mysterious interruptions to radio, have badly rattled the puzzled British Navy authorities:

> "I can get no British naval or air officer to pass any comment on *ufos*. I find that the 'edge' of these radio cut-offs is only around 500 yards from my house and does not affect the east of S . . . at all. It seems to happen around 9 P.M., and a woman friend of mine did not find any interference, but she lived beyond this 'edge.' One thing I can tell you: every time I mention the phenomenon, or speak of *ufos* to one particular naval officer-friend of mine, I come against a wall of silence. He turns the subject aside, and won't say a word. I am sure the subject of *ufos* is definitely taboo in naval and air circles."

Nevertheless, I got myself a stream of curious airmails from all over Western Europe, U.S.A., South America and Australia and New Zealand, about saucer and other mysteries. Here is a typical report:

In the lonely region of the wooded and mountainous Auvergne, Puy-de-Dôme, in south-central France, on June 5, 1955, a flying saucer actually came down from an altitude of about 1,300 feet, where it had hung silently in the sky, to the ground. There it hovered fewer than four-and-a-half-feet above the head of an astounded farmer,

268

Jean-Baptiste Collange, aged 70, who was, at the moment, looking after cows in a meadow. He said:

"It came down vertically and hung about four-and-a-half-feet from the ground. It was silent. I saw that the machine was about six feet in diameter and gave out a vivid light. I went all around it, but saw no signs of any sort of porthole. Then, as silently as it came, the eerie thing turned around on itself, rose up and vanished into the sky. When I saw it first, in the sky, about 1,300 feet up, it had come from the west, and it was its shining so brightly that drew my attention."

Collange is said, locally, to be quite a sane and sensible man, not given to flights of imagination.

June 7, 1955: At Fécamp, about twenty miles from the port of Havre, western France, M. Comus, a marine inspector and director of a school of hydrography, followed for fifteen minutes, through binoculars, the flight, high in the sky, of a mysterious shining *ufo*. It was no cosmic body like a meteor, nor any sort of plane, and it moved relatively slowly, southwest to northeast, for about 3½ miles. Shape like a disc, and an orange glow from the center. Several people also saw it.

June 14, 1955: On the terrace of his Manhattan apartment in New York, Warren Siegmond, a TV technician, was about to give a test to Mlle. Jeanine Boullier, of the French Office de Tourisme, when noticing that her gaze was fixed on the sky, he turned around, and in the sky saw a *ufo* moving. He grabbed his camera and for some seconds trained the lens onto it. It was noiseless, and its speed was fantastic, while it seemed to be under the control of a very experienced entity. The editor of the Swiss saucer journal, "Le Courrier Interplanétaire," believes that this *ufo* was identical with the one referred to by radio network Europe I, on May 24, 1955, when the *ufo* was sighted at 7:30 A.M. He found that it had flown all over Washington, D.C., and had been photographed on May 15, 1955. But he says: "The U.S. official censorship has given orders, and this *ufo* news has not been repeated, either by radio or press. Truly, information and liberty have become very rare and beautiful things."

While this book is going to press, the censorship clamps on tighter. Correspondents tell me that their reports are ignored by defense authorities and by the press, apparently on an understanding from these authorities. Nevertheless, reports continue to reach me from all over the world —an average of 200 reports each month. They prove one thing beyond any shadow of doubt:

The Truth of the Existence of Flying Saucers Cannot Be Censored!

Mr. Harold T. Wilkins will be very happy to correspond with any readers who wish to share their flying saucer experiences with him. His address is:

Colomberie
29, Bean Road
Bexleyheath
England.

Correspondents are requested to send self-addressed envelopes with International Postal Coupons for reply. Mr. Wilkins will be unable to answer letters lacking these enclosures.